HOW THE IRISH WON THE WEST

MYLES DUNGAN

NEW
ISLAND

How The Irish Won The West
First published 2006
by New Island
2 Brookside
Dundrum Road
Dublin 14
www.newisland.ie

ISBN 1 905494 11 4

British Library Cataloguing in Publication Data. A CIP catalogue record for
this book is available from the British Library.

Cover design by Anú Design
Printed in the UK by MPG

New Island received financial assistance from The Arts Council
(An Chomhairle Ealaíon), Dublin, Ireland

10 9 8 7 6 5 4 3 2 1

CONTENTS

For Stacey, Best Western Gal

PRE-CREDIT SEQUENCE

This may look like a book. But don't be fooled: it's really a movie. In the 1960s, when I was growing up, the western ruled our TV screens. It's hard to believe now but it seemed like every second programme back then was set in a saloon, a ranch or a sheriff's office. A lot of the films shown on TV were westerns as well, so, naturally enough, this was where we escaped to as kids in the school-yard or the back garden. There was a time (in between wanting to be a train driver and preparing to climb Mount Everest) when I yearned to be a cowboy. Of course, if I'd known how dangerous, dirty, dusty, badly paid and uncomfortable a job it was, I would have stuck with train driving.

The Wild West had a hold on the imagination of boys (it was an almost entirely male obsession) of a certain age. Few under the age of fifty and no one under the age of forty would have been similarly fixated. We thought we knew all about Billy the Kid, Jesse James, Butch Cassidy, the Sundance Kid and the Hole in the Wall Gang, the Wild Bunch, Cochise, Geronimo, Crazy Horse, Sitting Bull, Custer, Wyatt Earp, Bat Masterson and the Union Pacific Railroad. The fact that their stories always seemed to vary wildly depending on what film you were watching was of minor importance. We trusted John Wayne, James Stewart and Gary Cooper to get it right. (We'd have known precious little about Howard Hawks, Henry Hathaway or probably even John Ford at the time.)

Of course, we knew precisely nothing. What we were getting was black and white situations in Technicolor. Before our gawping eyes, America was inventing its mythic past while projecting the contemporary preoccupations of its society (McCarthyism, Vietnam) in the guise of simple boys' adventure yarns.

Ed Buscombe, in his *BFI Companion to the Western,* has described the genre as 'a site for the dramatization of the formation of America's evolving national identity'.[1] This is undoubtedly the case, assuming that Buscombe was referring to white America. The westerns we saw were largely mono. When it came to the portrayal of virtue and heroism, they were racially monochrome and monocultural. Not that we were bothered at the time. The only dark faces we saw were Native Americans (though nobody had thought of that designation back then) and Mexicans. Both filled the role of antagonist. They were the dark, sinister forces preying on innocent settlers and plucky cowboys and attempting to roll back the manifest destiny of the white man to tame and settle the West.

That is why the western is dead. Although he kept faith with the genre himself, Sergio Leone's *Once upon a Time in the West* was as much a farewell to the western as it was a hymn to the death of the old West. Despite occasional one-off revivals such as *Dances with Wolves* or *Unforgiven,* and despite latter-day attempts to atone for previous sins, it will not be coming back. In the 'modern' western, 'the stories of men and women who both entered and created a moral wilderness have begun to replace the simple contests of savagery and civilisation',[2] acknowledges historian Patricia Limerick. But it is too little, far too late.

The classic Hollywood western spoke to the myths and illusions of one race. Films like *Broken Arrow* or *Soldier Blue* will never make up for the innumerable westerns that slandered a conquered people subjected to virtual genocide. In addition, Mexican Americans must find the depiction of their forefathers particularly offensive. For others, the sins are those of omission. Although there have been attempts to make the western relevant to the African American experience, with films such as *Posse*, and to point out that African Americans went west in huge numbers, the genre is as fundamentally alien and irrelevant to black culture, as is country and western music.

So if you have been waiting patiently for a resurgence of the western, you will have to be content with its bastard children: the action movie and the science-fiction adventure. It ain't comin' back, Ma. Given that the inheritors of the 'Gunfighter Nation', of which Richard Slotkin has so memorably written, are currently in the political ascendant in the USA, I could be wrong, but America doesn't strike me as a nation that thrives on metaphor any more.

Even within the context of the prevailing template, the brave and oppressed white cowboys/farmers/settlers realising their American dream, there was very little diversity. All the accents seemed to be American. Granted, there was the occasional sing-song Scandinavian lilt, the slurred, drunken Irish slobber, the indecipherable Chinese patois or the oily, aristocratic English drawl, but they were usually only trotted out when a little light relief was required. So we might have been forgiven for thinking that the trans-Mississippi American 'frontier' was tamed exclusively by native-born Americans. That's what I thought until I began researching a book called *Distant Drums* in the early 1990s and discovered that more than thirty of the men who died with Colonel George Armstrong Custer at the Little Bighorn had been born in Ireland. About the same number again had been born in the USA of Irish parents. Nearly 140 members of Custer's 7th Cavalry (out of a total of 800 men) had been born in Ireland.

That discovery led to a desire to find out whether there were other Irishmen and women who hadn't just stopped in New York, Philadelphia and Boston after they emigrated from Ireland in the nineteenth century. There were. Lots of them. They have turned up in all sorts of places. One or two are principals in some of the great mythical stories of the American West. The rest are peripheral, but nonetheless colourful for that. The time has now come to stop collecting.

In this survey of nineteenth-century Irish migration to the American West, I have, by and large, concentrated on stories rather than on analysis, though I have benefited greatly from the writing of scholars of New Western History such as Richard Slotkin, Patricia Limerick and John Mack Farragher. Most of the material contained within these covers is based on secondary sources, on more than 120 books collected over a period of six years from the United States and on four visits to the USA – to Wyoming, California, New Mexico and Minnesota.

I am sorry to disappoint military-history fans, but I have deliberately avoided dealing with the experience of the Irish in the US Frontier Army. This is because this book is already far too long, because it is a subject I have already dealt with in a sketchy fashion in a previous work (*Distant Drums: Irish Veterans of Foreign Armies*, Belfast, 1993) and because it is one that I hope to deal with in far greater detail in the future.

I have also signally failed to deal adequately with the experience of Irish miners and railroad workers in the American West. This is because they were, mostly, unlettered men who left little account of themselves and whose lives, though relentlessly hard and often brutal, were often otherwise unremarkable. Some of those who achieved success or great riches in either field have been acknowledged and I hope that a little of the flavour of the lives of ordinary Irish miners and railroad builders can be gleaned from their experience. After all, they began at the bottom too – they just got lucky.

If this book has a thesis of any kind, it is not seriously attempting to suggest that the Irish actually won the West. It is merely pointing out that, contrary to the Hollywood version of the truth, the exploration, subjugation, development and exploitation of the West was multicultural and multifaceted. There are many mansions in this particular house. The Irish room happens to be very lavishly and flamboyantly furnished.

Enjoy the movie.

Roll it!

OPENING CREDITS

A NINETEENTH-CENTURY WESTERN TIMELINE

1803	Talleyrand offers 'whatever we took from the Spanish' to American negotiators for $15,000,000. The USA gets half of the 'West' for a few dollars more than it was prepared to offer for New Orleans in the Lousiana purchase.
1804	Lewis and Clark begin their epic voyage of exploration.
1806	Lewis and Clark return with the Corps of Discovery after they had been given up for dead.
1807	Manuel Lisa sets up the first permanent American fur trading post, Fort Raymond, at the meeting of the Yellowstone and Little Bighorn rivers in Montana.
1808	John Jacob Astor secures a charter from the State of New York, setting up the American Fur Company.
1811	Astor's men establish a trading presence at the mouth of the Columbia River.

1823   William Henry Ashley's newly recruited trappers journey up the Missouri River in search of fur pelts.

1824   Discovery of South Pass by Thomas Fitzpatrick and other Ashley employees.

1831   Jedediah Smith killed.

1843   John C. Fremont's influential account of his expedition to the Rockies is published by Congress.

1844   The Stevens–Murphy party blaze an emigrant trail to the West.

1846   Mexican–American War begins.
The Donner party set out for California.

1847   Twelve people murdered by Cayuse Indians at the Whitman settlement in Oregon.

1848   Gold discovered near Sutter's Fort in California, sparking an unprecedented gold rush the following year.

1851   First Fort Laramie Treaty negotiated by Thomas Fitzpatrick with Plains Indian tribes.

1859   Comstock lode discovered.
Henry McCarty (aka Billy the Kid) born in New York.

1861   American Civil War begins.

1864   Sand Creek Massacre of a Cheyenne encampment by Colorado militia.

1865   End of American Civil War.

1866   Goodnight–Loving Trail opens route for cattle drives from Texas to the Midwest.

1867   Fetterman Massacre – Red Cloud and Oglala Sioux on warpath – three Union officers and ninety men killed in ambush.

1868   Red Cloud signs Fort Laramie Treaty, ending his war on relatively favourable terms.

1869   Union Pacific and Central Pacific railroad lines meet at Promontory Point in Utah.

1874   Custer-led expedition to the Black Hills discovers gold and starts another gold rush.

1876   Two hundred and sixty-eight officers, men and camp followers are killed by combined Lakota/Sioux and Cheyenne forces at the Battle of the Little Bighorn.

1878   The Lincoln County War erupts. The murder of John Tunstall, the killing of Sheriff Brady by Billy the Kid and the 'Big Killing' of July all happened in this year.

1881   The Earps and the Clantons shoot it out at the OK Corral in Tombstone.

Pat Garret tracks down and shoots Billy the Kid.

1882   Oscar Wilde arrives in the USA for his celebrated lecture tour.

1883   'Buffalo' Bill Cody stages his first travelling Wild West Show.

1889   Johnson County War: Wyoming beef barons hire killers and take vigilante approach to rustling.

1890   Sitting Bull killed by Lakota policemen.

Ghost Dance movement comes to abrupt and bloody end at Wounded Knee massacre – resistance of the Plains Indians ends.

1896   Gold strikes in the Yukon start another gold stampede.

1903   Edwin S. Porter's *Great Train Robbery* (a western) becomes the first American feature film.

REEL ONE

INTRODUCTION:
HOW THE IRISH REALLY WON THE WEST

Sorry to disappoint, but ... the Pony Express went out of business after nineteen months, the gunfight at the OK Corral lasted less than thirty seconds, the Stetson was invented in Philadelphia, farmers outnumbered cowboys in the Old West by a thousand to one, Billy the Kid did not kill one man for each year of his short life, Frederick Remington never actually saw any cowboys in action because he was much too fat to get on a horse, Zane Grey was a New York dentist ... and so on.

The American 'Wild West' has been successfully mythologised over a period of a hundred years or more to the point where reality and

1

fiction have become interchangeable. A young emerging American nation needed an heroic past of its own. Its very size, remoteness and harshness, as well as the hardy, independent characters who inhabited its space, meant that the American West was ready-made for hyperbole. Even before memories of significant historical events had begun to fade, storytellers were creating a mythic past from those very sources. It was 'a past that never was and always will be', as one student of the frontier has put it.[1] Certain elements of that past were undeniably ground breaking and 'heroic'. But the nineteenth-century American West has been over-mythologised. Buffalo Bill, Frederick Remington, Hollywood and the 'dime' novel have seen to that.

Just as there are countless myths about the American West, there are many preconceptions about the Irish in the USA. They derive from convenient over-simplifications. One version of the Irish American story would have us believe that Irish nineteenth-century immigrants settled almost exclusively in the great eastern conurbations of New York, Boston and Philadelphia. Of course they did so in great numbers, but an interrogation of this particular myth quickly dispels it. Many, having acquired the urban skills they lacked on arrival, moved on from the stifling Irish ghettoes of the eastern seaboard. A significant percentage of those who did so settled in the West. In 1850 there were 900,000 Irish-born immigrants in the USA, only 0.4 per cent of whom lived in the western states. By 1920, one million US residents were Irish-born, 9 per cent of whom lived in the West.[2] As historian David Emmons has put it in his monumental work on Butte, Montana, *The Butte Irish: Class and Ethnicity in an American Mining Town 1875–1925*:

> Contributing to the historical neglect of these westering Irishmen has been the assumption that the American West was the exclusive province of native-born Protestants who wished to farm or graze their cattle on it. Farmers and cattlemen there were, but there was also an urban West, filled with miners and smeltermen, loggers, railroad workers, longshoremen, and industrial tradesmen of every sort. Many were Irish.[3]

There is a natural tendency to equate the words 'West' and 'frontier' and indeed they are often interchangeable. But while the 'West' was clearly the 'frontier' at one point in American history, the 'frontier' was as much an eastern as a western phenomenon. Arguably the American 'frontier' was to be found east of the Mississippi for far longer than it was located to the west of that great river. From the time of the landing of the Pilgrim Fathers until the late 1700s, American expansion was west-*ward* but the West itself was *terra incognita*. When Thomas Jefferson became president of the USA in 1801, two-thirds of the American people lived within fifty miles of the Atlantic Ocean. The USA itself ended on the eastern bank of the Mississippi River. Many of the men who had expanded the land area of the USA even that far had been Irish. They were the so-called 'Scotch-Irish', Protestant pioneers who had also played such a huge part in winning American independence and in formulating the US Constitution.

However, as the USA poured across the Mississippi and pushed, punched, cajoled, fought and cheated its way to the Pacific Ocean, the Irish pioneers who played a part in making a garden out of that wilderness were very different from the men who had helped bring America thus far. For a start, they were almost all Catholic. They were also, largely, from more impoverished backgrounds than the Scotch-Irish Protestants and Presbyterians who had preceded them. Mines, railroads and the army were the principal employers of the Irish in the American West. Most never rose above the status of lowly wage earner, but few became indentured wage slaves like many of their eastern counterparts. In states such as Montana there were no indentured employees. No company stores or company boarding houses ensured that the employee never escaped the economic grasp of the employer. There was also an abundance of land for the thrifty former miner, soldier or railroad worker who might decide to return to the avocation of his Irish ancestors.

In a newly minted society with few barriers to upward mobility, NINA (No Irish Need Apply) attitudes were not allowed to prevail. The Irish who moved west managed to avoid much of the bigotry and Know-Nothing[4] spirit that pervaded many of the mid-nineteenth-century eastern cities. In New York, Boston and Philadelphia, the Catholic Irish from the 1840s onwards faced organised and improvised racism on a considerable scale. The Irish in the West faced no such condescension or discrimination in western cities, primarily because the cities didn't exist, at least not on the scale of the eastern seaboard. Institutionalised racism cannot thrive in the absence of institutions, and the West of the mid-nineteenth century lacked an entrenched WASP establishment of the kind that directed the suspicion and scorn of their stooges towards the immigrant Irish in the East. And where cities did begin to flourish, such as San Francisco, Butte or St Louis, they did so with a healthy proportion of Irish first-generation inhabitants who were not about to be dictated to by Know-Nothings or vigilantes.

Furthermore, the environment in which the western Irish lived was more rough and ready than the one they abandoned (or avoided altogether in the rare cases of direct migration to the West) on the east coast. Despite many attempts to civilise the towns and cities of the West, middle-class, Protestant American values were slow to take hold in places that might not exist the following week if the gold/silver/copper gave out, the army fort closed down or the promised railway line went elsewhere. Without wishing to reinforce certain familiar ethnic stereotypes, there was an elemental wildness about the West that suited the rebellious anti-establishment streak in the post-Famine Irish who were uncomfortable and often unwelcome in the Nativist Protestant enclaves of the East until they banded together and learned to manipulate the politics of the big cities.

Aside from which, everybody in the West was a migrant except the indigenous peoples. *They* would become far more plausible scapegoats for the tribulations of the region than the Irish had ever been east of the Mississippi. And when the Indian threat was gone, if the Irish had ever been an underclass in the West, they had been replaced by the Chinese and the Mexicans.

In his highly influential essay 'The Significance of the Frontier in American History', Frederick Jackson Turner proposed that 'in the crucible of the frontier the immigrants were Americanised, liberated and fused into a mixed race'.[5] He was referring to the eighteenth-century frontier but applies his proposition to the trans-Mississippi frontier as well. Was this true of the Irish? How quickly did those who ventured west become American?

Far more quickly than in the eastern cities, where they faced anti-Irish and anti-Catholic bigotry. In a milieu where the Nativist had replaced the English as the oppressor, it was difficult not to cling to one's ethnicity and band together with one's countrymen for protection and in pursuit of political influence. But in an environment where preoccupations and priorities were somewhat different, it was not so essential to coalesce and cleave to one's Irishness. Granted, a remote

California mining town like Bodie (population 10,000 at its height) might boast a branch of the Ancient Order of Hibernians and the Irish Land League, but that can be ascribed as much to nostalgia as to any distrustful clannishness. The Bodie Irish, comprising as they did 30 per cent of the town's transient population, did not need to band together for protection. In the book *Irish Settlers on the American Frontier*, Michael C. O'Laughlin suggests that the reason relatively little attention has been paid to the Irish story in the American West is because rapid assimilation became the norm. Because the Irish were more readily accepted, their own ethnicity became less significant. 'Being an American proved more important than being Irish. Becoming a successful part of this new nation, their older heritage was often set aside.'[6] Perhaps 'new region' would be more appropriate than 'new nation' in this instance, but the nature of the assimilation of the Irish into western society has, ironically, led to their achievements often being overlooked. This is because they were not at the margins. Their experience was seldom at odds with the western narrative.

Although this study will concentrate on a few significant individuals, it is worth making some more general observations before launching into their stories. The classic image of the nineteenth-century Irish immigrant to the USA is of the peasant fleeing economic and political serfdom and sailing to North America in an unseaworthy 'coffin ship' – the indigent vassal on a leaky vessel. He (for the stereotypical Irish emigrant is male) would arrive in Boston or New York, stick close to his own, settle in an eastern urban ghetto and endure poverty and bigotry at the hands of the dominant WASP culture. He would become political fodder for an Irish Democratic Party ward heeler, probably become a trade-union activist and his children and grandchildren might, slowly and painstakingly, climb the political and economic ladder.

Like most stereotypes it has more than a grain of truth. But it can be challenged and questioned. What is outlined above *was* the experience of many nineteenth-century Irish immigrants to the USA (except for the gender balance – it was much closer to fifty–fifty). But, as we will see, a significant percentage didn't remain on the eastern seaboard. Many moved into the Midwest, to cities like St Louis and Chicago. Some even moved to the South, though there was a marked disinclination to do so because of the perception of antipathy towards Catholicism in the states below the Mason-Dixon line. What has gone largely unremarked is the significance of the American West to the Irish immigrant and vice versa.

The experience of the Irish in the West challenges certain axioms. It puts in some doubt, for example, the notion that the Irish did not engage with the land because the land had betrayed them. Aside altogether from the fact that many of the post-Famine Irish, despite their agricultural backgrounds, were not competent to work American farmland (assuming they could afford to buy it even on generous government terms), there is evidence that a significant percentage of the Irish who moved westwards did opt for the agricultural life. Work done on the 1870 and 1880 census in two Washington counties (Clarke and Spokane) shows that between 50 and 60 per cent of a substantial Irish population was working the land.[7]

It also challenges the notion that in an industrial dispute the Irish were more likely to be on the side of labour than of capital. The West was good to Irish enterprise. Unshackled by the Freemasonry and exclusivity of the eastern capitalist cabals, many newly arrived Irish immigrants were able to stake their claim to wealth, literally and metaphorically. The 'Silver Kings' were merely the most famous of a range of rich mine-owning Irishmen (and women). In a town like Butte, Montana, where most of the miners were Irish, as were most of the mine-owners, ethnic cohesion and some element of fair dealing seems to have blunted the tendency towards industrial action. Between 1878 and 1916, the Irish-dominated Butte Miner's Union never led its workers out on strike.[8] According to David Emmons:

> there were times when ethnic nationalism and working class protest reinforced one another. But there was a far tighter seam that marked the place where the rights of Ireland were joined only with the rights of *Irish* workers and there were more times when that ethnic exclusivity was used against rather than in defense of the rights of all workers.[9]

Confronting anti-Irish and anti-Catholic bigotry and racism was something many Irish were forced to do in the East and Midwest. This phenomenon was less prevalent in the West. In fact, if anything, the western experience reinforces the unpalatable fact established by the New York draft riots of 1863, namely that the Irish were just as capable of racism and bigotry as their oppressors. This is borne out by their treatment of the Native American, the African American and the Asian American.

The role of the Irish in the subjugation of the Native American population is largely beyond the scope of this work (because it is mostly associated with the US Army), but the evidence of Irish complicity in this nineteenth-century form of ethnic cleansing is compelling. Suffice it to say that the charity of a virtually destitute Choctaw nation in the mid-1840s in sending a large sum of money for the relief of famine in Ireland was not reciprocated in kind in the years that followed by Irish officers and soldiers in the western army.

The attitude of Irish communities on the eastern seaboard towards the issue of slavery has also been well advertised. In the near west and Midwest, the opposition of Irish settlers and labourers to the emancipation of slaves was hardly less virulent than was evident from the lynching of black men by Irish mobs in New York in 1863. As one historian of the Midwest has put it, 'There were antislavery Irish people, but contemporary observers agreed that the bulk of the Irish population in the 1850's was not moved by the abolitionists arguments.'[10] An Irish Midwesterner in the pivotal 1860 election wrote home, 'All Catholics here is Democrats or for slavery and all Republicans is prodestants [sic] or not for slavery but it is not known yet which will beat.'[11]

In the far west the Irish had a highly ambiguous relationship with the Chinese. Thrown together on the Central Pacific Railroad in huge numbers, relations between the Irish navvies and the Chinese coolies were often strained and occasionally burst into open violence. In the city of San Francisco a strange paradox can be seen at its most stark. There

> the Chinese presence was of great importance to the Irish. The cultural gulf between Chinese and white society ... was so great as to diminish, by comparison, almost to vanishing point the differences between the natives of Cork and Boston, Limerick and New York.[12]

The point being made by historian R.A. Burchaell here is that the Irish were, to some extent, beholden to the Chinese for their own status in San Francisco society. The Chinese were a ready-made underclass that discharged the Irish from their recurring obligation to be society's footstool.

This fact, however, did not prevent the Irish in San Francisco from discriminating against the Orientals in a mirror image of their own treatment in the mid-nineteenth-century in the eastern cities. Their colour meant they could make common cause with white groups who might, conceivably, have discriminated against them had the Chinese not been available as an alternative. Denis Kearney's Workingmen's Party of the 1870s, which advocated the expulsion of Chinese from the USA, was an egregious example of this phenomenon. Kearney himself was an immigrant, but that did not prevent him inciting violence against Chinese communities in the Bay area. Sadly, the same intolerance was often true of Irish trade-union activity: 'anti Oriental racism became the cement for labor union organization'.[13] Ironically, the closest a No Irish Need Apply sign got to San Francisco was on a mill owned by a migrant New Englander in Mendocino County. The Irish riposte was to cover the sign in graffiti.

Because the West lacked a social register (money determined social status) and because there were more resources to be distributed amongst fewer people, the Irish race fared relatively well there. Cities such as San Francisco had a 12 per cent Irish population in the 1850s, with a far higher percentage in highly paid professional employment in the 1870s than in eastern cities. Individual Irishmen, such as the 'Silver Kings' of Virginia City or 'Copper King' Marcus Daly of Butte, made huge fortunes and became first-generation 'lace curtain' Irish. Protected from Nativist bigotry by their relative prosperity and the existence of ethnic groups more vulnerable to racism than themselves, the Irish made a better home in the American West far more rapidly than they did in the East. Their strange lack of political cohesion was a function of this assimilation. As James Walsh, who has made a particular study of California, has put it, 'In California Irish-Americans had never built a consistent political machine … In San Francisco, Irish-American politicians acted as individuals for the most part.'[14] There was little need for them to do otherwise. They had none of the impetus for self-protection that spawned Tammany Hall and other eastern 'Irish' political machines.

But just because the Irish relationship with the western economic and political landscape was less fraught than it was in the cities that had been their first ports of call on reaching the USA does not mean that the story of that relationship lacks interest. The focus of this study will be on individuals and small groups who intersected with those landscapes in a fascinating and often violent manner. They are every bit as colourful and influential as the Irish icons of the eastern seaboard. As befits the Land of the Big Sky, they are also somewhat larger than life.

REEL TWO

MOUNTAIN MEN:
IRISH PIONEERS OF THE FUR TRADE

The iconography of the American West may not survive long into the third millennium, but the imagery from that period, laced with dollops of jagged romanticism, left a permanent mark on the twentieth century. Whether it was the poncho-clad Clint Eastwood extracting the last measure of revenge in a 'spaghetti western' or the Marlboro Man encouraging the association between the ruggedness of the great outdoors and the banal act of smoking a cigarette, there was no escape from the imagined and romanticised Wild West long after the more mundane reality itself had petered out.

One of the West's most enduring icons is the grizzled, beaver-hatted, buck-skinned and aromatic 'Mountain Man'. He is the quintessential loner, closer to nature and to the Indians amongst whom he lives than he is to the 'society' that he has rejected in favour of the simple, nomadic life of the hunter.

As with all such western images, there is an element of myth and of truth about this depiction of the lonely fur trapper or 'voyageur'. They were tough, independent (and unhygienic) men who opened up the West through their explorations, through their pursuit of the beaver and by trading with the indigenous population. But they weren't all native-born Americans and neither were they necessarily illiterate, uncultured nomads who shunned the society of all but other courageous misfits like themselves.

To put the significance of the Mountain Men in western history into perspective, it is important to understand the relationship between the United States of America and its vast hinterland in the early part of the nineteenth century.

America before the Louisiana Purchase

When Thomas Jefferson became president of the USA in 1801, two-thirds of the American people lived within fifty miles of the Atlantic Ocean. The USA ended on the eastern bank of the Mississippi River.

Others, who were not American, had explored the vast interior of the continental USA. French and Spanish fur traders had moved up the Missouri River. Employees of the British-owned Hudson's Bay Company had moved down from Canada as far as the Mandan Indians in what is now North Dakota. But to most, the area west of the Mississippi was a vast white space on the map of North America, a sort of Unfoundland.

Jefferson himself had never been much farther west than the Shenandoah Valley and he believed that

a) The Blue Ridge Mountains were the highest in the USA.

b) Somewhere in the West was a tribe of blue-eyed Indians who spoke Welsh. They were the mythical descendants of Prince Madoc, who was supposed to have settled in the New World in the twelfth century.

c) The Northwest Passage actually existed. This was a theoretical river series that would connect the east and west coasts of the continent. Whoever had control of this mythical river system would be able to realise the economic potential of the enormous land mass that was North America

Jefferson was committed to exploration and to pushing the uncertain boundaries of the USA, but not at the risk of war with the European nations with which the USA shared the continent – Britain, France and Spain. In 1804 he sent an Irish-born engineer, Thomas Freeman, with a group of thirty-five scientific and military personnel to the southwest border with Spain to explore the Red and Arkansas rivers upstream towards their sources. Freeman began his explorations on the Red River in two flat-bottomed boats. On 29 July his team encountered a force of Spaniards under Commandant Francisco Viana, who ordered the Irishman back downriver, claiming that he and the men under his command had strayed into Spanish territory. As Viana had a complement of 150 soldiers and Freeman had been warned not to engage or even antagonise the Spanish, he did as he was ordered.

Jefferson had already made two attempts to persuade explorers to search for the Northwest Passage. Those had come to nothing. In 1803 he secured authority for a 'scientific expedition' to cross French and British lands in a journey to the west coast. Spain refused permission, but this time Jefferson was prepared to ignore Spanish objections. The man Jefferson appointed to lead this expedition (christened the Corps of Discovery) was his own personal secretary, Meriwether Lewis, a twenty-eight-year-old former soldier given to occasional bouts of depression and not universally approved of as commander of such an enterprise. Lewis appointed as co-commander his thirty-two-year-old friend William Clark, an extrovert Virginian with an army background and much experience on the Kentucky and Ohio frontiers. It was probably the best executive decision he made. Ironically, it was Lewis who insisted on describing Clark as his co-leader – the War Department refused to recognise him as such.

With the sort of consummate timing which often seems to separate momentous historical events from mere footnotes, just the day before Lewis, Clark and their Corps of Discovery were due to leave for the West, on 4 July 1803, Napoleon Bonaparte signed a treaty selling off the Louisiana Territory to the US government for $15 million (twice the then federal budget). Bonaparte made the gesture to American delegates who had sought, merely, to purchase New Orleans itself. He needed the money for further hostilities against England. Jefferson's plenipotentiaries got the 820,000 square miles (far greater than what we know of today as Louisiana) for three cents an acre and doubled the size of the USA with the acquisition. Some thought it was a bad idea. The Boston *Columbian Centinel* exhibited considerable foresight when it observed that 'We are to give money of which we have too little, for land of which we already have too much.'[1]

The USA now bordered on Texas and California (Spanish owned) and the Oregon Territory (whose ownership was disputed with Britain). Suddenly Lewis and Clark were going to be crossing American, as well as British and Spanish, land. Their mission took on a diplomatic as well as a scientific purpose: contact had to be made with the indigenous tribes of the region to bring them the joyful news that they were now 'American'.

Probably not until the era of space exploration would Americans again take such a leap into the unknown. The Corps (which consisted of about fifty men) sailed up the Missouri on 14 May 1804. Slow progress was generally made against the five-mile-an-hour current by rowing. The river was 'resistant' in that it was muddy, full of logs and other snags. The expedition wintered at the village of the Mandan tribe on the banks of the upper reaches of the Missouri in what is now North Dakota.

The Mandan (a sedentary, farming people, quite unlike the stereotype of the nomadic Native American) were accustomed to white traders and trappers – both from St Louis and from Canada. The Corps had no problems either with adjacent tribes such as the Otoe, Missouri and Arikara. They made their way west, bestowing gifts on the Native American population as they went. Their first problems were with the Brule Sioux/Lakota, who threatened them with death, but Clark faced them down with his own threats of greater force to come if anything happened to the Corps of Discovery. The confrontation was a prelude to the ongoing tension between the white man and the powerful Lakota that would persist throughout the nineteenth century.

On 26 May 1805 the Corps saw the distant Rockies for the first time. They continued their journey along the upper Missouri to its source then beyond that to the Continental Divide, from where the rivers began flowing westwards. The Northwest Passage remained elusive and they were further from the Pacific than they thought with a second winter closing in. Also, they were beyond the boundaries purchased by Jefferson's $15 million and were in territory claimed by Britain.

They had also picked up one of the most famous French-Canadian fur trappers of the day, Toussaint Charbonneau, and one of his Indian wives, Sacagawea – a fifteen-year-old Shosone who had been kidnapped from her own tribe and sold to Charbonneau. She was to prove crucial to the safety of the Corps as the winter of 1805 set in. Lewis needed to buy horses from the Shosone to avoid getting caught in the mountains during the winter. The Shosone were reluctant. Sacagawea saved the day when she recognised the Shosone chief as her brother. After they were reunited he agreed to give the Corps the horses they needed. The very presence of Sacagawea served as a guarantee of the friendly intentions of the Corps of Discovery as, according to Clark, 'no woman ever accompanies a war party of Indians in this quarter'.[2]

Later, as they struggled through the snows of the Rockies, they were saved from starvation by the Nez Perce, who took pity on them and fed them. They also helped them build the canoes used to descend the Clearwater, Snake and Columbia rivers to the sea and looked after the horses of the Corps until the following spring. Lewis and Clark reached the Pacific coast of California on 3 December 1805. They began their return journey the following spring and in September 1806 were back where they had started twenty-eight months before. They returned as heroes, having been given up for dead.

Mountain Men

When Lewis and Clark reached the Mandan villages in August 1806 on their return journey to St Louis, they saw two white men paddling up the Missouri in the opposite direction. They were trappers, lured by the prospect of the fortune to be made from hunting beaver. At the time, demand for beaver pelts was huge in Europe. They were used to make felt hats. (For the record, the two men were Forest Handcock and Joseph Dickson and they were never heard of again.)

The fur trade had operated for years before the USA laid claim to the area west of the Missouri. It had involved Indian trappers supplying

English, French and Spanish traders with furs. But the Americans decided to do it for themselves. In 1807 Manuel Lisa, a Spaniard who was based in St Louis, set up the first permanent American trading post. Fort Raymond was at the meeting of the Yellowstone and Little Bighorn rivers in Montana. In 1809 Lisa and William Clark, now a national hero, formed the Missouri Fur Company.

Its great and enduring rival, the American Fur Company, owes its very existence to a piece of advice given on board a US-bound ship. The identity of the adviser is lost to history. The nature of the advice was to invest profits (from the sale of musical instruments in New York) in the purchase of furs. The man who accepted the advice was one of the most famous businessmen of the nineteenth century, John Jacob Astor. Those few words started him on the road to becoming the richest man in the USA at the time of his death in 1848.

Astor was born in Germany in 1763 in the town of Waldorf, near Heidelberg (hence the name of one of the most famous hotels in the world, the Waldorf Astoria). An ambitious and confident type, he decided to try his luck in the USA. It was his brother's musical instruments (seven flutes) he was bringing with him to sell when he met his lucky counsellor. They were his share of the family business. He did buy the furs. Then he sold them at a huge profit in London. From that point he was out of the music industry and into the fur trade. In 1808 he secured a charter from the State of New York that established the American Fur Company

The Lewis and Clark expedition had revealed a profusion of beaver in the catchment area of the Missouri and west of the Rockies – this, and the fact that a presence on the west coast gave access to the Oriental market for furs, prompted Astor to attempt to establish a foothold on the Pacific coastline. The fact that the area in which he wished to operate was effectively under the control of Spain, Britain and Russia did not deter him. Neither did it concern Jefferson, who saw it, as he said in a letter to Astor, as 'the germ of a great, free and independent Empire on that side of our continent'.[3] Clearly Jefferson was developing an aversion to sharing the bounty of continental North America with any European states. A similar aversion would inform the policies of many of his successors.

Astor's plan was simple and financially risky. He invested $200,000 (about $4 million today) in a business colony (Astoria) at the mouth of the Columbia River on the Pacific coast. The intention was to resupply it each year by ship and have the supply ship take the furs accumulated during each year's trading with local Indian tribes to the Orient. There, a variety of marketable products would be purchased with the proceeds of the fur trading and the ship would return with them to New York.

To advance his plan, Astor established the Pacific Fur Company. His assault was to be two-pronged. As well as the ship that would sail to the Pacific coast, to arrive in the early months of 1811, an overland expedition would travel west with the intention of reaching Astoria at the same time as the supply vessel. This expedition included an Irishman called John Reed. (His place of birth in Ireland is unclear.) It fared badly, with the overland travellers suffering from hunger, thirst, exposure to extreme cold and periodic desertion by understandably disaffected employees, before members of a much-reduced group straggled into Astoria in February 1812.

The first ship chosen for the journey to Oregon was the *Tonquin*, which weighed in at 290 tons. It came to grief after a dispute with local Nootka Indians, exacerbated by the character of the ship's captain, a martinet by the name of Jonathan Thorn. The Indians, having already been badly treated by Thorn, managed to inveigle their way on board the ship and attacked and killed most of the crew. The last surviving sailors onboard locked themselves below deck and ignited the ship's gunpowder, blowing themselves, dozens of Indians and the ship into oblivion.

On 17 October 1811, some weeks after the *Tonquin* had set sail, the *Beaver* became the next Astor supply ship to make the journey west. On board was the second Irishman in the Pacific Fur Company, Ross Cox. Much more is known about Cox than about his compatriot John Reed. Cox described himself as having a 'cropped head, John Bullish face' and being a 'low and somewhat corpulent person'.[4] He was a Dubliner, born there in 1793 and so only eighteen years of age when he signed up for his great life's adventure with Astor's company. His youth meant that his annual salary, as a clerk with the Pacific Fur Company, was $100, when others doing the same work were paid $150. Cox's importance was that he wrote one of only three first-hand accounts of the Astorian experiment. He remained on the west coast until 1817, when he began his return to Dublin. Subsequently Cox worked for the Dublin Metropolitan Police and, until 1837, as the Dublin correspondent of the *London Morning Herald*. In 1831 he wrote *The Columbia River – or Scenes and Adventures during a Residence of Six Years on the Western Side of the Rocky Mountains among Various Tribes of Indians Hitherto Unknown*, a colourful but not entirely reliable account of life in Astoria.

The *Beaver* reached Astoria in May 1812 and augmented the traders and trappers already at the post. However, the Astorians' sense of isolation and paranoia, already running at a high level after the *Tonquin* débâcle, must have been greatly amplified by the failure of an overland party, sent east with despatches, to make it very far before being attacked by Indians and forced to turn back. Among the unhappy returnees was John Reed (Cox spells the name 'Read'). Reed was the member of the group who actually carried the despatches, in a tin case. According to Cox, 'Its brightness attracted the attention of the natives and they resolved to obtain possession of the prize.' They duly did so, almost killing Reed in the process. As the attack proceeded, the Irishman was left for dead and would never have survived had one of the leaders of the party not insisted on searching for him. Reed was found, badly wounded and minus the despatches, trying to drag himself to safety.

Cox includes a description of Astoria in his account. The fort was situated on a promontory known as Point George, close to the mouth of the Columbia River and another headland named, no doubt in a fit of pure pessimism, Cape Disappointment. It was a short distance north of the spot where Lewis and Clark had spent the winter of 1805–06.

> The buildings consisted of apartments for the proprietors and clerks, with a capacious dining-hall for both, extensive ware-houses … a provision store, a trading shop, smith's forge, carpenter's workshop, &c. The whole surrounded by stockades forming a square, and reaching about fifteen feet over the ground. A gallery ran round the stockades, in which loopholes were pierced sufficiently large for musketry.[5]

The fort also boasted a six-pound cannon. The Astorian diet was overwhelmingly carnivorous, consisting largely of elk, wildfowl and fish. Anchovies were in abundant supply. 'We had them generally twice a day,' wrote Cox, 'at breakfast and dinner, and in a few weeks got such a surfeit, that few of us for years afterwards tasted an anchovy.'[6]

On 28 June 1812, a party of nearly a hundred well-armed Astorians started up the great Columbia River in canoes, intent on trading for furs with friendly Indian tribes. Each member of the expedition wore leather body armour, a sort of heavy-duty shirt made of elk hide, which Cox insists was arrow proof and could withstand a musket ball fired from a distance of more than eighty or ninety yards. While portaging the set of rapids where Reed's party had been waylaid the previous month, a feeble attempt was made by two Indians to steal some of the trade goods being transported. This was repulsed. Clearly the local Indian tribe had no intention of taking on the entire group. The journey upriver continued without any interference. Contact was made with the well-disposed Walla Walla and the Nez Perce peoples. A smaller group stored their canoes and started for the country of the Spokane tribe. The expedition was going well. But on 17 August, Cox's own luck ran out.

On the afternoon of that day he became separated from the main group when he went off in search of fruit and fell asleep in the afternoon heat. When he woke up his companions were gone. 'My senses almost failed me,' he wrote. 'I called out, in vain, in every direction, until I became hoarse; and I could no longer conceal from myself the dreadful truth that I was alone in a wild uninhabited country, without horse or arms, and destitute of covering.'[7]

Over the following fortnight Cox attempted to track and overtake his party (which had divided into three sections, each one assuming that he was travelling with one of the others) without possessing anything other than rudimentary wilderness-survival skills. His account of his ordeal is highly colourful and, more than likely, highly coloured. There is no doubt that he experienced constant hardship and occasional moments of terror, but his reported encounters with 'a murderous brood of serpents', a raging bear who chased him up a tree (where he was forced to remain overnight), as well as hazardous brushes with wolves, must be treated with at least some scepticism. The privations from which he reported suffering, lack of food and water, are far more credible. In such an environment, without firearms or the means of creating fire, hunger and thirst would have been inevitable. In addition, his moccasins were not equal to the terrain and quickly became shredded, slowing his progress and making walking extremely painful. He survived mainly on wild berries and fruit, which was, at least, a contrast to the carnivorous diet of Astoria.

On the fourteenth day of his ordeal, Cox came across fresh horse tracks. He followed these and soon imagined he heard the neighing of a horse. Pursuing the sound, he found himself on the opposite side of a stream from a grazing herd. When he crossed the stream one of the horses approached him. 'I thought him the "prince of palfreys",' he wrote rather floridly, 'his neigh was like the bidding of a monarch, and his countenance enforced homage.'[8] The herd of horses was owned by a Spokane Indian family and, in an act of charity which would be repeated hundreds of times in the history of the West, the Indians fed Cox, offered him rudimentary medical attention and reunited him with his Astorian companions. It transpired that for a rookie Mountain Man the young Irish clerk had made an amazingly good fist of tracking his party in extreme circumstances. They were only a couple of hours away! When the Indians brought him to where some Canadian members of the expedition were chopping wood, he was greeted with frank astonishment.

> Away went saws, hatchets, and axes, and each man rushed forward to the tents … it is needless to say that our astonishment and delight at my miraculous escape were mutual. The friendly Indians were liberally rewarded; the men were allowed a holiday, and every countenance bore the smile of joy and happiness.[9]

Perhaps the same smiles also masked some small trace of guilt at having so carelessly 'lost' a fellow Astorian. When it was finally discovered that he was missing, the search for Cox had continued for six days, at which point it was assumed, not unreasonably, that someone as devoid of experience of the wild as the Irishman could not have survived.

Cox's Astorian compatriot was not as fortunate as the young Dubliner. John Reed had established himself as a trapper (Cox spent more of his time involved in trading activities with co-operative Indian tribes). In the summer of 1813 he was sent to what is now southern Idaho to trap along the Boise River. There, in January 1814, he, along with all the other trappers in his company, was killed by members of the Snake tribe. Cox's epitaph for Reed is appropriately extravagant:

> Mr Read was a rough, warm-hearted, brave, old Irishman. Owing to some early disappointments in life he had quitted his native country while a young man, in search of wealth among regions, *Where beasts with man divided empire claim/And the brown Indian marks with murd'rous aim*; and after twenty-five years of toils, dangers, and privations, added another victim to the long list of those who have fallen sacrifices to Indian treachery.[10]

Cox himself decided not to ride his luck too far. In 1813 he had proved his worth on a trading trip to the Flatheads, returning to Astoria with a healthy complement of furs. He was to make many more successful trading expeditions, so much so that his decision to quit Astoria in 1817 appears to have been received with regret by his employers. Cox had arrived by sea but departed by land. He left Astoria in April 1817, accompanying a party of eighty-six men, ascended the Columbia then crossed the Rockies into Canada. Five months after leaving the Pacific Ocean, Cox reached Montreal.[11]

Cox's significance does not lie in anything he did while he was in Astoria. His exploits, while they might have impressed a European 'salon' audience, were nothing out of the ordinary in the fur trade. His legacy is his 1831 memoir *The Columbia River*. Although elements of his story are often contradicted by two other first-hand accounts of Astorian clerks (Gabriel Franchiere and Alexander Ross), it remains a valuable document, overflowing with historical and anthropological detail in spite of its exaggerations, inaccuracies and Cox's occasional self-aggrandising excesses. Despite playing a more minor role in the opening of the West than other countrymen who would follow, Cox is one of the few Irishmen to have left any sort of literate, readable account of his life and times. For that alone we should be grateful.

The Birth of the Legend of 'Broken Hand'

The fur trade really became established in the West when the lieutenant governor of Missouri, William Henry Ashley, who had made a small fortune in the War of 1812 by manufacturing gunpowder, placed an advertisement in a St Louis newspaper, *The Missouri Republican*, in 1822. It read, 'To Enterprising young men: the subscriber wishes to engage one hundred men, to ascend the river Missouri to its source, there to be employed for one, two or three years.'[12] He got his enterprising volunteers and an expedition into the far West, under the command of Ashley's partner Andrew Henry (who had more than a decade's experience in the trade), left St Louis in April 1822 and built a trading post on the Yellowstone. It was a modest enough beginning. Ashley aimed to reinforce the limited success of that foray the following summer, so he recruited another hundred men with the intention of leading them upriver himself to reinforce Henry.

That expedition became legendary, not least for the personnel whose services Ashley managed to engage. Among its members was a western legend in the making, a twenty-three-year-old New Yorker, Jedediah Strong Smith. Smith helped Ashley recruit the rest of his troupe. Some were of sufficiently dubious origins for Smith to write 'a description of our crew I cannot give, but Falstaff's Battalion was genteel in comparison'.[13]

Another member of that battalion would, like Smith, become a western hero. Jim Bridger would come to be known as 'Old Gabe', but at the time that he answered Ashley's advertisement he was only eighteen years old. His is a name that continually crops up in stories with Irish links right up to the 1880s. His first Irish 'connection' was one of his associates on that groundbreaking Ashley expedition of 1823.

Thomas Fitzpatrick, born in County Cavan in 1799, is probably the single most significant Irish-born figure in western history. He is described in one account as 'a slender Irishman full of drive and intelligence'.[14] According to his biographer, Leroy R. Hafen, 'No other man is so representative of this epoch.' His life story is 'the epitome of the early history of the Far West'.[15] Little is known about his life in Ireland other than his mother's maiden name (Mary Kiernan), that he was one of a moderately well-to-do Catholic family of seven (three boys and four girls) and that he came to the USA armed with a decent education. He had left Ireland before his seventeenth birthday and had arrived in St Louis in the winter of 1822–3.

In the spring of 1823 Ashley set out with his group on what proved to be a disastrous expedition. He lost thousands of dollars' worth of supplies when one of his boats collided with a snag on the Missouri. He was then attacked by the Arikara tribe, who were angry at white men because a number of fur trappers had sided with their traditional enemies, the Lakota, in a dispute. In the battle at the Arikara village on the banks of the Missouri, he lost twelve of his men and was forced to retreat. Worse still, he had to accept that the Missouri was no longer a viable conduit for his trappers. There is no record of the part played by Fitzpatrick in this infamous encounter, but Ashley was clearly impressed with the qualities of leadership and resourcefulness displayed by the Irishman because he made him second in command of a group. That helped Ashley salvage something from the apparent wreckage of his enterprise.

Logically, what could not be accomplished by water had to be achieved by land. Jedediah Smith came to the rescue when he agreed to try and find an overland route to and through the Rockies. Thus began a decade-long odyssey that took Smith into parts of the West that no American had ever traversed. It continued until his death, in 1831, at the hands of a hostile Comanche band in the southwest. Despite being attacked and almost having his head, quite literally, bitten off by a grizzly bear shortly after detaching from a small group of men from the Ashley contingent, Smith was spectacularly successful in his journey into the unknown. For the first months, Fitzpatrick was his able lieutenant.

Ironically, Smith may not actually have made one of the more significant discoveries with which he is credited. There was no more important event in the 1820s in the exploration of the American West than the discovery of South Pass in modern Wyoming. South Pass, a gently rising corridor through the high mountains, was the key that unlocked the Continental Divide and allowed safe passage through the Rockies. Its real significance came twenty years later when it became the conduit for emigrant wagon trains travelling to Oregon and California. The Continental Divide is the spine of the great Rocky Mountains. To the east of the divide, rivers such as the Missouri flow eastwards. Once you cross the divide they flow west. In March 1824, Jedediah Smith's trappers were told about South Pass by Crow Indians. Beyond it, said the Crows, 'you can throw away your traps and kill all the beaver you want with clubs'. In the years that followed, South Pass would be 'trodden into a pathway by the trappers and missionaries, and broadened into a great avenue by the Oregon emigrants, the Mormon colonizers of the Salt Lake Valley and the swarms of California Argonauts of 1849'.[16] Smith went in search of this trapper's nirvana.

However, it is possible that the Smith brigade was actually being led by Fitzpatrick when South Pass was explored by Americans for the first time. (A caveat – some of Astor's employees may already have travelled through it in 1811 or 1812.) Smith, it appears, may have been feeling the continuing effects of his dispute with the bear and, according to some accounts, was incapacitated at the time of the discovery. In 1847, when westward migration was well underway and South Pass was proving invaluable, an article appeared in the 1 March issue of the St Louis *Weekly Reveille* entitled 'Thomas Fitzpatrick – the discoverer of South Pass'.

According to the western poet John Niehardt, who lovingly recreates the era in his historical work *The Splendid Wayfaring*, Smith became aware that some of his troupe's horses would be unfit for the journey, so he decided to rest them, and himself. Accordingly, he divided his forces and sent Fitzpatrick in search of the area described by the Crow.

Jim Bridger's biographer, Stanley Vestal, doesn't even mention Jedediah Smith in the context of South Pass. His version of events has Fitzpatrick in charge of the group, with Bridger as his second in command. The only source he quotes, however, is the St Louis *Weekly Reveille*. The same is more or less true of Niehardt. The latter recounts the Irishman's vision of the significance of their discovery.

> That night by a cheerful fire, Fitzpatrick indulged in what must have seemed extravagant prophecy to many of his companions, telling how ox-drawn wagons would one day be seen trundling up the valleys of the Platte and the Sweetwater to this place, thence to the headwaters of the Columbia and down that river to the sea.[17]

If this monologue did indeed take place, Fitzpatrick's assessment of what he and his men were initiating was a shrewd one. He could not have known at the time that he would act as guide to many of those ox-drawn wagons and, later still, as guarantor and protector to many more in his capacity as an Indian agent.

Beyond South Pass, the Smith/Fitzpatrick group spent the rest of the spring of 1824 on the Green River. They divided in two, Fitzpatrick taking his men northwards, Smith moving south. Beaver was in plentiful supply, but the Irishman's section suffered a severe setback when its horses were stolen by a band of Shosone in late March or early April. Without horses, their chances of making it back across the Continental Divide with their furs were marginal. But Fitzpatrick's luck was in. On the day they started that potentially hazardous journey on foot, they ran into the Indian band that had stolen their mounts and 'repossessed' them. They headed east through South Pass. According to Fitzpatrick's biographer:

> His days of apprenticeship were passed; he had been successful in his first hunt for beaver, and a loss that had seemed irreparable disaster had been overcome by the recovery of his stolen horses. From now on he was to be a leader among men.[18]

After meeting up with Smith on the Sweetwater River in modern Wyoming, Fitzpatrick, accompanied by two companions, then began an epic journey east. He and Smith had decided that it was imperative to get the fruits of their successful 1824 season back to the Missouri. The Irishman constructed a 'bullboat' (which looked like an upturned umbrella) and ventured onto the treacherous Sweetwater – a river whose dangerous rocks and rapids belied its inoffensive name. After a few close shaves Fitzpatrick decided not to risk the valuable cargo any further and 'cached' the furs in a dig near the distinctive Independence Rock. This is a tortoise-shaped hill in Wyoming that would later become a monument for western emigrants on the California and Oregon trails and upon which hundreds (including Fitzpatrick) etched their names. The three men would have dug a hole more than large enough to store the furs in the driest possible soil. This would then have been lined with sticks and dry leaves before being filled in. According to Hiram M. Chittenden, one of the great chroniclers of the Mountain Men, 'the greatest difficulty in the preparation of a cache was its concealment after completion. From the sharp eyes of the sons of the prairies no trace, however minute, would escape.'[19]

After the 'cache' (which would prove successful), Fitzpatrick and his men continued down the Sweetwater and the North Platte in their makeshift craft. They survived the canyons and rapids, the loss of much of their ammunition and their own exhaustion to arrive in Fort Atkinson on the Missouri in September of 1824. From there Fitzpatrick wrote to the financially beleaguered Ashley that the hunt of that year had been a spectacular one. To his intense relief Ashley discovered that actual income, as opposed to mere expenditure, was to be had from the mountain trade. For two more years the politically ambitious St Louis businessman took large profits from the trade he had helped pioneer. He then sold out to Smith and William Sublette and, effectively, launched the Rocky Mountain Fur Company (RMF) – the title itself wasn't used until later but the personnel didn't change much.

The era of the fur trapper had properly begun in 1807 with Manuel Lisa, but that was something of a false start. From 1823 onwards the trade gathered momentum, competition became ever more cut-throat and the men who participated in the enterprises of the Rocky Mountain and American Fur companies became quite simply 'the most significant group of continental explorers ever brought together'.[20] The age of the fur trapper lasted barely twenty years, but it gave birth to a new breed of American, the Mountain Man. These were the men who effectively opened up the West to white (and some black) Americans. Those who survived the harsh life of the mountains were tough, resourceful and lucky. They also relied heavily on a number of Indian tribes, such as the Flatheads and the Nez Perce, while giving others a wide berth. Traditional enemies of the trappers were the Blackfeet and the Arikara (or the 'Rees', as they were nicknamed).

Much of the trappers' activity was in the Montana, Wyoming and Idaho areas along rivers such as the Powder, Bighorn and Yellowstone, which were either tributaries of or adjacent to the upper reaches of the Missouri. Later, attention switched to the far side of the Continental Divide, as the rivers across the Rockies were also discovered to abound in beaver.

Early trappers faced many dangers. Their work was difficult, as the best beaver fur was the lush winter coat of the animal, and this meant spending hours in ice-cold meltwater streams in spring setting traps for beaver and retrieving others that had been caught. Hypothermia, therefore, was a regular occurrence, as was death from wild animal encounters – bears in particular were much feared. There was also little love lost between the American trappers and the officials of the British-run Hudson's Bay Company (HBC). The latter had a number of Indian tribes and groups in its 'sphere of influence' and they were often encouraged to deal violently with American trappers who strayed into British or jointly claimed territory (much of what is now Washington state and northern Oregon was disputed during this entire period).

Various scams and ruses, short of outright theft (and not always short of it either), were employed by either side in attempting to secure as many pelts as possible. One typical instance involved Fitzpatrick and a group of Hudson's Bay Company trappers under their wily and redoubtable leader, Peter Skene Ogden. Ogden liked to make things as difficult as possible for rival trappers, so it was, no doubt, with great pleasure that Fitzpatrick and his men succeeded one night in getting a party of the HBC's Rockway Indians wildly drunk after opening a keg of whiskey. Under the influence of the hooch, the natives were persuaded to trade their pelts to the RMF rather than the Canadians.

Companies such as the RMF, who sent trappers into the wilderness (there were many independent trappers as well), operated in a number of ways. Forts and fixed trading posts were established at strategic points along rivers (often at the confluence of two rivers). Some of these developed into towns; others were taken over by the army. Fort William is an example. It was named after William Sublette, who was with Ashley in 1823 and who became a leading fur-trapping entrepreneur. When it was taken over by the army it became Fort Laramie. (Sublette, along with his Irish partner Robert Campbell, of whom more anon, realised early on that there was more money to be made from supplying fur trappers than from trapping for fur pelts).

From the mid-1820s the fixed forts, by and large, were abandoned as a means of carrying out the trade. Instead, large travelling groups of trappers would be resupplied once a year, in the summer, at a prearranged rendezvous point. The first of these famous gatherings took place, largely by accident, in the summer of 1825 at Henry's Fork on the Green River. Fitzpatrick had guided General Ashley and a supply train into the Green River area in the spring of that year. The general decided to explore while most of his men trapped. The supplies brought to keep the trappers alive were cached along the banks of the river at a site whose location was identified to the trappers. The general moved downriver in a bullboat, indulging his sense of his own significance by his investigation of the countryside around the river. When he returned to the supply cache he found the first informal 'rendezvous' already underway. He was quick to realise the usefulness of such a gathering. Because of the poor quality of the pelt, summer beaver wasn't worth taking, so his men were often idle anyway at that time of year. Summer was also an easier time to get supplies to the trappers. So the 'rendezvous' was born.

Though Ashley had brought them out as employees, many trappers were already, in effect, free agents. But despite their rapid metamorphosis into Mountain Men, they still needed or wanted some of the trappings of civilisation. Guns and ammunition kept them secure and a few shots away from their available food sources. Fripperies such as ribbons and mirrors were important for the only available sexual outlets ('perfect enticements for enchantable squaws') and tobacco and alcohol were the luxuries that offered a pleasurable antidote to the environment. The first rendezvous was 'dry'; thereafter, draconian federal laws about bringing alcohol into Indian lands were bypassed via a loophole which entitled boatmen to a liquor allowance – this despite the fact that the supply trains moved overland rather than up the Missouri. After that they got very 'wet' indeed, becoming an excuse for much drinking, the telling of towering tales, fighting and all-round debauchery.

The second thing that Ashley realised was that there was money to be made from the rendezvous. Furs could be bought from free trappers at a price that would still allow for a profit back in St Louis. Still more impressive sums could be made from selling goods to the trappers. Because of the cost of transporting goods such a huge distance and over such difficult terrain, prices were about ten times higher than in St Louis. Meanwhile, Ashley could sit at home in St Louis and make money while he planned the political campaign that would, ultimately, get him elected to Congress.

Thomas Fitzpatrick was by far the most significant Irishman numbered among the ranks of the Mountain Men, but there were others. One, by the name of Maloney, earns a single mention in the entire trapper literature. By 1826 Jim Bridger was leading his own group of trappers and proving to be something of a despot. He was known for his martial discipline at a time when the military-style structures Ashley had put in place with his early battalions in 1823–4 had relaxed considerably. In one encounter with Blackfoot Indians, Bridger lost his gun. Under fire, as he tried to get his horse under control, he managed to get away from danger but without his weapon.

According to Stanley Vestal, Bridger's biographer, some time later he was inspecting the guns of his trappers and found that one belonging to an Irishman known only as 'Maloney' had not been properly cleaned. Bridger admonished the Irishman. 'What would you do with a gun like that if the Injuns war [*sic*] to charge this camp?' 'Begorra,' the Irishman is said to have replied, 'I would throw it to thim and run, the way you did.'

A rather more consequential figure was Robert Campbell, who first appears in the mountains in the mid-1820s. Campbell, born in 1804, was a native of Aghalane in County Tyrone. He was one of the twelve children of Hugh Campbell, Sr. and Elizabeth Buchanan (her American relatives produced a president of the USA in James Buchanan). The Campbells were a fairly well-to-do family. One chronicler of the period even refers to Robert Campbell as 'an Irish aristocrat'.[21] The family home, Aghalane House, built in 1786, forms part of the Ulster American Folk Park. It was acquired in 1985, as it was about to be demolished, dismantled and then rebuilt in the park near Omagh in County Tyrone. Robert Campbell left Ireland in 1822 and followed his older brother, Hugh Jr. to the USA. Because of failing health (he was tubercular) he had moved west in the mid-1820s to where it was felt the climate suited him better.

In 1870 Campbell dictated a memoir to William Fayel, who had accompanied him on a mission to Fort Laramie to negotiate with the great Lakota chief Red Cloud. Fayel, in a preface, writes that when Campbell arrived in Missouri

> He was an invalid, pale and subject to hemorrhages [*sic*] of the lungs. He saw old Dr. Farrar, who advised him, saying: 'Young man your symptoms are consumptive, and I advise you to go to the Rocky Mountains. I have before sent two or three young men there in your condition, and they came back restored to health and as hearty as bucks.'[22]

When he signed up with Ashley's group, Campbell got into a profession far more hazardous to his general well-being than tuberculosis. He is first seen in the mountains in the spring of 1826 in a group of fifty men led by Ashley and Jedediah Smith.

Campbell, like his fellow Ulsterman Thomas Fitzpatrick, was quickly entrusted with considerable responsibility. He spent a decade in the field (although he remained in the trade for twenty years), during which time he was exposed to the hardships and vagaries of fur trapping. On one occasion, for example, while leading a group of about thirty men moving furs down the basin of the Bighorn and Yellowstone rivers, a member of the party (his name was George Holmes) had the misfortune to be bitten by a rabid wolf. The wolf also bit one of the cattle travelling with the trappers. That night Holmes heard the animal bellowing and ventured the hope that he would not similarly go mad. 'Holmes soon developed hydrophobia and had to be carried across streams in a blanket. He got worse until one day he ripped off his clothes and ran into the wilderness and was never seen again.'[23]

Ashley's last rendezvous was in 1826. He had made a comfortable income from the fur trade without becoming obscenely rich and had political ambitions to pursue. He sold out to Smith, William Sublette and a third partner, David Jackson (after whom the town of Jackson and the Jackson Hole ski resort in Wyoming are named). Fitzpatrick and Campbell remained on as employees (or 'partisans') of the new company. Ashley continued to act as banker for the new partnership and advanced credit for their activities. He was still making money out of the fur trade while leaving most of the risk to others.

Because Ashley's men had been forced to seek out new territory from the outset of their enterprise, they had not faced too much competition from Astor's American Fur Company (AFC). Towards the end of the 1820s that situation changed, with the AFC making a strong bid for control of the trade in what is known as the 'interior West', namely the Wyoming/Idaho area where most of Ashley's successors were trapping. The AFC began an aggressive policy of building trading posts, and agents were sent through the region to entice Indians and free trappers away from Smith, Sublette and Jackson. Maybe they saw the writing on the wall or perhaps they had realised where the real money was to be made in the fur trade, but the three partners sold their interest in 1830. Fitzpatrick and Bridger were among the purchasers. The new entity was the first to actually use the name Rocky Mountain Fur Company.

The other major realignment that took place around this time was the partnership, formed in December 1832, of Sublette and Irishman Robert Campbell. They proved that they had learned the essential truth of the fur trade and were more evident in the business of supply than of trapping. The new partners undertook to transport goods to the annual rendezvous and resupply the trappers of the Rocky Mountain Fur Company. This virtually guaranteed that most of the RMF turnover ended up in their pockets. For four years, before Campbell moved to St Louis to develop his entrepreneurial talents, he and Sublette shared hardship, danger and immense riches. Another family member, Hugh Campbell, Jr., later moved from the east coast to join his younger brother's businesses in St Louis. (After his retirement from the trade, Robert Campbell, in his capacity as an Indian commissioner, was involved with Fitzpatrick in the negotiation of the Fort Laramie Treaty of 1851).

The history of the far West has traditionally been represented as a struggle between the indigenous Native American and the white American invader. It has become a cliché in the twenty-first century to point out that this is an oversimplification. The invaders were not all white and many of the indigenous tribes fought against each other at least as often as they did against the invader. For decades after the Louisiana Purchase, the US Army did not have sufficient resources to establish the sort of garrisons in the West that might have antagonised the Indians. As long as American migrants merely passed through Indian land on their way to Oregon or California, they generally faced little worse from the aboriginal population than occasional petty thievery. It was only when the migrants began to settle the plains and American miners moved into areas of cultural significance to the Indians, such as the Black Hills, that conflict began. By the time that happened, the US Army was more visible and active on the frontier and the trading of atrocities was the norm.

But in the 1820s, that lay in the future. Relations between the fur trappers and the Native Americans were often symbiotic in nature. In some instances there was animosity and latent hostility, but this tended to be confined to certain tribes. Relations between the trappers and the Indian population were largely pragmatic and dictated by a mutual economic interdependence. A crude diplomacy also governed their intercourse. The principle that 'the enemy of my enemy is my friend' was applied. The Blackfoot nation, for example, was antagonistic towards voyageurs because trappers traded with their traditional adversaries.

But even 'friendly' Indians were not entirely trustworthy, especially when it came to the property of whites. Most tribes, given an opportunity by careless trappers, could be relied upon to steal horses or badly cached furs. The mounts were of huge practical value and the furs could be traded as their own. The Crows were the Indian nation best disposed towards the Americans, but that alliance would not be allowed to get in the way of honestly appropriated booty. In 1828 Robert Campbell was trapping along the Wind River in Crow country in modern Wyoming. No trapping or trading had taken place in the region for two years. He made a large cache of beaver pelts that was subsequently found and raided by a Crow war party. The braves returned to the Crow village of which an elder called Long Hair was principal chief. As it happened, when they did so Campbell was enjoying Long Hair's hospitality. When he discovered what had happened the Crow chief threatened his people that he would go on hunger strike until all the pelts were returned. Campbell got most of his cache back.

The relationship between White and Red found one of its expressions in the annual rendezvous. This interaction between the Native American and the interloper, though usually peaceful, was not altogether positive. Although the Indian came to trade as an equal and had something the white man valued (furs), he lost something in the transaction. As historian Bernard de Voto has put it:

> The first step in the white man's exploitation of the Indian, and it was the inevitably fatal step, was to raise his standard of living. From the moment when the Indians first encountered manufactured goods they became increasingly dependent on them. Everything in their way of life now pivoted on the acquisition of goods.[24]

Of course there was a further complicating factor in the always-delicate relationship between the two civilisations – the introduction of the Native American to alcohol. For all practical purposes its importation was banned in the 'interior' West and for all practical purposes that ban was ignored. This was not done specifically to encourage Indians to consume a product to whose effects they were unaccustomed (it was sold primarily to trappers), but that was the upshot of this particular infraction of the law.

Fitzpatrick's aforementioned alcohol-induced coup against the HBC was about as good as it got for the Rocky Mountain Fur Company from 1830 onwards. Increasing competition from Astor's powerful American Fur Company made it difficult for Fitzpatrick and Bridger's RMF to function and survive, never mind turn a profit. Initially the style of the two main rival companies had been quite different. The RMF stuck to the Ashley model: send your own men into the mountains, resupply them once a year and avoid clashes with Indian tribes along the Missouri by taking supplies in and furs out along well-tested overland routes. The AMF, on the other hand, relied heavily on Indian trapping, stuck to the Missouri River for its shipments and introduced steamboats (principally the *Yellowstone* and the *Assiniboin*) onto the upper reaches of the Missouri to reduce the Indian threat and transfer pelts more efficiently.

By the time Fitzpatrick, Bridger and their partners in the RMF had bought out Smith and Sublette, the strategy of their rivals had begun to change. Two new figures became prominent in the trade (one very briefly) and a new philosophy was introduced. One of these representatives of the AMF is the third and final remarkable Irish figure in the western fur trade. His name was Andrew Drips and his involvement in the business predated that of the more celebrated Fitzpatrick, Bridger and Smith and would continue long after their lives had ended or their interest had ceased.

Drips was born in Ireland in 1789.[25] His parents emigrated when he was very young and he was brought up in Pennsylvania. There is some evidence to suggest that the family had once been named Seldon and had moved from Scotland to settle in Northern Ireland. Drips himself moved west in 1817 and by 1822 was a partner in the powerful Missouri Fur Company. In the late 1820s, as many fur trappers did, he married an Otoe Indian woman named Macompemay (she took the English name of Margaret) and they had four children together. He is reputed to have taken quite a few Indian wives, both concurrently and consecutively.

He threw in his lot with the American Fur Company in 1830 and was outfitted by them for a moderately successful expedition into the mountains, remote from the usual AMF sphere of influence. Logistical problems forced him to abandon plans for a repeat expedition the following year. He next appears in Wyoming/Idaho in the summer of

1832 with his long-time partner William Henry Vanderbergh, bound for the rendezvous that year at a place called Pierre's Hole.

The American Fur Company had sent Drips and Vanderbergh into beaver country to get a piece of the RMF action. They didn't know the country so they fastened on the best way to locate good beaver streams – follow Bridger and Fitzpatrick wherever they went and trap on the same streams. Despite the earnest and ingenious efforts of the Rocky Mountain trappers to evade Drips and Vanderbergh, the American Fur Company's men proved surprisingly tenacious. Finally Bridger and Fitzpatrick tried an extreme solution. They simply abandoned all plans of their own to trap and led the employees of the American Fur Company across hundreds of square miles of territory entirely devoid of beaver. Eventually Drips and Vanderbergh realised that they had been duped and were forced to abandon the close pursuit of Bridger and Fitzpatrick.

But time was running out for the RMF. Although the 1831 season had been a good one, the RMF had been unable to get its furs to St Louis. Fitzpatrick spent the winter of 1831 there trying to gather supplies for the following year based largely on a promise – two years of furs in return for resupply of the trappers. William Sublette was the only taker and the bargain he drove was a hard one, hard enough to ensure his subsequent control of Fitzpatrick's enterprise. He agreed to extend credit to the RMF and he, Campbell and Fitzpatrick set out with a supply pack in April 1832. Sometime towards the end of June the Cavan man decided to strike out for the rendezvous on his own, to let his colleagues know that aid was at hand. However, when Sublette and Campbell arrived at Pierre's Hole on 8 July, there was no sign of Fitzpatrick. A search party was sent out to look for him and he was found by two men. According to one account, 'He was hardly recognizable; his body was a mere skeleton; his eyes were sunken; his face was drawn and emaciated, and his hair seemed to have turned white.'[26]

The story he told his rescuers fully accounted for the pale hair colour. On his way to the rendezvous, shortly after crossing South Pass, he had been set upon by a group of hostile Indians, probably Gros Ventres. He was fortunate not to have met the fate of his friend and colleague Jedediah Smith. He headed for the mountains but his horse was not up to the task of outstripping the Indians and he was forced to dismount and follow a mountain path on foot. Before his pursuers could catch up with him he managed to crawl into a hole and close its mouth with leaves and rocks. The Indians contented themselves with the capture of his horse but remained in the general area searching for him fitfully. It was two nights before it was safe for him to continue his journey, in darkness and on foot. Not daring to fire his rifle for fear of attracting more unwelcome attention, like Dubliner Ross Cox before him he survived on berries. On one occasion he was attacked by wolves and was forced to climb a tree to avoid being savaged. He managed to survive only because he came across the carcass of a dead buffalo which had been half eaten by animals, but that only sustained him for a couple of days. He was unable to walk and had given up hope when he was discovered, more dead than alive.

The rendezvous to which he was carried offered him some physical comfort but little consolation of any other kind. The pack train of Sublette and Campbell had arrived before that of the American Fur Company so the latter were now going to have problems with resupply. But the mountains were getting crowded that year. In addition to the two main players, smaller groups under New Englander Nathaniel Wyeth and Captain B.L.E. Bonneville had arrived ready to trap the ever-dwindling stocks of beaver. Bonneville had in his ranks a man by the name of Tom Cain, described in Washington Irving's *The Adventures of Captain Bonneville* as 'a raw Irishman, who officiated as cook, whose various blunders and expedients ... had made him a kind of butt or droll of the camp.' He did little to shake off this status when he decided to participate in a buffalo hunt and proceeded to lose his horse and then himself in the mountains. (It was becoming something of a recurring Irish theme.) Bonneville despatched a party of men to find the hapless Irishman, who was located after about twenty-four hours

> in a complete state of perplexity and amazement. His appearance caused shouts of merriment in the camp – but Tom for once could not join in the mirth raised at his expense: he was completely chapfallen, and apparently cured of the hunting mania for the rest of his life.[27]

Pierre's Hole, the site of the 1832 rendezvous, is located at the headwaters of the Snake River in the shadow of the exquisitely sculpted Teton Mountains on the borders of modern Wyoming and

Idaho. The gathering was augmented by free trappers and friendly Indians of the Nez Perce and Flathead tribes ready to trade furs, mostly with the voyageurs of the Rocky Mountain Company, given the failure of the AFC resupply team to arrive.

By mid-July all the trading that could have taken place had happened and all the liquor that was not going to be removed to the mountains had been consumed on the premises. Small groups began to head into the hills for the autumn trapping. One such party became involved in a dispute with a large party of Indians, variously identified as Blackfoot or Gros Ventre (in some accounts the two different tribes are almost interchangeable), ending in the RMF party retreating under a hail of bullets.

This action triggered a pitched battle in which Indians allied to the Mountain Men also played a pivotal role. Initially the Gros Ventres set up defensive breastworks in a wooded area while the trappers sent to the main Pierre's Hole camp for reinforcements. It was Fitzpatrick who, according to most accounts, took command of the offensive operation. William Sublette and Robert Campbell took part in the attack on the Gros Ventre position, each informing the other of his last will and testament as they crawled towards the Indian defences. The trappers lost one man in the attack and William Sublette was wounded by a bullet in the shoulder. But they were successful in surrounding the Gros Ventre lines. The trappers proposed burning the Indians out of their protective wooden shield but the Nez Perce and Flatheads objected. They reasoned that their enemies could not escape and they did not want any potential plunder incinerated.

With the Gros Ventre totally encircled and besieged, the propaganda war began between the Indians on both sides. As de Voto puts it in colourful fashion:

> Custom required them to taunt and deride one another in their
> own languages and such others as they knew. You shouted that
> your enemy was a boy, a squaw, a homosexual, or that hares or
> other timid animals were in his ancestry, that he and his tribe
> ate dung and carrion and could not fight – and so on.[28]

The Gros Ventre also informed the Nez Perce and Flatheads that reinforcements would arrive soon. Somehow this was mistranslated as a claim that the main rendezvous camp, about eight miles away, was already being attacked by Gros Ventre forces. Dozens of the besieging Indians rode off to do battle with this new threat. But it didn't exist. The camp basked peacefully in the July sunshine. By the time the redeployed force had returned to the main action it was already dark and no further attack would be launched that night. As it happened the battle was over. During the night the Gros Ventre withdrew, leaving ten dead behind them (their total dead was probably closer to thirty). These were quickly scalped by the exultant Nez Perce and Flatheads. The trapper casualties have been variously reported but probably amounted to about five dead and the same number of wounded.

The battle was to make things even more difficult for the rival trapping companies in the mountains that year, but a more significant event for the RMF took place far away from the heat of battle. Fitzpatrick and William Sublette (despite having his arm in a sling) signed an agreement that gave Sublette authority to sell the RMF product of two years in the mountains (169 packs of beaver fur) on the open market and recover the money owed to him and Campbell. The Rocky Mountain Fur Company, by the end of the rendezvous in July 1832, owed Sublette $41,000. The furs would fetch $58,000, but with a transport bill of $7,000, as well as sundry other charges and interest owed on the loan of 1831–2, there was little profit for Fitzpatrick and his partners from two hard but good years in the mountains.

After the Battle of Pierre's Hole it was 'business as usual' for Drips and Vanderbergh. An attempt had been made by Fitzpatrick and Bridger to arrive at an agreement to divide up the beaver country between the Rocky Mountain and the American Fur companies, but Drips had rejected the notion. He preferred to stick to his original plan. Consequently the stalking of Fitzpatrick and Bridger continued. The latter now took a calculated risk: they headed into Blackfoot country in the hope that their deadly enemies would run into Drips and his men before they met up with the forces of the RMF. This is precisely what happened. Vanderbergh was unaccustomed to Indian warfare. He would not live to become any better acquainted with it. He led his men into a Blackfoot ambush and was killed.

If Fitzpatrick and Bridger derived some macabre pleasure from this, they had little time to enjoy it. New tactics employed by the AFC were ruthless and calculated to bring the competition to its knees. This included setting previously friendly Indians against their rivals. In the autumn of 1833 Fitzpatrick, entering a Crow village to seek permission to trap, was set upon and had all his party's horses and pelts stolen. He had no doubt that the previously friendly Crow had been put up to it by Drips and his lieutenants. (The AFC later offered to sell him back the skins!) By this time, according to the first major historian of the trade, Hiram Chittenden:

> unrestrained competition had filled the mountains with rival companies, each using every effort, regardless of honour, to undermine the power of the rest ... it is stated that murders were committed on account of these rivalries. The Indians were utterly demoralised by the strange conduct of the whites towards each other and of course lost all confidence in them. They became more lawless and less industrious, and even the friendly tribes could no longer be depended upon.[29]

The RMF struggled on for two years after the bumper 'crop' of 1831–2 had been sold with little profit for the partners. It gradually became clear that the Rocky Mountain Fur Company did not have the financial resources to compete with the AFC. They might have had an intimate knowledge of the mountain streams that flowed between the riverbanks, which were the natural habitat of the beaver, but the employees of the American Fur Company had a far more detailed knowledge of the cash streams that flowed from the St Louis banks that kept their company in business. When Drips and Vanderbergh had arrived in the Rocky Mountains they had been forced to play a cat-and-mouse game with Fitzpatrick and his partners. Two years on it was clear that, all along, Drips had really been the cat while his fellow Irishman had been the mouse.

By 1834 some sort of economic reality was brought to the western fur trade with the amalgamation of the American Fur Company and the Rocky Mountain Fur Company. But it was a double-edged reality. The merger was not just based on the insanity of cut-throat competition. A worm was eating away at the fur trade from without. A silkworm. The American Fur Company that combined forces with its great rival was no longer owned by John Jacob Astor. He had observed from London that year, 'I very much fear beaver will not sell very well soon unless very fine. It appears that they make hats out of silk in place of beaver.'[30] By the time of the 1834 merger he had already sold out his interests to a group of businessmen from St Louis.

Though Fitzpatrick and Bridger were not pleased to be working for the company exemplified on the frontier by Andrew Drips, they still had their work cut out, despite the merger. The new organisation continued to face stiff competition from the Hudson's Bay Company. The beaver itself was becoming played out. It was more difficult to come by pelts. In an environment where demand continued at 1820s levels this would have led to greater rewards, but prices were falling as well. When supply and demand are both in decline the future is not bright. Little by little the fur trappers were forced to find other livelihoods. The trade continued for many years, first decelerating then declining, but the best years were over by the time the British adventurer William Drummond Stewart brought the artist Alfred Jacob Miller to the rendezvous of 1837 to capture the way of life of the Mountain Men. Miller managed to convey some of the vibrancy of the occasion, but while the trappers may have retained their powers of celebration, by the end of the 1830s they had little enough to be pleased about.

The three Irishmen with the most noteworthy involvement in the trade proved to be highly resourceful in the years of decline. Campbell, as we have seen, became a prosperous St Louis-based businessman. His and Fitzpatrick's subsequent careers will be dealt with in more detail elsewhere. Drips proved to be the most tenacious of the three, in that he stuck to the fur trade for the bulk of his working life. Aside from a brief period when, like Campbell and Fitzpatrick, he became an Indian agent, he remained an employee of the American Fur Company. He died in Kansas City in 1860 at the age of seventy-one.

The era of the fur trapper was colourful but short. The trapping economy relied on a demand for beaver fur that was dependent on the fickleness of fashion. The trapper's lifestyle depended on a solitude and remoteness that was shattered by large-scale westward migration and the irresistible development of the West.

First, in the 1840s, came the emigrants. The trappers were forced out of economic necessity to guide them across the Rockies to California and Oregon. They brought with them the ethos and prejudices of the East. They also carried eastern diseases, which decimated the Native American population and rendered them increasingly restive and mistrustful of whites. The migrants were followed by the miners, with the 'quick buck' mentality and an imperative that showed scant regard for ecology or indigenous culture. If all that wasn't enough, the railroads finished them off entirely. If you could get on a train in New York and make your way across the continent to San Francisco without getting your feet wet, you didn't need an anti-social, pungent throwback to guide you over South Pass. Some tenacious Mountain Men clung to their livelihoods, but they were the remnants of a brief and thoroughly romanticised era in American western history. It had lasted barely twenty years and had produced a short-lived breed of pioneers who had progressed 'from a cock of the walk to a smelly old relic in half a lifetime'.[31]

REEL
THREE

THE DONNER PARTY:
CANNIBALISM ON THE WESTERN TRAIL

Today it's the most heavily populated state of the union. But in the 1830s there was a surprising amount of resistance in the US to the notion of migrating to California. Despite its acknowledged climatic advantages, it had attracted a mere 200 American settlers by 1842.[1] If you wanted to get there, you had two choices. You could travel overland or take a boat. The downside of the former route was that no safe passage had been discovered for migrants over the Sierra Nevada. The alternatives were the scalding deserts to the south or a hazardous and circuitous journey through Oregon Territory. By sea you had the option of death by drowning somewhere near Cape Horn or, if you preferred a shorter maritime journey, you could opt for death by any number of tropical diseases in the malarial jungles of uncanalised Panama. So you had to be a doughty soul to be bothered making the effort.

What made California equally unattractive to prospective migrants was Mexican rule over the entire area. It wasn't until the defeat of the political rulers of California in the Mexican–American War in the late 1840s and the subsequent discovery of gold in the area that the first real immigrant wave began. But throughout that decade the search continued for a route through the vast range of mountains that protected California's eastern flank.

Some trails had been discovered but they were too narrow to accommodate wagons and were only negotiable by pack animals. Wagons were too integral a part of western migration. Leaving them behind was not practicable. They carried the possessions of entire families and any trail that was inaccessible to this particular form of transport was not viable. In 1844 a party of about fifty migrants, led by one Elisha Stevens (sometimes spelled as Stephens) and including County Wexford-born Martin Murphy and his extended family, followed a newly discovered route through Nebraska, Wyoming, Idaho and Nevada which (barely) allowed the passage of wagons. Progress was, to say the least, tortuous. In places the oxen that towed the wagons were unable to get a proper purchase on the trail. In that event, and it was frequent, cargo had to be unloaded and the wagons hoisted over ridges with a combination of pulleys, ropes and manpower. Stevens proved that it was possible to cross the Sierra Nevada; what he failed to demonstrate, however, was that it was any sort of attractive or even tenable proposition. Nonetheless, within two years hundreds of American families were attempting the hazardous trip west. One account puts the number in 1846 at over 500 wagons.[2]

There were those who were prepared to talk up the attractions of California and talk down the perils of undertaking the journey required to get there. One such man was Lanford W. Hastings, who had travelled widely in the West. He had a book to promote, a career as a western guide to launch and a plan. His book was entitled *The Emigrants Guide to Oregon and California*, the career, as a guide, was dependent on the book's success and the plan was nothing short of the annexation of California from Mexico and the installation of one

Lanford W. Hastings as leader of a new colony. To achieve this he had to persuade western migrants to opt for California rather than Oregon. Unfortunately for this twenty-three-year-old entrepreneur, the US federal government later deprived him of the opportunity of a potentially lucrative personal confrontation with Mexico by taking on the task itself in the Mexican–American War.

Hastings toured extensively in the East promoting himself and his book and making the journey west sound suspiciously like a summer ramble along the Appalachian Trail. His descriptions of California's mild and short winters proved a powerful selling point with sturdy Midwestern farmers inured to, but not overly fond of, harsh, brutal and lengthy winters. In addition, they were experiencing one of America's periodic agricultural depressions at the time.

The reality of the journey west was of an arduous and perilous trek. Time became an important element. Time saved meant less risk incurred. Hastings suggested a short cut to California to those who could not afford or were not interested in his services as a guide. Knowledge of this potential alternative route played a crucial role in the westward journey of at least one party. Three families, two of Swiss German origin and one of Irish patriarchy, had begun the westward journey on 14 April 1846 from Springfield, Illinois. They formed the nucleus of what would be known as the Donner party and the basis of what was to become the most tragic and notorious episode in US migrant history.

The tragedy of the Donner party is not the only one that involves major loss of life on a westbound wagon train. In 1856 a group of impoverished Mormons, pushing handcarts because they could not afford wagons, were caught by early snows before they could reach the newly established Salt Lake City. Seventy-seven of them died before the remainder were rescued.[3] But what is especially notable about the Donner party is the circumstances in which they staggered into their plight and the fact that many of the survivors were forced to eat the bodies of the dead in order to make it out of their snowy Californian mountain prison alive.

The Donner party story comes laden with caveats. The truth about the unfortunate group is buried as deeply in flurries of partiality and misinformation as the Donner wagons were in the snows of the California mountains in the winter of 1846. Many of those who survived had to resort to dubious means in order to do so. As a consequence, many first-hand accounts as well as second-hand narratives based on information supplied by participants are so full of special pleading, self-justification, self-aggrandisement and downright lies as to make them approachable only with a pair of rubber gloves and a fistful of salt. A number of twentieth-century publications have merely built on the misinformation and prejudice of the nineteenth-century accounts and, while frequently well researched, often fail to exhibit the levels of even-handedness, scepticism and lack of bias required of the historian.

At the time the journey was undertaken George Donner was sixty-two years of age and his brother Jacob Donner was sixty-five. They were of German descent. Both their wives, Tamsen and Elizabeth, were forty-five. In a colourful but often inaccurate account of their western migration, *Ordeal by Hunger*, written in 1936, George R. Stewart describes George Donner as a prosperous farmer of 'a gentle, charitable spirit'. His prosperity was such that, according to Stewart, he carried a quilt in one of his wagons into which Tamsen Donner had sewn 'bills to the amount, it has been reported, of ten thousand dollars'.[4]

Accompanying the Donners was the family of James Frazier Reed, a sometime miner, merchant, carriage maker and railroad contractor. Reed was Scotch-Irish; he was Protestant-born and from County Armagh. The Reed family had originally come to Ireland from Poland to escape Russian rule and was actually named Reednoski.[5] His family had emigrated from Ireland to Virginia when he was quite young and he himself had moved to Illinois in the 1820s, where he had served in the same militia company as an obscure young lawyer named Abraham Lincoln. Reed was a businessman but one who had suffered some reverses in his more recent business interests. Nonetheless, like the Donners, he was a prosperous man of substance in his own community. These were not desperate, starving emigrants.

Reed might well have been a more appropriate leader of the wagon train than the ageing Donners but his aristocratic manner had a way of alienating those around him. He was described by one of his female fellow travellers as 'an overbearing Irishman'.[6] Although George Donner was the nominal leader of the group, Reed's energy and competence meant that he had huge influence on decision making.

Virginia Reed, twelve years old at the time and Reed's stepdaughter, had been brought up on tales of the ferocity of Plains Indians by her septuagenarian maternal grandmother, Sarah Keyes. Grandma Keyes had an aunt who had been taken captive by Indians in one of the early Virginia settlements. 'When I was told that we were going to California and would have to pass through a region peopled by Indians, you can imagine how I felt,' she wrote. 'But right here let me say that we suffered vastly more from fear of the Indians before starting than we did on the plains.'[7]

The Reed family wagon, or 'prairie schooner' as they were known, was large and luxurious by the standards of western migration. According to Virginia Reed, 'no family ever started across the plains with more provisions or a better outfit for the journey'.[8]

Amongst the Reed retinue (transported by three wagons) were the three children from James Reed's marriage to Margaret Keyes Backenstoe, Patty, James Jr. and Thomas, aged eight, five and three; Virginia Reed, Margaret's daughter from a prior marriage; Grandma Keyes (who left with the group against the appeals of her two sons); three drivers in their twenties, James Smith, Walter Herron and Milt Elliott; and a brother and sister, Eliza and Bayliss Williams, also in their twenties, who worked their passage as servants. Reed himself was forty-six years of age on 14 April 1846 when the party left Springfield, Illinois. His wife was thirty-two and in 'delicate health'.

The two Donner families had six wagons between them. George and Tamsen Donner travelled with five children, Jacob and Elizabeth Donner with seven. An English-born friend, John Denton, aged twenty-eight, travelled with them as well as three drivers, Samuel Shoemaker, Noah James and Hiram Miller.

The party was augmented by a number of other less well-to-do families. The Murphys, as the name suggests, were Irish American and consisted of a widow travelling with seven children, two sons-in-law and a number of grandchildren. William Eddy, an Illinois carriage-maker and a useful man with a rifle, travelled with his wife and two small children, James, aged three, and Margaret, aged one.

Many of the other travellers were more directly European in origin. Patrick Breen and his wife Margaret, who joined the Donner party after Springfield, were Irish Catholics from County Carlow. He was fifty-one; she was eleven years his junior. They had emigrated to

Canada in the 1820s and had moved to the USA in 1834. They finally settled on a farm in Keokuk, Iowa, with their seven children. There Breen was granted US citizenship in 1844. Accompanying the Breens was a family friend, Patrick Dolan, a native of Dublin. In his homespun, non-PC style George Stewart informs us that 'Breen was no mere bog-trotting Paddy of the type which was flooding America in the forties. He could read and write (no common accomplishments for an Irishman of his day) and his diary remains as a unique historical record.'[9] Dolan appears to conform more to Stewart's stereotype of the Irish: he was 'a merry light-hearted Irishman given to being a comedian for the company'.

Breen and Dolan, according to Breen's son John, spent a lot of time discussing California. They would have been aware of the trail blazed by the Stevens–Murphy party in 1844. That group had made the 2,000-mile journey from Iowa to Sacramento without the loss of a single life. Breen had also read John C. Fremont's account of his celebrated 1843–4 exploratory expedition and, according to his grandson Patrick, may also have met the famous scout and Mountain Man Jim Bridger. By this stage of his long life, Old Gabe ran a trading post and settlement with his partner Louis Vasquez on one of the possible routes to California. Listening to some of Bridger's notoriously tall tales, if indeed they did meet, might have fired Breen's imagination further. The sale of his farm meant he could afford to leave Keokuk with three wagons, seven yoke of oxen as well as some cows, horses and (according to John Breen) $500 cash. Dolan travelled in his own wagon.

There were also two German families, the Kesebergs and the Wolfingers, in the 'extended' Donner party, as well as a number of other disparate individuals and families, including an unattached elderly man called Hardcoop, who was originally from Antwerp in Belgium. Altogether the size of the group varied from the low seventies to the high eighties and included, at different times, fourteen family groups and twenty-two unattached individuals.

Depending on where in the USA they were coming from, the journey westward usually took the travellers from St Louis to Independence, Missouri, near the Kansas–Missouri border. From there they would generally traverse a small portion of Kansas as far as the Big Blue River before crossing into the state of Nebraska and thence along the Platte River to Wyoming. Here they would tend to rest for a while in Fort Laramie before heading south to the Wyoming–Utah border, skirting the Great Salt Lake to the north before making for Nevada. Then it was a trek to the daunting Sierra Nevada, which lay between them and the promised warm, luxuriant valleys of California. Provided the Sierra Nevada could be crossed before the onset of winter, the migrant stood a good chance of surviving the trip, though hunger, thirst, Indians, accidents, wild animals or sheer boredom might make it an unpleasant experience.

Virginia Reed's account of the early days of the journey suggests that it was uneventful. However, the Reeds experienced their own personal setback when the entire party was delayed by the high water level in the Big Blue River, which they reached at the end of May. The venerable Sarah Keyes died there and was buried on the trail. At the time of the account written by her granddaughter, the grave of Grandma Keyes still survived.

The Donner party reached Fort Laramie in time to celebrate the Fourth of July. Virginia Reed's account of their stay there and of the resumed journey illustrates the fact that migrant wagon trains faced little threat from indigenous Indian nations. They were far more preoccupied with fighting each other. She wrote of a party of Sioux at Laramie which was on the warpath, 'going to fight the Crows or Blackfeet', and some of whom attempted to trade for her pony, Billy (and for her – they got neither). On 6 July

> the Sioux were several days in passing our caravan, not on account of the length of our train, but because there were so many Sioux. Owing to the fact that our wagons were strung so far apart, they could have massacred our whole party without much loss to themselves. Some of our company became alarmed, and the rifles were cleaned out and loaded to let the warriors see that we were prepared to fight. But the Sioux never showed any inclination to disturb us.[10]

The Native American tribes still viewed the westward migrants more as a curiosity than a threat. That view would change as the great buffalo herds declined due to over-hunting by the wagon trains.

Beyond Fort Laramie the terrain was somewhat tougher. About two weeks after leaving the fort the group came, via the Sweetwater River, to the Rockies and South Pass. This would take them across the

Continental Divide. Shortly thereafter they had a decision to make. On 17 July a lone rider had handed them a letter addressed 'To All California Emigrants Now on the Road'. It told them something they already knew, that the USA was at war with Mexico, and urged them to head for Fort Bridger (which was not on the most travelled route to California) where Lanford Hastings would be waiting to guide them along the short cut he had recently identified.

The choice came down to a right or a left turn. A right-hand turn (the so-called 'Fort Hall Trail') would take the migrants along the route travelled by the Stevens–Murphy party in 1844 and favoured by most of those who had made the journey in 1845. A left turn, striking out almost due west and passing along the southern shore of the Great Salt Lake, meant putting their trust in the adventurer Hastings and hoping that his trail would get them to California sooner. Hastings was enthusiastic about the new route, claiming that it would lead to savings of up to 400 miles on the journey. The members of the Donner party debated and disputed amongst themselves the wisdom of following the untested route that was rumoured to include a forty-mile stretch without water. Most of the 1846 travellers opted for the tried and tested route. James Frazier Reed wanted to try the potential 'Hastings' short cut. Breen and Dolan went with their fellow countryman. The Donners were persuaded. It would be untrue to say that from that point there was no turning back but, as it transpired, the die was cast.

According to most sources, the party members also listened to the advice of Jim Bridger and his partner Vasquez, of whom James Reed had a very high opinion ('two very excellent and accommodating gentlemen … they can be relied upon for doing business honorably and fairly'[11]). Hastings himself was not at the fort. He was escorting another group of sixty travellers on the road ahead but left word to any other migrants to follow after him. Journeying to Fort Bridger did not commit the party absolutely to the Hastings route but the traders advised them to take it, telling Reed that it was 'a fine, level road with plenty of water and grass'.[12] Because most of the migrants travelling west that year were reluctant to follow the Hastings Cutoff, there was the added advantage of the potential reduction in the amount of dust on the trail. It was in the knowledge that Hastings himself was 'out ahead, examining sources for water' and guiding other migrants that the Donner party took its decision. There was some dissension, though: one of the Donners' own drivers, Hiram Miller, left the party, refusing to take the alternative route.

The decision-makers within the Donner party would not have been so sanguine had they been aware that the counsel of Bridger and Vasquez was not entirely disinterested. Both men were partners of Hastings and, like the great advocate of Californian immigration, had a financial stake in attracting travellers to the Hastings Cutoff. Those who took this direction would be obliged to stop at Fort Bridger. However, Bridger and Vasquez may have been even more directly responsible for the disaster that overtook the Donner party. A friend of James Reed's, Edwin Bryant, had scouted ahead and returned to Fort Bridger full of misgivings about the Hastings Cutoff. He had left a letter at the fort warning the Donner party to avoid the cutoff. Either knowing or suspecting what was in the letter, Bridger and Vasquez failed to deliver it. The Donner party choice was made without this vital piece of intelligence from a concerned and informed source ever being included in the decision-making process.

The Donner party members gathered at Fort Bridger consisted of families and individuals with a common goal but it was not an altogether happy camp. There were personality differences and perhaps even covert racial tensions. There is evidence that the three dominant nationalities amongst the party, the Americans, Germans and Irish, tended toward a certain clannishness, only co-operating when necessary. According to George Donner's daughter Leanna, twelve years old in 1846, there was 'a great deal of unnecessary trouble, confusion and jealousy … when they would meet at the campfire morning and evenings'.[13]

Even within the Irish group there may have been tensions. Reed was an imperious, prosperous Americanised Irishman and a Master Mason. Breen and Dolan were Catholic, more recent immigrants and not nearly so well-to-do. Reed's ostentatious wealth, independent ways and often arrogant behaviour had not endeared him to other members of the party and, despite their common nationality, Breen and Dolan had few reasons to be any fonder of him than the Germans and Americans. Later *in extremis* the Breen and Reed families would be drawn closer together but at a time when the journey was simply becoming harder and more frustrating, Reed, with his four teamsters and his cook, might well have been an object of jealousy to his less prosperous compatriots.

Blissfully ignorant of what lay ahead, the Donner party left Fort Bridger on 31 July 1846. The party had grown to seventy-four in number. The group had remained at Fort Bridger for four days. In retrospect that can be seen as another mistake. Though wagons were repaired and stock was rested, the Donner group was well behind most other migrant parties as it set out on a journey that would take it across an almost unbroken landscape of deserts and mountains. Failure to begin that journey until August meant that time was not on the Donner party's side. Nonetheless, according to Virginia Reed:

> without any suspicion of impending disaster, we set off in high spirits. But a few days on the road proved that the cutoff was not as it had been represented. This road had not been well marked or worn smooth by hundreds of wagons as our old trail had been. Instead at times it was hard to find any trace of the cutoff.[14]

Things became even worse when they reached a landmark along the trail called Weber Canyon. A note awaited all travellers who had followed Hastings along his much-vaunted 'cutoff' warning them that the canyon was impassable for all but the smallest wagons. It was written by Hastings himself and included a rough outline of *another* alternative route to the Great Salt Lake through the Wasatch Mountains. The directions were far too imprecise and vague to be followed by travellers unfamiliar with the territory. The Donner party now faced a dilemma. If they turned back, they would not make California that year. If they pressed on, they risked getting lost in the mountains and being overtaken by winter.

While the rest of the group waited, James Reed and two fellow travellers decided to go in search of Hastings himself. When they found him they insisted that he return to guide their party to safety. He refused to accompany them. Instead he retraced some of his steps with them and from a mountain-top tried to show them how they could circumvent Weber Canyon and find the new cutoff trail. Reed then struck out alone for the Donner party wagon train. The Irishman literally 'blazed a trail' to help him guide the travellers out of the impassable canyon. He burnt trees and took note of landmarks in a journey that took him five days.

Reed persuaded the party to follow his trail. In doing so he left himself wide open to discontented mutterings when the way proved almost impenetrable. The days that followed the resumption of their journey were harrowing for the ill-prepared travellers. They were forced to hack their way, painstakingly, through matted undergrowth. Tempers rose in inverse proportion to the amount of ground being covered.

While carving out its own 'trail of tears', the Donner party was joined by another group of hapless migrants who had chosen the Hastings option, a group led by W.F. Graves, which consisted of Graves, his wife, their eight children, his son-in-law Jay Fosdick and a young man called Jay Snyder. The enlarged group now numbered eighty-seven people. In all it took them a month to claw a way through the Wasatch Mountains to the Great Salt Lake. It was supposed to have taken a week. The day they reached Salt Lake Valley, Edwin Bryant, whose letter might have tipped the balance against the Hastings Cutoff, crossed the Sierra Nevada and began his descent into the Sacramento Valley.

Next the party laid in supplies of water and grass that they assumed would be adequate for what they had been told lay ahead. Their next challenge was the Great Salt Desert. This had been represented to them as being forty miles wide. It turned out to be closer to eighty. 'It was a dreary, desolate, alkali waste, and not a living thing could be seen. It seemed as though the hand of death had been laid upon the country,'[15] wrote Virginia Reed. After three days they had little water left and there was still no end of the wasteland in sight.

The tireless James Reed (now effectively the leader of the party, though it was still nominally in the charge of George Donner) scouted ahead in search of water. Finding some he returned to the wagon train and instructed his drivers (ill-advisedly as it transpired) to unhook the oxen from his family's three wagons and drive them towards the water, which was about ten miles away. The other wagons moved on, leaving Reed's family waiting beside their stationary prairie schooners. The Reeds waited for twenty-four hours. When a second night in the open loomed and there was still no sign of the drivers and oxen returning, the family was forced to start walking. They had to find the wagons belonging to the other members of the party or face certain death.

They were fortunate in catching up with the wagon of Jacob Donner, but that was where the Reeds' luck ran out. At daylight James

Reed went off in search of his drivers and stock. Without the latter he had no prospect of rescuing his redundant wagons from the desert. When he was finally reunited with his drivers the news was bad. The only livestock accounted for were one ox and one cow. The rest had stampeded towards the water when they smelled it from far off, outdistancing the drivers. Reed's employees assumed that the animals had been rustled by local Indians and taken into the hills.

Further delay of a week was incurred by the party in a futile search for Reed's animals (though some opportunity was taken to rest as well) until Graves and Breen offered the Reeds two yoke of oxen that allowed them, with their remaining ox and cow, to get one of their wagons moving again. This was filled with the barest of necessities. Surplus food was distributed amongst the other wagons with no guarantee that in emergencies it would be returned. The rest of the family's belongings were buried in a cache in the desert for possible later retrieval. The wagon that Virginia Reed described as 'our two story palace' was abandoned in the desert. Their relatively sumptuous mobile penthouse had given way to a travelling outhouse. The Reed family circumstances had changed dramatically.

At around this time it was realised what effect the lengthy delays (mostly blamed on Reed) were having on the expedition. An inventory of the remaining food was taken and it was concluded that there would not be enough to get the party to California. Someone would have to go ahead and make the journey to Sutter's Fort near Sacramento to purchase provisions. Two members of the party, Charles Stanton and William McCutchen, volunteered to make the journey.

Sutter's Fort was a settlement that had been established by a former Swiss Army officer, Captain John A. Sutter. It was a Californian colony set up with land grants from the Mexican government. Sutter was noted for his generosity toward American travellers who made the journey to California. The members of the Donner party were now dependent on that generosity.

By early October the party was back on the old Fort Hall Trail, the traditional way west. They reached the Humboldt River on 5 October. They were still in Nevada, with more than a hundred miles of rough terrain to cross before they would even reach the High Sierras. Pasture was scarce so the party divided, agreeing to make camp in different places at night in order to eke out the scant grass available to the livestock. The Donners, taking three of Reed's teamsters, went ahead and made good progress. The group following consisted of the Reed, Breen, Graves, Murphy and Eddy families. As if they had not been dogged by sufficient misfortune, an incident took place shortly after the party divided that would greatly impact on the Donner history. Once again it involved James Frazier Reed. There are various accounts of what happened, though ironically there is none from Reed himself, despite his own narrative of the Donner episode written in 1871.

Faced with a steep hill, the decision was taken to yoke as many oxen as possible to the wagons to get them over the top. The Reeds' driver, Milt Elliot, and John Snyder, who drove one of the Graves' wagons, became involved in a dispute about how best to manage the ascent. Snyder insisted on yoking and driving his oxen his way, although it was palpably obvious after a short period that his 'way' was ineffective. Frustrated, losing face and angry, Snyder, according to Virginia Reed's account, began to beat his cattle with the butt end of his whip. James Reed remonstrated with him, reminding him of how utterly dependent they were on the animals.

The scolding served only to further infuriate Snyder, who turned his anger on Reed instead. He struck out at the Irishman, hitting him over the head with his whip and drawing blood. Margaret Reed saw what was happening and ran to intervene. Before she could do so Reed had almost been felled by two more blows. Blood was pouring from the wound in his head. When Margaret Reed stepped in between the two men Snyder either failed to notice or didn't care that a woman had intervened. He continued to lash out, striking Reed's wife. Enraged by this the Irishman whipped out his hunting knife and lunged at Snyder, wounding him in the chest. Only at this point did the other travellers arrive to break up the fight. It was already too late for Snyder.

Virgina Reed, aged only twelve, had witnessed the assault on her mother and stepfather and the stabbing of the Graves' driver.

> My father regretted the act, and wiping the blood from his eyes, he went quickly to the assistance of the dying man. I can see him now as he knelt over Snyder, trying to staunch the wound, while the blood from his gashes, trickling down his face, mingled with that of the dying man. A few moments later, Snyder died.[16]

Reed's regret at the killing of Snyder seems to have been genuine. He and Snyder had been friendly but Reed seems to have had a highly interventionist sense of justice and fair play. His dangerous intrusion on Snyder's rage mirrored an earlier dispute with another member of the party that was to have a profound influence on his immediate future.

Reed had made an enemy of a German named Louis Keseberg. Keseberg had joined the Donner group on the plains. He was in his early thirties and was married to twenty-three-year-old Phillipine Keseberg, whom, according to Virginia Reed, 'he was in the habit of beating until she was black and blue'. Reed had issued a threat of some kind to Keseberg that had resulted in an end to the beatings, but as a result

> he [Keseberg] hated my father and nursed his wrath. When Papa killed Snyder, Keseberg's hour for revenge had come. But how a man like Keseberg, brutal and overbearing, although highly educated, could have had such influence over the company is more than I can understand.[17]

If the malign influence of Keseberg was indeed at play (as the hardly impartial Virginia Reed suspected), then it carried the day. After the burial of Snyder a meeting was convened to decide Reed's fate. Little notice was taken of the Irishman's pleas of self-defence or his insistence that he had been protecting his wife from serious injury. There was talk of lynching Reed, who responded to the threats (again according to his stepdaughter's account) by baring his neck and inviting anyone who wished to step forward and hang him. No one moved. Instead he was banished from the train without food or arms. In that wilderness it was effectively a sentence of death. Reed at first refused to go, claiming that he had done nothing wrong, but was persuaded to leave by his wife after a guarantee was extracted from the remainder of the group that his family would be looked after. She also assured him that, separated from the group and travelling light, he would be able to get to Sutter's Fort and return with provisions for them. Given the distance involved and the fact that he was unarmed and unprovisioned, such a possibility was remote in the extreme.

As regards his stepdaughter's bafflement over how someone like Keseberg could have exerted any influence over the company, the simple explanation may lie in growing disenchantment with Reed and the absence of the Donner wagons. The Donners were several days in advance of Reed's group and played no part in the decision to banish the man who, along with themselves, had been a motive force in initiating the move west in the first place.

Rather than see him fall prey to starvation, wild animals or hostile Indians, Virginia Reed, with the help of Milt Elliot, smuggled a rifle, pistols, ammunition and some food to her father. When Reed caught up with the Donners, one of his former drivers, Walter Herron (or Herren – the different versions of the spelling of the Donner party names is worthy of a minor thesis!), decided to accompany him into the wilderness. Sutter's Fort was 600 miles away and such supplies as they had ran out rapidly. The two men were able to support themselves from game as long as they travelled along the Humboldt River, but for a period of seven days after they left the Humboldt behind them their only food was wild onions. Over a seven-day period they ate only twice. During that time they covered 180 miles, but their rate of advance slowed from thirty-five miles on the first day to seventeen on the last. At one point Herron became delirious with hunger and Reed describes how 'while walking, I found a bean and gave it to him and there never was a road examined more closely for several miles than was this. We found in all *five beans*. Herren's [*sic*] share was three of them.'[18]

On reaching the Bear River valley they came across another party of migrants waiting to be reprovisioned. Herron, unable to continue, elected to stay with them until he had regained his strength. His companion was given some supplies and pushed on. Periodically, Reed would leave letters along the trail for his family to assure them that he was healthy and in good spirits. Eventually, as he outdistanced the following party, these fizzled out.

In his absence, Reed's family did not fare well. Their animals became too weak to draw their remaining wagon. It was abandoned and a sparse few of their belongings were loaded onto other wagons. Their two remaining horses, almost on their last legs, were used to ferry the youngest children, James Jr. and Thomas Reed. The rest of the family members were forced to walk.

Shortly after the departure of Reed, an incident took place that prefigured some of the self-interested and fractious behaviour that would regularly mark the enforced sojourn of the Donner party in the Sierras. One of the older, unaccompanied travellers was a European known only as Hardkoop or Hardcoop, a Belgian from Antwerp aged in his sixties who had owned a farm in Ohio. Finding it difficult to keep up with the group, he had been given a place in Keseberg's wagon. Then the German threw him out. Hardcoop subsequently became separated from the party.

Some members of the group, led by William Eddy, wanted to help the ailing old man and approached Breen and Graves. They were the only others with horses in that section of the travelling party (the Donners being further ahead on the trail). Breen and Graves were asked to go and search for the Belgian. Both declined. Breen reckoned that Hardcoop was already dead, 'that it was impossible, that he must perish'.[19] Graves said he wasn't going to kill his horses searching for an old man who might die anyway. Eddy, Milt Elliot and William Pike then offered to go back on foot, but the rest of the party refused to wait. The three would-be Samaritans could not risk going it alone, without horses, in Indian country and reluctantly abandoned their rescue mission before it began.

Like some sort of judgment for their lack of humanity, within two days all Graves's horses were stolen and Breen had a mare trapped in the mud. When he asked Eddy for help in rescuing the horse, the latter 'referred him to poor Hardcoop, and refused'.[20]

The incident casts the Irishman in a negative light and it was one of many decisions made by Breen over the months to come in which he put his own family first to the detriment of others. The fact was that Breen, unlike many of his fellow travellers, reached the California mountains with his possessions and his stock relatively intact. His family was one of only two to survive without any loss of life. (Reed's was the other.) In order to protect those dear to him, Breen was forced to make decisions that were less than admirable but entirely human.

Breen was regularly faced with such dilemmas and appears to have operated on an ad hoc or pragmatic basis on each occasion. He refused to go back for Hardcoop, reasoning that to do so would only briefly prolong the old man's life at risk to his own. Later Eddy claims that Breen refused him and his family water, which Eddy goes on to allege he took anyway, at gunpoint. That winter, in the extremities of cold and starvation that were to come, Breen refused food to others on the grounds that he had nine mouths to feed. Yet he took in two of the Reed children in mid-December and he and his wife looked after them as if they were their own. As was the case with virtually all the members of the hapless Donner party, Patrick and Margaret Breen displayed generosity and small-mindedness, bravery and weakness, in about equal measure.

On 19 October 1846, while travelling along the Truckee River in the Sierra Nevada foothills, the party was heartened by the return of Stanton from Sutter's Fort with two of Sutter's Indian herdsmen, Luis and Salvador (these are the only names by which they appear to have been known). McCutchen had been too weak to make the return journey but Stanton brought welcome provisions and welcome news for the Reeds. He had met James Reed on the trail, not far from Sutter's Fort. Reed hadn't eaten in three days and the condition of his horse forced him to walk beside rather than ride the animal. Stanton had given him food and a new horse and had no doubt that he would have made it to the fort. He had arranged with Stanton to seek extra supplies and to meet up with the party in the Bear River valley in California.

However, as news went, that was as good as it got. First the Donner party had to get to the Bear River valley. The Sierra Nevada still intervened and the signs were ominous. Although it was only late October, there was already a considerable depth of snow on the trails in the higher reaches of the mountains. This meant that the trails themselves had simply disappeared, making passage difficult. In spite of this the party decided to let the cattle graze for five days and regain some condition. Added to the week spent chasing Reed's lost stock, it meant a delay of twelve days. Twelve days that might well have seen the Donner party become just another footnote in migrant history, as well remembered as the Harlan party that had preceded them (guided by Lanford Hastings) or the countless wagon trains that would follow them.

On 25 October the party moved off towards the summit, travelling in three groups to Truckee Lake (since renamed, for reasons that will become apparent, Donner Lake). Stanton, who had already made the trip, reckoned it would take five days to get through the summit pass. From the outset, however, the wagons of the two Donner families were having trouble keeping up. By 28 October they had made it as far as Alder Creek, a few miles from Truckee Lake, before an axle broke on one of George Donner's wagons. While they tried to fix the axle it began to snow. Further up the mountain, snow was falling more heavily. Three feet fell that night and there was no going forwards or backwards. The entire Donner party was stranded in the Sierra Nevada.

The distance from Donner Lake to the summit of the Sierra Nevada is about two miles as the crow flies and not much more than three along the wagon route. In decent conditions an averagely healthy person could walk the path in an hour. It is a pleasant trek amid tall pines. But that winter it became a ghastly prison for the Donner party.

Virginia Reed wrote about the night spent on the mountainside that sealed the fate of the Donner party.

> That night the dreaded snow came. The air was so full of great feathery flakes that one could see objects only a few feet away. The Indians knew we were doomed, and one of them wrapped his blanket about him and stood under a tree all night. We children slept on our cold bed of snow with a white mantle falling over us so thickly that every few moments my mother would have to shake the shawl over us to keep us from being buried. In the morning, the snow lay deep everywhere. We were snowbound in the Sierras.[21]

Two years previously the Stevens–Murphy party had come to this point in far better physical and mental condition than the Donner group and had been forced to leave more than half their wagons behind. Three members of the group remained guarding the six wagons and built a cabin by Truckee Lake that still stood in October 1846. This was immediately occupied by the Breen family. Others started to build two new cabins near the Breens. For their part, the Donner families, still situated about five miles down the trail at Alder Creek, relied on tents to ride out the storm. The entire party hoped (and some prayed) for a let-up in the weather.

Meanwhile, Reed had reached Sutter's Fort, where the ever-generous Sutter had offered him more provisions, twenty-six horses and a number of Indians. The Irishman, accompanied by the greatly recovered William McCutchen, set off to, as he thought, rendezvous with the Donner party in the Bear River valley. Within two days of leaving the fort in late October, it began to rain heavily. However, what was falling as rain on the approach to the Sierra Nevada from the western side was clearly falling as snow on the upper slopes of the mountains themselves. Reed must have known how difficult passage across the slopes was going to be for the Donner company. When Reed's own party reached the Bear River valley there was no one waiting for them.

The Irishman and McCutchen opted to push on towards the higher slopes, hoping to link up with their party. When this expedition brought them to snow thirty inches in depth they were quickly deserted by the Indians but they pushed on with seventeen horses. Next to give up were the wretched animals. The two men attempted to continue on foot but, lacking snowshoes, sank continually and were forced to abandon their journey less than twelve miles from the mountain summit.

Reed retreated to Johnson's Ranch. This was the first settlement that California-bound travellers reached after traversing the Sierra Nevada. Here he was advised that, winter having set in, it would be impossible to reach his family. He returned to Sutter's Fort to seek help but was advised against a rescue attempt until February at the earliest. Furthermore, every available male was fighting in the rebellion against Mexican rule that had begun while the Donner party was on the trail. It was suggested that if he wanted help he was going to have to offer his own first. Reed duly enlisted in a company of riflemen and fought in the Battle of Santa Clara shortly afterwards. It was little more than a skirmish in which the American forces prevailed but it effectively ended hostilities in the area. Reed's unit returned to San Francisco and disbanded.

Only then was Reed able to get minds focused on the plight of the migrants. Money was raised in San Francisco to despatch a supply launch commanded by a naval officer, Selim Woodworth, to the mouth of the Feather River, the nearest navigable point to the Donner encampment. The rest of the relief fund was used by Reed to hire men and buy horses to meet the launch at the river and transfer the food to the overland rescue party.

And the food would be badly needed. Many of the families (the Reeds and the Eddys in particular) had reached Truckee Lake with very little left. Winter meant that there was little game remaining in the highlands, though William Eddy (by his own account) managed to shoot a grizzly bear that kept his family going for a while. The shortage of livestock was exacerbated by the storms. Many of the cattle strayed and died but their bodies were quickly covered by the snow so their meat was lost to the stranded travellers. Little by little, the sixty or so people in the camp became debilitated by malnourishment. In her account Virginia Reed wrote that

> the lack of food made us weak. Some could scarcely walk, and the men had little strength to procure wood. Men, women, and children dragged themselves through the snow from one cabin to another in order to barter for food or other supplies. Little children cried with hunger, and mothers cried because they had so little to give their children.[22]

Within weeks malnourishment would give way to outright starvation.

If the Donner party hoped that the winter weather would let up sufficiently to allow for any sort of escape attempt, they were to be disappointed. Every week a new storm would deposit ever-greater volumes of snow, making movement impossible. Virginia Reed remembers some of them as lasting up to ten days.

> The snowfall was so heavy on occasion that we had to shovel out snow from our fireplaces before a fire could be made in the morning. When the storms were at their worst, we dared not leave our shelters, and we had to cut chips from the walls of our log cabins for fuel.[23]

The only contemporaneous diary of events and conditions at Donner Lake was kept by Carlow man Patrick Breen. He began his record on 20 November. It is a remarkable document in that it was compiled by a man of limited education in unbelievably adverse circumstances. Breen had the energy and self-discipline to maintain an account of the privations of the party while he shared in those same privations. Between 20 November, three weeks after their arrival at what was then called Truckee Lake, and the end of February 1847, there are sixty entries out of a possible 102. Most are only a line or two; some are more detailed. It is not a florid, revealing testament. It is matter-of-fact, almost devoid of insight and stylistically unadorned. It is a sparse famine diary, recorded by Breen at a time when, ironically, his fellow-countrymen were trapped in similar privation in Ireland, albeit without experiencing the extremes of cold to which the Carlow man's family was being subjected.

Breen only aspires to the metaphysical in his piety (or pietism).

> Dec.31 Last of the year; may we with the help of God spend the coming year better than we have the past, which we propose to do if it be the will of the Almighty to deliver us from our present dreadful situation. Amen.

The following day his entry is in the same vein.

> Jan 1, 1847 We pray the God of mercy to deliver us from our present calamity, if it be his Holy will.[24]

It had not been His holy will to deliver Bayliss Williams or William Pike who, in December, had become the first Donner Lake fatalities. Pike died as a result of a shooting accident while, ominously, Williams, one of the Reeds' hired men, died of malnutrition.

Two unsuccessful attempts to escape on foot (through what would soon be named Donner Pass) were made on 12 and 21 November. By mid-December a party of seventeen, twelve men and five women, wearing improvised snowshoes, were ready for another attempt to escape the Donner camp. Included in the party were Stanton and the two Indians from Sutter's Fort, Luis and Salvador; the energetic and resourceful William Eddy; Sarah and William Foster; Harriet Pike and her brothers Lemuel and William Murphy (aged twelve and ten); Franklin Graves, his daughters Mary and Sarah and Sarah's husband Jay Fosdick; a Mexican known only as Antonio; Karl Burger, a German and one of Keseberg's teamsters; and Mrs McCutchen and Dubliner Patrick Dolan. Dolan, according to later accounts from members of the Breen family, joined the Snowshoe party so that there would be one less mouth to feed in the Breen cabin. He left his dried beef to the Breens, thus increasing their survival chances.

After five days the group had managed to travel upwards through Donner Pass and had then made about twenty-five miles towards safety in twelve-foot snowdrifts. The first casualty was the selfless Stanton. Although he had no dependants amongst the members of the party, he had left the security of Sutter's Fort to rejoin his travelling companions in the mountains along with Luis and Salvador. He must have wondered why he had bothered when he found himself at Donner Lake without food and forced to beg from the starving emigrants. Patrick Breen recorded in his very pithy and matter-of-fact journal on

9 December (with his usual pragmatism and customary lack of generosity), 'Stanton trying to make a raise of some [beef] for his Indians and self ... not likely to get much.'[25]

Stanton had been finding it more and more difficult to keep up with the rest of the party. On the morning of the sixth day, as the group made ready to leave their camp, Stanton showed no inclination to move. He was suffering from snow-blindness as well as exhaustion and starvation. Mary Graves asked was he coming with them and he replied, 'Yes, I am coming soon.' But Stanton had no intention of moving. He had made up his mind to die there and his assurance to Mary Graves was designed to relieve the party of the burden of having to make any decision to abandon him. His sacrifice was not unlike the well-publicised act of bravery on the part of Captain Oates at the end of the ill-fated Scott Antarctic expedition in 1912.

The others continued. They used up the last of their provisions that day, and that night Stanton simply did not arrive at camp.

For two days they plodded on through the snow without food. Unknown to themselves, and without the guidance of Stanton, who had made the journey twice, they had already taken a wrong turning that would ensure they didn't reach their medium-term destination of Bear River valley, where they had hoped to get some relief before moving on to Johnson's Ranch. On the night of 23 December 1846, trapped by a fierce storm, they spoke for the first time about steps that might be taken to ensure the survival of some. According to contemporary accounts, it was the Dubliner Patrick Dolan who first raised the subject that was on more than one mind. He proposed drawing lots, killing the unfortunate loser and eating his or her remains. William Foster opposed the measure and in the absence of unanimity it was dropped. But a Rubicon had been crossed: the most compelling human taboo of all had been discussed openly.

During the storm, which lasted two days, four more members of the party died. The first to go was Antonio. Then Graves, a sixty-year-old man who had done well to last as long as he had, followed soon after. Patrick Dolan, the Dubliner who had wished to make his home in the American West, was next. One account has the Irishman losing his mind shortly before his death, pulling off his boots and clothing and having to be restrained. Finally, the youngest member of the party, Lemuel Murphy, gave up the ghost.

With these deaths, and with the presence of corpses among the group, the time for honouring cultural taboos had now passed. Dolan, who had been the first to suggest the consumption of human flesh, was, appropriately enough, the first to be eaten. Though not everyone had the stomach for it. William Eddy and the two Indians refused to cannibalise the Irishman's body. The others cut the flesh from his arms and legs, roasted it over an open fire and ate it.

They remained in that particular camp for three more days, eating the bodies around them. On 30 December the ten who remained alive set off again. They were in bad shape. They were lost, without any food source (unless someone else died), and they had also managed to lose the head of the axe that had provided them with fuel for their night-time fires. Furthermore, their snowshoes were beginning to fall apart and their feet were bleeding from the beginnings of frostbite.

For the next four days, the twenty-three-year-old Jay Fosdick, son-in-law of Franklin Graves, proved to be the main encumbrance. He held the group back to the point where on the fourth day they covered only two miles. Clearly he would not last long. Unless, suggested Foster, an Indian was sacrificed to save the life of a white man. The proposal to kill and eat the two Native Americans was made covertly to Eddy. Eddy, ever the hero and the conscience of his own narrative (he subsequently left a detailed account with a Californian journalist, J. Quinn Thornton), was having none of it. Instead he warned Luis and Salvador what was brewing and recommended flight. They didn't stand upon the order of their departure. Fifteen had now become eight and one of those was on his last legs. Fosdick died that night.

The two men (Foster and Eddy) and the five women pressed on. The next chapter of their adventure was an act of brutality. The remains of the Snowshoe party came across their erstwhile guides Luis and Salvador on the trail. Both men were in a bad way (having refused to eat human flesh) and were reduced to dragging themselves along the ground. This time Foster wasn't going to be denied and on this occasion Eddy didn't intervene, rationalising that the two Indians would not survive much longer anyway. He averted his eyes while Foster despatched Sutter's two employees.

On 17 January, after a demoralising and utterly debilitating thirty-three days exposed to the elements and racked with hunger and indescribable fatigue, the seven survivors of the Snowshoe party staggered, more dead than alive, into an Indian village where they were fed with acorn bread. Eddy was unable to keep the food down and survived by eating grass instead. The other six were unable to move any further but Eddy, spurred on by the knowledge that his wife and child were still trapped in Donner camp, dragged himself (or was dragged by friendly Indians) to Johnson's Ranch. The settlers there quickly brought in the six other survivors and the epic 'Snowshoe' journey was over. The escape attempt had been a long shot and for some members of the party it had proved fatal. Ironically all of them were male. None of the female members of the group, although they experienced the same suffering and privation as the men, died en route to their objective, Johnson's Ranch.

Back in the Donner camp, unaware that her husband had already tried and failed to reach his family, Margaret Reed managed to hoard a few dried apples, some beans, the stomach of an ox and a small piece of bacon for Christmas Day. The effect of this comparative feast was not just to sustain the dwindling strength of the Reed family but to raise morale. Virginia Reed wrote that 'the relief of that one bright day, ending weeks of misery, was a great blessing, and whenever I sit down to a Christmas dinner now, my thoughts go back to that special day at Donner Lake'.[26] But the meal served up on that day was the exception.

In early January 1847, Margaret Reed decided that there was no hope of survival without help and there was no sign of that on the horizon. She elected to make an attempt to cross the mountains. Leaving her three smallest children with the Breen, Keseberg and Graves families, she set off on 4 January with the faithful Milt Elliot, the family's hired girl, twenty-five-year-old Eliza Williams, sister of the late Bayliss Williams, and twelve-year-old Virginia. Milt Elliot wore snowshoes and the three women followed in his footsteps. Their only guide was a compass. Within three days, unable to find any landmarks to guide them and with toes and hands close to frostbite, they were forced to turn back. It turned out to be a wise decision. Shortly after their return one of the worst storms of the winter began. Had they continued their attempted escape they would certainly have died on the mountains.

But the Reeds were now faced with a stark choice. Their only food source was the rawhide covering the roof of their shelter, obtained when they had butchered their cattle. They had no option but to tear down the hide roof and boil the skins, producing an unappetising but edible glue-like liquid. They were now left, not halfway through the winter, with no roof over their heads. Patrick Breen took pity on their plight and took them in. Virginia Reed wrote that Margaret Breen saved her life in the months that followed 'by slipping me a piece of meat now and then and making sure that I ate it'.[27] The Breens still had supplies of meat because, anticipating a lengthy imprisonment at Donner Lake, they had begun by eating their hides rather than their meat.

Patrick Breen's diary continued to itemise the daily hardships in his very basic, unsentimental style. It recorded the deaths and the further degeneration in the spirit of co-operation that had already been eroded on the trail west. On 10 February Breen refers to the death of Milt Elliot at the Murphy family cabin.

> Mrs Reid [sic] went there this morning to see after his effects … all are entirely out of meat but a little we have our hides are nearly all eaten up but with Gods help spring will soon smile upon us.[28]

It was probably Breen's religious faith that allowed him to retain a certain amount of optimism. But the death of Elliot was a huge blow to the family of Armagh man James Frazier Reed. Virginia Reed helped to bury Elliot.

> Mother and I dragged him out of the cabin to bury him. Beginning at his shoes, I patted the pure white snow down softly until I reached the collar on his jacket. Poor Milt! It was hard to cover his face from sight forever, for with his death, our best friend was gone.[29]

But some relief was at hand. The arrival of the Snowshoe-party survivors confirmed the location of the Donner party. Volunteer rescuers were called for at a rate of three dollars a day. On 5 February a party of fifteen men left Johnson's Ranch heading for Mule Springs, Bear Valley, the pass above Truckee Lake and, it was hoped, Truckee Lake itself where, it was now known, the settlers were held captive by the winter. This party, led by one Aquila Glover, who had met the Donners on the California trail, is known as the 'First Relief'.

Simultaneously James Frazier Reed and William McCutchen were organising a second relief effort.

Glover's party (depleted by defections) reached the settlers' camp on 18 February 1847, with supplies for some and the promise of rescue for others. 'Are you men from California, or do you come from heaven?' was reportedly how one of the physically and mentally exhausted migrants greeted Glover's team.[30] Glover had left a number of food caches along the route and was confident that he could handle a group of twenty-three of those fittest to travel. Among the migrants taken out by the First Relief were six from Alder Creek, Edward and Simon Breen and Margaret Reed and her four children. Almost straight away the party's numbers were reduced by two, when Margaret Reed realised that two of her children, Patty and Tommy, would not survive the journey. With natural maternal reluctance she allowed them to be sent back to the Breens who were, by all accounts, not unduly pleased to see them. Before doing so she extracted a promise from Glover that he would return to rescue the two children.

The First Relief suffered a number of vicissitudes (discovering at least one of the food caches had been half consumed by animals) but lost only three of the twenty-one migrants in its charge – a minor miracle when their condition before setting out is taken into consideration. Along the route they met the members of the Second Relief, led by Reed and McCutchen. After many months James Frazier Reed was reunited with his wife and two of his children. He still had a powerful incentive, however, to continue his journey into the mountains. His other two children were back in the Breen cabin at Donner Lake, where straitened circumstances were becoming increasingly desperate.

On the far side of the crest of the High Sierras, after three months of privation, the remaining inhabitants of the cabins and shelters at Alder Creek and Truckee Lake were beginning to think the unthinkable, just as the Snowshoe party had two months before. Their minds were already beginning to dwell on the sustenance that might be provided by the bodies of those who had already died. On 26 February Breen wrote in his diary:

> Mrs. Murphy said here yesterday that [she] thought she would commence on Milt and eat him. I don't think she has done so yet, it is distressing. The Donnos [*sic*] told the California folks

[The First Relief] that they would commence to eat the dead people 4 days ago, if they did not succeed that day or next in finding their cattle then under ten or twelve feet of snow & did not know the spot or near it, I suppose they have done so ere this time.[31]

Mrs Murphy was probably as good as her word. On 1 March an advance party from the Second Relief reached the camp and found that the remains of Milt Elliot had indeed been consumed. At Alder Creek Jacob Donner and Shoemaker, the teamster, who had been among the early deaths, were similarly consumed. They were not to be the last victims of cannibalism.

On 1 March Patrick Breen, in his last diary entry, recorded the arrival of Reed and his group. 'Froze hard last night there has 10 men arrived this morning from bear valley with provisions we are to start in two or three days'.[32] With that he put away his diary and no more is heard from him. The single-most remarkable document to emerge from the Donner party travails ends with the words 'they say the snow will be here untill June'.

Breen's diary is not discursive and betrays relatively little emotion, despite the catastrophic nature of the events it describes. However it does, by constant repetition of the diurnal misery, chronicle the deteri-oration in the conditions, the general health and the morale of the members of the party and their descent into hunger and despair. It is, understandably, self-serving, at least by omission. There is no reference to any of the acts of neglect or unkindness of which Breen has been accused by other members of the party. He records the younger Reed children being left behind during the December breakout but mentions no unwillingness on his part or on that of his wife to take them back. While ignoring the beam in his own eye, he does use the pages of his diary to point out the mote in others'. He cites Mrs Murphy for uncharitable behaviour towards the Reed family. 'Feb 15 … Mrs. Murphy refused to give Mrs. Reed any hides; put Sutter's pack hides in her shanty and would not let her have them.'[33]

In general Breen sticks, turgidly, to the facts. He records the weather conditions on almost a daily basis and such events as took place in the camp. As the mortality rate begins to climb, deaths are rarely commented upon. This gives the diary a somewhat clinical and detached air.

On the day the diary ended, Patty Reed was sitting on the snow that topped the Breen's cabin when she saw her father in the distance. She had enough strength to begin to run towards him but was so weak that she fell before he could get to her. When James Reed reached her, according to one account, she began babbling, asking after her mother and Mr Glover, the man who had made the promise to rescue her (Reed had met Glover and relieved him of his pledge). Reed was more concerned about the fate of his young son. When Patty assured him that Tommy was still alive he descended through a snow hole into the Breen's cabin. The boy was skeletally thin and on the verge of delirium. He did not recognise his father and had to be assured by his sister that they were safe.

Leaving bread for his own and Breen's children, Reed went to Keseburg's cabin, where he found the occupants (including two children) in dire straits. Reed washed the children and did the same for Keseburg himself, despite their past history. It was only after feeding and washing the inhabitants of the cabin that he commented on the first signs of cannibalism: 'the mutilated body of a friend, having nearly all the flesh torn away, was seen at the door – the head and face remaining entire. Half consumed limbs were seen in trunks. Bones were scattered about.'[34] They found further evidence of cannibalism in the Donner camp. 'Around the fire were hair, bones, skulls, and the fragments of half consumed limbs.' The members of the family of George Donner were consuming their last available body, that of his own brother Jacob:

> The children were sitting upon a log, with their faces stained with blood, devouring a half roasted liver and heart of the father [Jacob Donner] unconscious of the approach of the men … Mrs. Jacob Donner was in a helpless condition, without any thing whatever except the body of her husband, and she declared that she would die before she would eat of this.[35]

Reed and the other members of the Second Relief picked out seventeen of the remaining emigrants as strong enough to be taken to safety. Among those left behind were Tamsen Donner and her dying husband George at Alder Creek and Keseberg, Lavina Murphy and three Donner children at Donner Lake. The remainder of the Breen family were to accompany the Second Relief, although the eldest child,

John, aged fifteen, was extremely weak. Breen, in order to keep spirits up, brought a fiddle with him that he played in camp at night.

The Second Relief, which set out from Donner Lake on 3 March, had a far more difficult time of it than had Glover's party. Their first food cache had been robbed by animals and on 5 March they were caught in a storm which lasted for two nights. They were forced to seek shelter in what would become known in Donner lore as 'Starved Camp'. In the course of the storm the campfire they had lit almost went out. Had it done so few, if any, of the group would have survived. Only the strength and courage of McCutchen kept it alight (Reed was suffering from snow-blindness). Despite this, the following morning little Isaac Donner was found dead. He had been lying between his sister Mary and Patty Reed. When the storm abated Reed wanted to press on with the entire party. But Patrick Breen made his own judgement. He concluded that he and most of the members of his family were too far gone to continue. Another relief party was known to be on the way and Breen decided that his family's best chance was to wait until it arrived with food. Reed remonstrated with him. In his own account of the Donner debacle, written in 1871 for the *Pacific Rural Press*, the Northern Irishman wrote that Breen

> stated that if he had to die, he would rather die in camp than on the way. A strange proceeding of Mr. Breen, when he and his family were all strong enough to travel ... I asked some of the men standing by to witness, that I then told Mr. Breen, 'that if his family died, their blood be upon his head, and not ours.'[36]

The confrontation is a fascinating one. The Protestant, aristocratic Northerner, the courageous and resourceful Reed, exercising his inalienable right to lead, versus the simple, Catholic Southerner doggedly clinging to his right not to be led. Two Irishmen meeting in a battle of wills in the American West. Being the better judge of his own and his family's condition, Breen stuck to his guns. He was not alone. Mrs Graves, with four of her children, also opted to remain behind. Young Mary Donner was left with them, as was the body of Isaac Donner. Reed allowed them three days' supply of fuel but no food and continued on the trail towards the security of Johnson's Ranch.

The Breen and the Graves families settled in for an indefinite wait at Starved Camp. Margaret Breen had managed to hold on to some seeds, a small amount of tea and coffee and a one-pound ball of sugar. She needed most of the latter to save her son James from lapsing into a fatal coma. Mrs Graves and her five-year-old son Franklin succumbed quickly. They died the first night after the rescue party left. Patrick Breen, who, up to this point, had resisted any urge towards cannibalism, now realised that there was no alternative. The bodies of Isaac Donner and Franklin Ward were eaten first and then the body of Mrs Graves was consumed.

In the meantime, William Eddy and William Foster, the two male survivors of the Snowshoe party, were heading back to the mountains in the hope that their children were still alive (in fact they were already too late). They teamed up with a group that had been operating in support of Reed's rescue attempt to form the Third Relief party. Before they got near Donner Lake they came across the survivors of Starved Camp, who had waited for a week to be rescued. Eddy and Foster left it to three rescuers to get them back down the mountain. Two of those three, in a display of self-interest prompted by the offer of a bonus of fifty dollars to anyone who would carry to safety a child not his own, took one child each (baby Elizabeth Graves and Mary Donner). The third man, variously named as John Stark or John Starks, was more sympathetic. Stark was a giant of a man with great physical strength. He was to need all of it in order to convey the Breens to safety. Years later James Breen, who had almost died at Starved Camp, wrote of Stark:

> to his great bodily strength, and unexcelled courage, myself and others owe their lives. There was probably no other man in California at that time, who had the intelligence, determination, and what was absolutely necessary in that emergency, the immense physical powers of John Stark.[37]

Miraculously the seven members of the Breen family, as well as Nancy and Jonathan Graves, were brought to safety by a single guide.

For Eddy and Foster, however, there was to be no comfort. By the time they got to the camp their children had already died and been eaten. Keseberg, one of the last survivors left at the lake camp, was either demented or completely insane by this time because, according to some accounts, he quite openly boasted to William Eddy that he had eaten his baby son. Keseberg was left to his own devices. Eddy had, by his own account, been tempted to kill him on the spot (later he actually tried to but was prevented from doing so), therefore he was not disposed to take any risks on the German's behalf. For his part, Keseberg showed no inclination to move.

There now enters into the story the mysterious figure of William Fallon (or O'Fallon or Fellun), leader of the Fourth Relief. He was a Mountain Man who had earned the nickname 'Le Gros'. One account describes him as 'an Irishman of enormous bulk, and one of the most dangerous breed of Rocky Mountain trappers'. As was the case with a number of other would-be rescuers, Fallon's group, and its leader in particular, appear to have been motivated as much by the desire for personal enrichment as by any altruistic inclinations. Much to their surprise, they came across a survivor, the tenacious Keseberg.

Fallon published his own account of the rescue attempt in the *California Star* on 5 June 1847. It was, in all likelihood, at least partially ghost-written. As far as he was concerned, this final relief effort was designed to bring out any remaining survivors and to secure the property of the living and the dead.

> April 17. – Reached the cabins between 12 and 1 o'clock. Expected to find some of the sufferers alive, Mrs Donner and Kiesburg [*sic*], in particular. Entered the cabins and a horrible scene presented itself – human bodies terribly mutilated, legs, arms, and skulls, scattered in every direction. One body, supposed to be that of Mrs. Eddy, lay near the entrance, the limbs severed off, and a frightful gash in the skull. The flesh was nearly consumed from the bones, and a painful stillness pervaded the place.

After chasing off three Indians who were concealed nearby, some of the members of the Fourth Rescue journeyed to the camp of Jacob Donner at Alder Lake. There, according to Fallon:

> At the mouth of the tent stood a large iron kettle, filled with human flesh, cut up. It was from the body of George Donner. The head had been split open, and the brains extracted therefrom, and, to the appearance, he had not been long dead – not over three or four days, at the most ... [They] discovered Kiesburg [*sic*] lying down amidst the human bones, and beside him a large pan full of fresh liver and lights ... In the cabin with Kiesburg were found two kettles of human blood, in all

supposed to be over one gallon. Rhodes [one of Fallon's companions] asked him where he had got the blood. He answered 'There is blood in dead bodies'. They asked him numerous questions, but he appeared embarrassed, and equivocated a great deal.[38]

Fallon's implication was that Keseberg had killed some, or all, of the last survivors in order to feed himself.

Fallon and his men started for the Bear River on 21 April, bringing Keseberg with them. Their accounts of the Fourth Relief would lead to the German receiving a very bad press and living for the rest of his life with the stigma of having killed to cannibalise. There is no evidence that he actually did commit murder – he certainly strenuously denied it and later won a defamation action against one of the rescuers who made such a claim. (Though in common with a number of controversial verdicts in favour of the plaintiff in the twentieth century, he received only $1 in compensation.)

Keseberg was the last member of the ill-fated Donner group to emerge alive from the mountains. Altogether eighty-seven people had made up the party that had crossed the Wasatch Mountains. They had later been augmented by the two Indians from Sutter's Fort. Of those eighty-nine, a total of forty-one died on the trail or in the Sierra Nevada. Interestingly, only 42 per cent of the males survived while 74 per cent of the females made it to California.

The only two families that achieved a 100 per cent survival rate were those belonging to the two Irishmen, Reed and Breen. After the events of the winter of 1846–7, they had no occasion to continue their harrowing acquaintance. Like the other survivors of the Donner party, they were quickly absorbed into Californian society. The Reeds settled in San Jose, the Breens in San Juan Bautista, forty-five miles away. Reed, with money he had managed to take with him when he was banished from the wagon train, bought a large tract of land near what was then the 'village' of San Jose. When gold fever struck the state he became a forty-niner and further increased his wealth. He was said to have spent $20,000 in a campaign to have San Jose named as capital of the state. This can be seen as an investment rather than as altruistic benevolence. He owned a lot of land around San Jose and would have benefited had the town been named capital of California. Mrs Reed died in 1861 while James Frazier Reed survived until 1874.

Many of the families and individuals who survived the ordeal at Donner Lake in the winter of 1846–7 were dogged thereafter by stories of cannibalism, many of which were exaggerated in the telling. Some defended themselves in print; one (Keseberg) went to law to preserve his reputation; some denied to themselves and to others that it had ever taken place; others simply glossed over it, wishing to put behind them the awful circumstances in which they had been forced to eat human flesh. But whatever they did, the survivors of the Donner party became objects of prurient curiosity while they lived.

This was especially true in the case of the Breens, who had been able to avoid eating human flesh until their sojourn in Starved Camp. In February 1848, they became the first English-speaking family to settle near the Mission at San Juan Bautista in North Central California. Their house quickly became a stopping-off point for forty-niners seeking their fortunes after the first discovery of gold near Sutter's Fort in 1848. It was sometime in 1862 that the final Irish contribution to this story took place.

John Ross Browne was born in Dublin in 1821 and moved with his family to the USA in 1832. He became a sailor but discovered a skill for travel writing and it was in the course of his wanderings in California that Browne crossed the paths of the (now elderly) couple from Carlow. He put up for the night in the Breen household, which by then had become a fully fledged inn. He admits in an article published in *Harper's New Monthly Magazine* that he was drawn to the Breens' inn because he was aware of the owners' history. Like a latter-day practitioner of 'New Journalism', most of the piece he wrote about their meeting concerned his own reaction to the proximity of two cannibals. The Breens themselves, though described in unflattering terms, do nothing menacing, threatening or even vaguely out of the ordinary. Browne, however, admits to an awful fascination with the couple, especially Mrs Breen (he erroneously exonerates Patrick Breen from having consumed human flesh). He says:

> I could not but look upon this woman with a shudder. Her sufferings had been intense; that was evident from her marked and weather-beaten features. Doubtless she had struggled against the cravings of hunger as long as reason lasted. But still the one terrible act, whether the result of necessity or insanity, invested her with a repellant [*sic*] atmosphere of horror.

Browne found that he was unable to eat anything placed in front of him. Neither was he able to sleep. In a fit of Gothic exaggeration he ascribes his insomnia to 'an unfounded suspicion that she might become hungry during the night ... I was glad when daylight afforded me an excuse to get up and take a stroll in the fresh air.'[39]

Patrick Breen died on 21 December 1868 at the age of seventy-three. He died a wealthy man, leaving an estate valued at over $100,000 behind him. His wife Margaret followed him to the grave six years later. She never forgot her homeland. In 1869 she donated £8 ($40 at the time) towards the erection of a belfry and bell for the church at Ballymurphy in County Carlow. When she and James Frazier Reed died in the same year, the last direct Irish link to one of the most famous and tragic stories of the American West was severed.

In historical terms the Donner party is not much more than a foot-note in the story of western settlement, albeit a distressing one. It did nothing to slow the process of westward migration that proceeded apace once the snows of the winter of 1846–7 had melted. But it is a story which, understandably, has a firm hold on the American imagi-nation in that it serves to underscore the courage of those trapped in the Sierra Nevada that winter and the resourcefulness and bravery of those who followed and who were not put off by the fate of the unfor-tunate Donner party.

REEL FOUR

INDIAN AGENT:
THE LATER CAREER OF THOMAS FITZPATRICK

y the 1840s, including disputed territory, much of the American West had belonged to the USA for more than thirty years. But were you to travel westwards you might easily think otherwise. Few but the most intrepid of Americans would venture across the Missouri. Reluctance to traverse the Great American Desert was finally overcome by stories brought back from California of fertility and abundance. One group of potential emigrants sought out the trapper and pioneer Antoine Robidoux, who sold them on the idea of settling in California. He was asked, 'Do they have fever out there?' His response was that 'there was but one man in California that ever had a chill there, and it was a matter of so much wonderment to the people of Monterey that they went eighteen miles into the country to see him shake'.[1] It wasn't a great basis upon which to begin a substantial demographic shift, but on such tall tales was the westward migration of the 1840s partly based. Thomas Fitzpatrick would contribute to the explorations that offered a more pragmatic foundation for the movement of population to California and Oregon and he would then help police the trails across which the migrants travelled.

Fitzpatrick guided an early missionary–migratory party in the summer of 1842, led by John Bartleson and the famous Jesuit priest Fr Pierre Jean de Smet. Fitzpatrick's participation, according to one of the travellers, John Bidwell, was vital. 'When we came in contact with Indians,' Bidwell wrote, 'our people were so easily excited that if we had not had with us an old mountaineer the result would certainly have been disastrous. The name of the guide was Captain Fitzpatrick.' De Smet was very taken with Fitzpatrick ('every day I learned to appreciate him more and more'), but one of his more sanctimonious travelling companions decided that Fitz had spent a few years too many away from civilisation. The Irishman was 'a wicked, worldly man, and is much opposed to missionaries going among the Indians'.[2] Fitzpatrick guided the group until it divided into two separate units, one bound for Oregon the other for California.

In 1843 Fitzpatrick came to the attention of the Missouri senator Thomas Hart Benton. Benton was a colourful character who had once fought a duel over a political row with one Charles Lucas on Bloody Island, a frequent venue for such encounters. At their first meeting, Benton severed a blood vessel in Lucas's neck and then waited until the latter had recovered. The two went at it again six weeks later and Benton finished the job by shooting his opponent in the heart. This was the man who recommended Fitzpatrick to his son-in-law John C. Fremont as a guide for his second expedition. The first excursion of the man who became known as the 'Pathmaker' had been guided by Christopher 'Kit' Carson and had been responsible for the mapping of large tracts of previously uncharted western land. Fremont's own published account of his expedition had been a huge success and had inspired many of the emigrants who had already been guided to their destinations by Fitzpatrick. The Irishman was taken on as a guide and also, effectively, served as the quartermaster to Fremont's corps.

With war against Mexico imminent (a pretext was found for one in 1846), Fitzpatrick's next role was also as a guide. This time he accompanied a force of dragoons led by Colonel Stephen Watts Kearny back to his old stamping ground of South Pass. The fear was that the northern Plains Indians would take advantage of any US military preoccupation in Mexico. Kearny's force was intended as a persuasive show of strength that would discourage the likes of the Sioux, Cheyenne and Arapahoe from attacking the increasing numbers of emigrants travelling west via South Pass in wagon trains. It was also despatched by way of experiment. One thesis held that westward travellers should be protected by a number of fixed military forts that would be established along the trail. The alternative was a more mobile cavalry force of the type Fitzpatrick was guiding into the Rockies. Kearny was known to favour the latter option.

Pour encourager les autres, Kearny addressed an assembly of Indian tribes on the plain between Fort Laramie and the river Platte (in modern Wyoming). A pipe of peace was smoked and platitudes were exchanged about loyalty and devotion to the Great Father in Washington, but what really impressed the Plains Indians was the loosing off of three shots from the dragoons' howitzer. That kept the peace for a while, but within a few months a number of trappers had been killed and the customary violent cycle of action and reprisal began again.

In his official report, Kearny advised the government against permanent forts along the emigrant trails and advocated occasional expeditions such as the one he had just commanded. He also sang the praises of 'Broken Hand' (the nickname comes from an old injury), 'an excellent woodsman – one who has as good, if not better, knowledge of that country than any other man in existence'.[3]

In 1846 the Mexican–American War began and Fitzpatrick was guiding Kearny again, as his force moved, more or less unopposed, into New Mexico. At the behest of Thomas Hart Benton, an Indian Agency was to be established for the Upper Arkansas and Platte region (a vast area covering thousands of square miles from New Mexico to Wyoming and beyond) and Benton recommended the appointment of Fitzpatrick as the first agent. The proposal was ratified by the Senate on 3 August 1846 and the Irishman was to take up the post after the small business of taking New Mexico from its rightful owners was accomplished. This was rapidly achieved thanks to the effective capitulation of the Mexican commander Governor Armijo in the face of a ten-thousand-strong American force.

Kearny's unit had passed through some difficult terrain and Fitzpatrick would claim in correspondence that had a detachment of even a thousand men trapped Kearny in one of the canyons through which he passed, they could have inflicted serious and possibly fatal damage to the expedition. But Armijo preferred to concede without a fight and take to the hills, where he conducted a sporadic and ineffectual guerrilla campaign that caused more hardship to Mexican American peasants than it did to the US military forces.

With his new appointment, Fitzpatrick would become the second Irish-born Indian agent. Andrew Drips had swapped the American Fur Company for an agency in the Upper Missouri some time before. The exact role of an agent was, like much else in the West, neither clearly understood nor plainly defined. In theory, Fitzpatrick was a sort of ambassador, given that the Plains Indian tribes were 'domestic dependent nations' as defined by the US Supreme Court. In reality, his role was underpinned by the authority and military might of the federal government. In essence, Fitzpatrick's job was to maintain peace and order in the region through which most of the Oregon–California migrants were travelling. He had to keep the Plains Indians quiet and do so at the least possible cost to the parsimonious federal government.

We also see an entirely new side of Fitzpatrick during this final phase of his extraordinary life. We discover a highly educated and articulate man. His letters and reports to his immediate superiors in St Louis and to Washington itself are well written and fluent. Most of his old trapper peers were semi-literate at best. Kit Carson only learned to read late in life; Jim Bridger never bothered. But Fitzpatrick did not simply rely on his literacy to impress his superiors. He approached his work with an intensity and a zeal that was, unfortunately, not always typical of his profession. What he wrote about the Indian peoples among whom he had lived for twenty years doesn't always make for pleasant reading in our politically correct times, but Fitzpatrick always seems to have acted with what he perceived to be the interests of his 'charges' at heart, however paternalistic his reports might seem.

His primary function was to ensure that peace reigned in the vast area covered by his agency. From that peace might flow the sort of government policies and assistance that would help the tribes whose welfare was his responsibility. One of his first expeditions was back to New Mexico where, in the aftermath of the Mexican–American War and in the absence of a single cohesive military force, hostile Indians had been wreaking havoc with white and Mexican settlers. The Irishman took with him an old associate, John Smith. Smith, a well-respected trader, had married the sister of a Cheyenne chief, Yellow Horse. His wife and four-year-old son Jack came with him. Courtesy of a Colorado militia unit exceeding its brief, John Smith, Jr. would not make it into his teens. In 1864 he was killed along with dozens of other peaceful Cheyenne in the notorious Sand Creek Massacre at the age of twelve.

Thanks to an administrative error, Fitzpatrick's 'big talk' with the Cheyenne and Arapahoe near Bent's Fort was not accompanied by the customary distribution of gifts to the Indians. Fitzpatrick had arrived there with one arm as long as the other. By way of atonement he used his personal credit with the fort's owner, William Bent, and bought enough bread and coffee to satisfy the Indian warriors that they were being feasted. Fitzpatrick's speech to the Cheyenne and Arapahoe was part harangue and part cajolery. He warned them against the 'murdering and plundering of his people – the perpetrators of which would be speedily and severely punished'. But he also tried to convey, as best he could, his own sense that, whether they liked it or not, their way of life was about to change completely. 'I reminded them,' he wrote, 'of the great diminution and continual decrease of all game and advised them to turn their attention to agriculture, it being the only means to save them from destruction.'[4]

The Cheyenne and Arapahoe listened politely but didn't seem to pay undue attention to his message. The issue of their long-term future was not addressed and, in his reply, one of the principal Cheyenne chiefs offered to help the white men deal with their real enemies and the hostile Indians who were behind *all* the attacks on white and Mexican settlements: the Comanche. A discouraged but not disconsolate Fitzpatrick declined the offer. The encounter, however, his first in his new capacity, may have brought home to him the difficulties he faced.

His report of the meeting also contains some scathing comments about the very nature of the people with whom he now had to deal on a level to which he was not accustomed. He wrote to Thomas Harvey, Superintendent of Indian Affairs:

I do not wish to be understood as placing much confidence in
the profession of the Indians of this country. Circumstances and
necessity may seem to change their disposition; but ingratitude,
low, mean cunning, cowardice, selfishness and treachery, are the
characteristics of the whole race.

This was from a man who, at the age of fifty-one, would marry an
Arapahoe woman. 'Yet I believe,' he continues,

the Cheyennes are serious in their professions of friendship;
they plainly see what must befall them on the extinction of
game, and therefore wish to court the favor of the United States
government hoping to obtain assistance.

He does his best by those Cheyenne who appear willing to adopt the
pastoral mode of farming. He points out that some members of the
tribe, recognising the obvious diminution in the scale of the great
buffalo herds, seem willing to grow corn. He warns, however, that they
will need help or they will simply abandon the practice:

If the government wishes those Indians to settle down, they must
give them some assistance, at least towards a beginning. A few
dollars expended with those who are now willing to commence,
might work some good and be the means of inducing others to
follow the example; and by the time the buffalo is all gone, those
Indians will be prepared to live without them.[5]

Fitzpatrick might have felt that he had a duty of care towards the
Plains Indians in his agency, but his letters during this final period of
his life reveal his real feelings about them. In a further letter to Thomas
Harvey, in October 1847, his analysis of what lies in store for the
Native American is harsh and chilling but, as it happens, not far wide
of the mark. He had been asked for what would be classed today as
anthropological information on the tribes in his area. On the subject of
financial provision for native peoples he opines:

I believe moreover, that all the aid from the wealthiest governments of Europe, united with that of the United States, could
not redeem or save those people, inasmuch as I consider them a
doomed race, and must fulfil their destiny. Yet, it is a generous,
and praiseworthy exercise in the government to do all it can for
them.[6]

Neither does he set much store by efforts to Christianise the Indians. He is sceptical of the much-touted claims by missionaries to have brought the word of God to the Native American. He seems to be saying that while the missionaries may have talked up a storm about deliverance and redemption, the attention of their childlike audiences may have been elsewhere. Their allegiance was still, as far as he observed, to their own gods.

This philosophical flexibility also extended to the negotiation of treaties. He observes drily in another missive to St Louis:

> There is not a single day in the whole year, that I could not make a treaty with any of the Indian tribes of this country, if I happen to have sufficient merchandise on hand to make presents worth the inconvenience and trouble of assembling the nation, and let the stipulations of that treaty be whatever I choose to propose, it would be solemnly and apparently (in good faith) ratified, and agreed to, but not for one single moment longer than a favourable opportunity offers for its violation. This they think will cause a renewal of negotiations by which means more and a still greater quantity of merchandise will be distributed in order to bind them more closely to the compact.[7]

But through all his scepticism and tempered realism, there remains a very nineteenth-century Irish sense of a huge injustice meted out by the strong to the weak. He points out to the Superintendent of Indian Affairs a single unvarnished truth: 'in accordance with strict justice, we owe them much, being instrumental in (almost) the entire ruin of their country as far as their immediate mode of subsistence is concerned'.[8] In a letter written in 1847 he (accurately) predicts the virtual extinction of the buffalo and warns of the effects this will have on the Plains Indian tribes who, as a consequence, 'must inevitably come to deplorable states of destitution'.[9]

The impression one gets from Fitzpatrick's letters would tend to undermine the received wisdom of the school of New Western History that emigrant wagons suffered hardly at all from Indian attack. On the basis of research into the thousands of letters sent home by western migrants and of other documentary evidence, latter-day historians have concluded that the Hollywood notion of wagon trains under constant threat from hostile Indians is another prized western myth.

On the basis of the only evidence that matters, they conclude that less than 5 per cent of migrant deaths were as a result of Indian attack (the rest came about as a result of disease, harsh weather conditions and accidents). However, on the strength of Fitzpatrick's reports, one might conclude otherwise. They are full of references to the increasing hostility between migrants and Indians. The anecdotal evidence from these narratives paints a picture of Indian tribes who were only too ready to prey on travellers in the absence of a US military threat. However, it must be remembered that Fitzpatrick had his own agenda. He was unhappy with the level and quality of military protection for the wagon trains and would, quite naturally, tend to highlight incidents where there had been clashes between local tribes and migrant groups.

Furthermore, many of the worst incidents he describes took place on the Santa Fe Trail and involved attacks by Comanche and Apache Indians rather than the Plains Indians of the northern part of his sphere of responsibility. The Santa Fe Trail was one used more by traders than it was by emigrants. In many cases these hardened traders displayed a scant regard for the welfare of indigenous tribes (especially when it came to the supplying of liquor) and attacks were often as a result of trading disputes rather than being well-planned ambushes on innocent travellers. As Fitzpatrick put it himself in a letter to the Superintendent for Indian Affairs in Washington in August 1848, 'It is the general opinion throughout the United States that Indians are very much imposed on by the white man who trades with them.'[10] He added in a letter to St Louis the following year that the Indians had good grounds for complaint against many of the migrants, who were responsible for

> The destruction and dispersion of game. The cutting down and destroying wood. And other minor cases hardly worthy of notice. I do not wish to be understood as believing their griev-ances to have ever been the cause of Indian hostilities in that particular section of country heretofore, but I do believe that the time is fast approaching when these very grievances will become a source of great trouble, unless a salutary remedy is speedily applied.[11]

Fitzpatrick's hard work was not going unnoticed. In 1849, Fremont, on yet another exploratory expedition, was writing to Thomas Hart Benton about this admirable agent, entirely educated for such a post … He will be able to save lives and money for the government, and knowing how difficult this Indian question may become I am particular in bringing Fitzpatrick's operations to your notice. In a few years he might have them all [by 'them' he means the Comanches, Apaches, Kiowas and Arapahoes] farming here on the Arkansas.[12]

The admirable agent's own plans were ambitious. He wanted nothing more or less than an enormous conclave, a gathering of Indian chiefs (though that word meant something entirely different to the Native American than to the European American) and representatives of the federal government. This assembly was to produce a solemn and binding treaty that would govern relations between the white man and the red man for years to come. It would involve the Native populations forgoing many of the practices and traditional pursuits that were at best an irritant and at worst a grave threat to the USA. On the other hand, it would involve concessions by the federal government and some measure of compensation from Washington for the effect that its citizens were having on the game and the hunting grounds that had been a part of the Indian culture and way of life for centuries.

In the context of his own recorded opinion of the efficacy of Indian treaties, this might seem a strange project for Fitzpatrick to undertake. Certainly others were sceptical. His trader friend, Solomon Sublette, for example, wrote to his wife that 'As soon as they get the presents they [the Indian tribes] would commence war.'[13] But by 1849 Fitzpatrick seems to have overcome his own cynicism and was so fired by the project that he travelled to Washington himself to make his case. It was supported by the Commissioner of Indian Affairs and the Secretary of the Interior but failed to pass muster with Congress in April 1850. (It was accepted by the Senate but thrown out by the House of Representatives.) What had brought about this change in the Irishman? Why was he so determined to negotiate a treaty that might bring lasting peace to a considerable portion of the American West?

Well, one could argue that his attitude hadn't actually changed that much. In a letter written to St Louis in September 1850, long after his efforts appear to have failed, he advises D.D. Mitchell, the local Superintendent of Indian Affairs, that until we show our strength and ability to protect ourselves, by giving some one of the most unruly tribes a good flogging, I much fear that any treaties which may be made or entered into with them will not be very lasting – at least not longer than they may consider it advantageous; because they have not the slightest idea whatever of the strength and power of the United States.[14]

Yet he persisted. He refused to give up on his campaign and would eventually succeed in getting what he wanted.

Might it have had something to do with the fact that, putting aside a life spent as a solitary bachelor, he decided to get married at the age of fifty? He had seen countless trapper friends take Indian wives in the course of a quarter of a century spent in the American wilderness (though some were wives added to a collection that included spouses in St Louis and elsewhere). Fitzpatrick, however, despite many opportunities, had never chosen to go down this road. Now, despite his regularly professed antipathy towards many aspects of Indian culture and at a time of life when most men have long since dealt with the question of whether or not to wed, he chose not only to marry but to marry an Indian woman.

Fitzpatrick's matrimonial intentions (which would have coincided with his sudden energetic pursuit of the prize of a major Indian treaty) gave him a far greater stake in the future of the West than his employment as an Indian agent by the federal government. He was marrying into the Arapahoe tribe (the half-breed daughter of a trader, John Poisal, and Snake Woman, sister of an Arapahoe chief, Left Hand – an interesting digital liaison between Left and Broken Hand!) and would, he must have assumed, be producing quarter-breed Indian children.

Did the personal begin to overlap with the professional for Fitzpatrick in 1849? He was, after all, from a national culture that had a long tradition of forging marital alliances for political ends. Is it conceivable that the Irishman's own marriage influenced the development of his political thinking? Unfortunately, his letters leave us no clue as to whether the fact that his seed and breed might soon begin to populate a territory over whose immediate future he had a major say played any part in his efforts to bring about what would become the Fort Laramie Treaty of 1851. Perhaps he just wished to make his mark on history rather than posterity. Perhaps it was a combination of both.

His wife's name was Margaret. She was probably only in her late teens at the time of her marriage. Photographs taken of her later in life reveal an attenuated, ascetic-looking woman with the high cheekbones and the dark eyes of her mother's race. Their union produced two children, a boy, Andrew Jackson Fitzpatrick, and a girl, Virginia Thomasine Fitzpatrick. The fact that he named his son after the former president, a famous Indian fighter and the architect of the Indian removal policy that had led to the infamous Trail of Tears in the 1830s, suggests that Fitzpatrick had not entirely made his peace with the Native Americans.

But he still cherished an ambition to be the architect of peace between the Indian tribes in his vast agency and the federal government. Finally, in February 1851, came the breakthrough he had been waiting for. An Appropriations Bill passed through Congress allocating funds for his plan of action. The date chosen for the huge convocation was 1 September 1851 and Fitzpatrick set about gathering together the *dramatis personae* for the watershed encounter.

At a preliminary gathering in the Southwest, the Irishman obtained the agreement of the Cheyenne and Arapahoe, but the Apache, Comanche and Kiowa refused to travel to the designated meeting place, Fort Laramie on the North Platte River in modern Wyoming, because they 'had too many horses and mules to risk on such a journey and among such notorious horse thieves as the Sioux and Crows'.[15] They agreed, however, to discuss a separate treaty provided the talks took place on or near the Arkansas.

Having secured that guarantee, Fitzpatrick headed back for the North Platte and his date with history at Fort Laramie.

The beginning was not propitious. D.D. Mitchell, the St Louis-based Superintendent of Indian Affairs, arrived without any provisions – the 'presents' the Indian tribes expected as their due for attending the gathering. Fitzpatrick, always the facilitator, patched things up by telling the Indian chiefs that the 'presents' were on their way. The Sioux (Oglala and Brule), Cheyenne and Arapahoe decided to accept his word (he was telling the truth) and remain. In addition to the Plains Indian tribes, there was a strong military presence, led by Colonel Samuel Cooper, Adjutant General of the army, and US civilian representatives, including Fitzpatrick's old friend and compatriot Robert Campbell and A.B. Chambers, editor of the influential *Missouri Republican* and the designated council secretary.

Although the conference had been called to sort out relationships between the white man and the Native American, as much tension was caused by the presence of a delegation from the Snake tribe as by the juxtaposition of Indian warriors and US cavalry soldiers. The Snakes, and especially their chieftain, Washakie, were well disposed towards the whites but were sworn enemies of the Cheyenne and Sioux. The situation was like the proverbial powder keg. All it would take would be a single spark for the conflagration to start.

Although the resulting treaty is called after Fort Laramie, the actual council itself took place some miles distant from the fort, at a place called Horse Creek. Such was the size of this unique gathering that a huge area of good grazing land was needed to accommodate the animals of all parties to the talks. The meeting place of these representatives of two great civilisations must have been an impressive site. Not even the greatest of the old trapper rendezvous would have been nearly as remarkable. There was a formality about proceedings that would not have prevailed at any of those rumbustious gatherings from an era that had already passed. The great council began on Monday, 8 September with the Indian tribes determined to outdo the whites and each other in display. Ceremonial robes were worn and faces were elaborately painted as they approached the circle around which representatives were to gather under a fluttering 'Stars and Stripes'. The nearby Platte itself would have been wider and fuller than it is today. There were no dams along its path and no consumption demands from farming and urban communities to reduce its water levels.

Tribal chiefs took their places around the circle, as did the federal delegation. Mitchell spoke first. His words of welcome were painstakingly translated into each native language by interpreters. A pipe of peace was passed from the superintendent to Fitzpatrick and on around the circle. Then Mitchell began to address the substantive issues that concerned the Indians. He accepted that the days of the buffalo were numbered and apologised for the depredations of the emigrants and their livestock on traditional tribal lands. But there would be financial recompense. In return for free passage for migrant wagon trains, the right to build forts along the trails, a definition of the boundaries of the Indian tribes and the appointment of a tribal chief responsible for his people and answerable to the federal government, Washington promised $50,000 worth of goods annually for the next fifty years.

Fitzpatrick then spoke and asked the tribes to go away for forty-eight hours and give serious consideration to the agreement on offer.

Two days later the assembly reconvened, this time with the addition of the Crows. Extraordinarily, these sworn and implacable enemies of most of the other tribes present were accepted into the fold without demur. Feuds and vendettas had, genuinely, been set aside, at least for the duration of the council. At around the same time, the famous Jesuit missionary Fr de Smet arrived with Assinboin and Arikara headmen and was greeted rapturously by the Indian delegations. The missionary's presence at the council was almost as important, psychologically, for the Indians as that of Fitzpatrick himself.

The Jesuit celebrated mass, baptised a number of infants (including Andrew Jackson Fitzpatrick) and zealously attempted to convert entire nations of pantheists single-handedly, while an Indian celebration took place on the fringes of the great assembly. However, supplies of dogmeat and other delicacies were running low and the site of the negotiations was becoming highly unsanitary, such was the scale of the event. The stench of human and animal waste was becoming unbearable and still the wagon train with $50,000 worth of provisions for the Indians had not arrived. Furthermore, the council was becoming bogged down in more than faeces. Disputes were arising among the Indians about tribal borders.

Given that there were no clearly defined boundaries and that various tribes had, at various times, occupied each other's territory or simply possessed themselves of the hunting grounds of other tribes by means of *force majeure*, it was never going to be easy to create sovereign entities for each nation. By 11 September Jim Bridger had joined the convocation, and together he, Fitzpatrick and Campbell drew and redrew the map until they came up with distinct and acceptable boundary lines between tribes. Thus did two educated Irishmen and an illiterate American trapper dictate the homelands of Native American tribes who had roamed as they saw fit (or as other tribes allowed them) over the North American landscape for thousands of years.

On 17 September the final treaty was presented to the council and accepted by the representatives of all those present. Three days later the wagon train arrived and one treaty obligation, at least, was honoured by the United States of America. The following day the Indians departed with their presents and the whites with their treaty.

Fitzpatrick had done his work well. He had managed to get the most warlike of the tribes, who offered a potential threat to the emigrant trails, to attend the council. He had then succeeded, by staking his reputation on it, in brokering an agreement.

Of course it didn't last. The story of the American West is a history of shattered treaties and dishonoured agreements. Within months the US Senate had reduced the annuity period from fifty to fifteen years and, in time, the Crow, the Snake, the Cheyenne and the Sioux resumed their old vendettas and blood feuds. It took somewhat longer for the great Plains Indian tribes, the Sioux and Cheyenne, to go back to war with the far more powerful federal government but, in time, those hostilities too would resume. By that time Fitzpatrick would be out of the picture.

The federal government's agenda and that of Fitzpatrick were at variance where the Fort Laramie Treaty was concerned. For the Irishman it was a simple trade-off: goods for peace. For the federal government it was the expression of a new policy, the notion of 'extinguishing' native title. In the minds of the Washington policy makers and bureaucrats, you extinguished Indian title to the land they occupied either by taking or buying it. The former option was no longer morally or politically acceptable, so Indians now had to be removed from 'their' land by some form of purchase agreement. In return they had to be offered defined (though not necessarily viable) portions of land to exploit as they saw fit. These would be smaller than the area they had previously occupied but adjacent to it (where practicable) and inviolable. It was a fur-lined version of the Jacksonian Removal policy.

In what turned out to be one of his final official reports, penned in November 1853, Fitzpatrick is his usual direct and opinionated self, except that in this instance he undermines the very basis of the Indian policy that would dominate the interaction between the USA and the Native Americans for the next four decades (and which survives in amended form to this day).

After apprising the Superintendent of Indian Affairs in St Louis of the fact that a treaty similar to that worked out at Laramie in 1851 had been concluded with the south-western tribes, the Apache, Comanche and Kiowa, he goes on to condemn the development of what would become the reservation policy. This strategy for dealing with Native American tribes would, as it turned out, blight relations between the white man and the Indian tribes in the West for generations to come. He makes the case against the removal and separation of Indian nations cogently and passionately.

He wrote of the reservations:

> If penned up in small secluded colonies ... they become hospital wards of cholera and smallpox, and must be supported at an immense annual cost to the government. If no alteration is effected in their present state, the future has only starvation in store for them.

As he had already pointed out to St Louis and Washington, the Indians were already close to starvation despite claiming vast swathes of territory. What was to happen to them? Were they to be stripped of most of their territory and squashed onto much smaller parcels of land? Fitzpatrick's own solution was a radical one – involving total assimilation of the white and native races:

> make such modifications in the 'intercourse laws' [designed to protect Indians from liquor and the prostitution of their women] as will invite the residence of traders amongst them and *open the whole Indian territory to settlement*. In this manner will be introduced amongst them those who will set the example of developing the resources of the soil, of which the Indians have not now the most distant idea ... Trade is the only civilizer of the Indian. It has been the precursor of all civilization heretofore, and it will be of all hereafter.[16]

Fitzpatrick's argument may not have been altogether sound, given the tendency of legal and illegal traders to exploit the Indians when they could do so (that is, when the native population was in a position of weakness), but his analysis of the potential ills of the reservation system was accurate and he knew that the so-called 'intercourse laws' were more honoured in the breach than the observance anyway. He seems to see Indians as the potential employees of white traders and even farmers. They would then be encouraged to grow their own crops on their own land. How exactly they would acquire that land, how the Native tribes might divide up their own land given the collective nature of their society and how their title to tracts of land would be defined given their nomadic way of life were, perhaps, issues he was leaving for another day.

If so he was, sadly, never going to get around to teasing out those issues. His 1853 report has more than a hint of the valedictory about it. It reads like the final throw of a man who knows that he has over-stepped the mark too often already and need no longer bother to moderate his language. He had been relieved of his post once before. In October 1850 he was told that Charles Keemle of Missouri had been appointed in his place. Keemle was a former trapper of the Ashley era who now owned a number of St Louis newspapers. The appointment was probably political, but before Fitzpatrick had been relieved of his responsibilities, Keemle declined the appointment.

It is possible that Fitzpatrick felt that official patience with his increasingly testy diatribes had worn as thin as it was going to and that he might need to seek an alternative form of employment. He could see the edifice of relative peace that he had carefully constructed being unstitched thread by thread as the awful truth of the approaching reservation system became apparent to the indigenous peoples of the West. And so it proved. Too many of the Indians refused to be corralled onto reservations and in the 1860s a state of almost perma-nent war began, which only ended three decades later with the massacre of the Lakota at Wounded Knee Creek. But had Fitzpatrick lived on into the next decade, he would have had no reason to reproach himself. For six difficult years he had kept the lid on a tense situation on the frontier and earned the respect of the tribes in his agency. He had not completely avoided bloodshed (in his first year, for example, forty-seven people were killed in the Upper Platte and Arkansas region in civilian and military wagon trains), but he had prevented the state of all-out war that would follow a few years after his untimely death.

It was the final great irony of his life that Thomas Fitzpatrick, born in the often unpromising soil of County Cavan and reared in the often hazardous mountains and unforgiving plains of the great American West, died not in a camp under the stars beside a gurgling mountain stream, but in the nation's capital, Washington, DC. It is another, and sadder, irony that he had just been reunited with the only member of his immediate family he had seen since his departure from Ireland. Mary Fitzpatrick was only an infant when her brother had emigrated, but reading reports of his visit to Washington in December 1853 to report on his treaty with the Comanche, Kiowa and Apache nations, she concluded that this must be the brother she had been told about who chose to live in the American wilderness. Hardly had they been reunited, in early 1854, than she received news of his death. On 7 February he died of pneumonia that had developed from a severe cold.

His old friend and associate Robert Campbell was on hand to act as executor and organise his fellow Irishman's funeral. He was buried in the congressional cemetery in Washington where his grave is to this day. He is, arguably, the most significant Irishman to have made his home and his living (he left more than $10,000 in his will) in the American West. He is certainly one of the most interesting and important men of any nationality to have done so. He lacked the dime-novel cachet of his friend and contemporary Christopher 'Kit' Carson and his life ended at a time when his other great friend and peer, Jim Bridger, still had many years ahead of him. But he was on a par with either as a trapper and a guide and that places him in the first rank of great westerners.

He also had something neither of the others possessed: an academic intelligence and a scholarship that he used to good advantage in the final phase of his career as an Indian agent. Perhaps he was not the greatest businessman in the world and, although comfortably off, he did not make a vast fortune like some of his fellow countrymen who struck it rich in the minefields of California, Colorado or Montana and became Silver Kings or Copper Barons. But his legacy lay in the treaty that he was instrumental in bringing about in 1851. His name is associated with that ultimately failed attempt to bring peace to the Great Plains. During his period as Indian agent, he was respected and trusted by the Native American tribes with whom he dealt. He was seen as an honourable representative of a culture that they must have realised intended to supplant their own. Yet he managed to keep a lid on a deteriorating situation. For how much longer he would have been able to hold the line will always be open to question, but the fact is that the treaty he brought about was still working at the time of his death. It more or less held for some considerable time after he was no longer there to guarantee its continuance. It would lapse into worthlessness only when the gold of Montana, the establishment of the Bozeman Trail and the building of army forts forced the Sioux back on the warpath in the decade that followed.

One of the great Cheyenne chiefs, Black Kettle, delivered his own epitaph for 'Broken Hand' some time after his death. 'Major

Fitzpatrick,' he said, 'was a good man. He has gone ahead of us, and he told us that when he was gone we would have trouble, and it has proved true. We are sorry.'[17] Ten years after the passing of 'Broken Hand', Black Kettle had good reason to be sorry and to regret even more the death of the Irishman. In 1864 his settlement on Sand Creek was attacked by the God-fearing Methodist minister John Chivington and his Colorado militiamen. They were coming to the end of a tour of duty and feared the derision of their neighbours because they hadn't managed to kill any Indians during their period of service. They made up for that omission with the slaughter of ninety-eight women, children and (mostly) old men. The atrocity went unpunished. Massacres like those at Sand Creek bear out the essential truth of Frederick Jackson Turner's definition of the frontier as 'the meeting point between civilization and savagery', though not in the way Turner intended when he wrote his famous thesis on the West at the end of the nineteenth century. The mistake he made was in his failure to identify the civilised and the savages.

The patient work that Fitzpatrick had done to try and broker some lasting form of coexistence between two antithetical civilisations was already fraying at the edges before Sand Creek, but after that massacre (which, to be fair, was roundly condemned by much of the American press and described, privately, by President Grant as murder), the West exploded and the legal edifice Fitzpatrick had created lay in shards. The fault lay elsewhere, of course, but the fruits of his legacy had been squandered. That fact does not detract, however, from his stature. He was, in the words of his biographer, 'an epic figure, unique and incomparable'.

REEL
FIVE

TOFFS:
IRISH ARISTOCRATS WEST OF THE MISSISSIPPI

The epic hunt of Sir St George Gore

The man known in the burgeoning West of the 1850s as 'Sir George Gore' or 'Lord Gore' and believed by some to be a member of the British Royal family was none of the above. He was, in fact, an Irish commoner who had succeeded to a hereditary title in 1842 and his actual name was the rather grandiose Sir St George Gore, Eighth Baronet of Manor Gore in County Donegal. He was 'a Victorian dandy'.[1] Although he spent less than three years in the American West, Gore came to epitomise the profligacy and mindless slaughter of animals that turned the stomachs of even the most hardened American hunters. Over three 'seasons' he cut a bloody swathe through half a dozen states, leaving behind an abiding legacy of place names and a massive pile of rotting carcasses. Gore's epic adventure provided excellent sport for an Anglo-Irish gentleman, such as was denied him even in the 'free fire zone' of the Scottish highlands. But it drew the ire of the indigenous Native American population and became so wantonly destructive of western wildlife that even a previously unconcerned official bureaucracy had to sit up and take notice.

Gore was born in Dublin in 1811 into an aristocratic family that had little connection with its former estates in Donegal but which was connected by blood to the famous Gore-Booths of Sligo and by marriage to the Farnhams of Cavan. He spent the early years of his life in Corkagh House in the Dublin suburb of Clondalkin before heading for the famous English public school of Winchester and then on to Oriel College, Oxford. There 'he went down without bothering the examiners at all'.[2] In the Valhalla of the Anglo-Irish, Gore was a very minor deity indeed, but his sporting instincts would lead him to become a more significant footnote in the American frontier narrative than he was ever likely to become in the history of his own country. His estates, with which he never bothered very much, gave him an annual income of between £3,000 and £4,000, a sum that would not have cut much of a dash in fashionable London but which (when translated into $20,000 a year) went a long way on the Western Plains and the Rocky Mountains. Gore never married and maintained no 'establishment' of any consequence. Devoted to hunting, he spent most of his time on the move and, with no fixed costs, was able to devote his income to his full-time hobby.

Gore, who left no personal record of any of his exploits, is known to have hunted extensively in Scotland and Europe. He is thought to have met the British adventurer William Drummond Stewart, who made him aware of the rich pickings in the forests and plains of the Americas. The Scottish nobleman pointed him in the direction of the American Fur Company, who undertook to supply his hunting and guiding needs from their western trading posts.[3] Gore arrived in St Louis in March 1854 and set about assembling an entourage for what was originally supposed to be a three-month expedition. The Irish baronet, by then a rather florid-looking aristocrat in his early forties, was described by a member of his party, Henry Bostwick, as of 'medium height, but rather stout, bald head, short side whiskers, a good walker, but poor horseman, a good shot from a rest but rather indifferent offhand'.[4] Bostwick, who was a guide, recorded his impressions of the hunt that followed when he was stationed at Fort Shaw in the 1870s. It is one of the few contemporary accounts of what was to become an epic expedition.

As it happened, merely equipping his entourage took Gore three months. When the party was finally assembled it consisted of forty-one men, six mule wagons, three ox wagons and twenty-one smaller carts. One entire wagon was reserved for Gore's private arsenal, consisting of seventy-five rifles and fifteen shotguns. Two more wagons were loaded down with his lordship's fishing tackle and he was attended at all times by a skilled fly maker. According to Bostwick, Gore himself travelled in style as well:

> He had a large linen tent, about ten by eighteen feet, hung throughout with striped lining, a brass bedstead that unscrewed and packed in a small space, a portable iron table, an iron wash-stand, and three milk cows.

His wagon

> appeared like an ordinary open box-spring wagon, but by putting cranks on four points near the corners and turning all at once a top was lifted into view out of the bed, which converted it into a comfortable carriage or a bedroom, as might be desired.[5]

Clearly the baronet was not prepared to make too many sacrifices or concessions to the outback, even in the name of sport.

Given the size of his retinue, westerners, not unreasonably, tended to elevate Gore well beyond his station. A biographer of Jim Bridger referred to him as 'the royal sportsman'[6] while a contemporary, Captain R.B. Marcy, who actually met the baronet, added a zero to his wealth, claiming that 'he possessed an income of some $200,000 per annum'.[7] There is, however, no denying the scale of his enterprise. Marcy, then an officer with D company of the 5th Infantry, wrote years later that 'The outfit and adventures of this titled Nimrod, conducted as they were upon a most gigantic scale, probably exceeded anything of the kind ever before attempted on this continent.'[8]

So, accoutred like some medieval monarch or an Indian Rajah, Gore headed for the hinterland. Despite the level of ostentation that surrounded him and his subsequent 'achievements', the Irishman might never have enjoyed the notoriety he does had his retinue not included Jim Bridger. As one of the original fur trappers of the Old West, Bridger's legend was already secure. Some seven years older than his employer, Bridger was simply 'the ablest hunter, mountaineer and guide of the West'.[9] By the time of Gore's arrival in the USA the fur trade had long since passed its peak and Bridger, whose career was never less than chequered, was reduced at this time to parlaying his expertise into dollars by undertaking guiding tasks for the government or for private employers like Gore. Some of Bridger's peerless celebrity seems to have rubbed off on Gore. Their association (Bridger was first hired in St Louis) made Gore's story more appealing to contemporary historians, thus guaranteeing the Irishman his place in western lore.

Bridger's attitude to his work with Gore must have been ambiguous at best. He was being well paid, but, as his biographer puts it, 'Bridger, like the Indians, hunted for meat or pelts. He never killed game for which he had no use. Hunting for horned heads was like going after scalps.' Nonetheless Bridger was always quick to defend Gore, describing him as 'a bold, dashing, and successful sportsman, a social champion, and an agreeable gentleman'.[10]

Bridger was down on his luck in 1854 because he had just lost his business, Fort Bridger in Utah, to the Mormons. Brigham Young and the elders of his Church of Latter-Day Saints had decided that they did not want Bridger as a neighbour and that they wanted to exact more profit from westward migrants for themselves. This profit, as the Latter-Day Saints saw it, was being creamed off by the likes of Bridger and his partner, Louis Vasquez, so they went after Bridger with a vengeance. In a letter sent to his senator, G.B. Butler, the famous Mountain Man claims:

> I was robbed and threatened with death by the Mormons, by the direction of Brigham Young, of all my merchandise, livestock, in fact everything I possessed, amounting to more than $100,000 worth, the buildings in the fort partially destroyed by fire, and I barely escaped with my life.[11]

But escape he did.

Bridger was not the only guide who accompanied Gore on his increasingly ambitious expedition. Bostwick has already been mentioned, and in addition to him, two St Louis brothers, the Chatillons, were hired. The elder brother, Henry, had reputedly killed more than thirty grizzly bears. At the instigation of Bridger, Louis Vasquez's son, Auguste Pike Vasquez, was also taken on. In the autumn of 1854 the party headed north for Fort Laramie, a military post (though only recently acquired by the army – it had once been jointly owned by Bridger and Thomas Fitzpatrick) at the junction of the North Platte and Laramie rivers in south-eastern Wyoming. Gore hoped to winter there.

Because Bostwick was not with the party in the summer and autumn of 1854, little is known about the activities of the Gore entourage during that time. The history of the army post at Fort Laramie records that the group 'went into North Park, at the headwaters of the North Platte, and continued westward over the continental divide to leave his name on the Gore range and the Gore pass of present north-central Colorado'[12] (where the names of members of the party were later found gouged into some of the park's trees). Given the vastness of the West and the relative paucity of travellers and explorers, it didn't take very much to have some geographical feature called after you, but Gore certainly left an extensive topographical legacy. Bearing his name today are the aforementioned Gore Pass (altitude 9,000 feet – it now bears a plaque placed there in 1956 by the Colorado Historical Society) and the Gore Range. But in addition he managed to bag Gore Canyon, Gore Lake, Gore Creek, Gore Mountain and the Gore Wilderness. Briefly, in 1905, he even had a town called after him. However, Gore City quickly became absorbed into the town of Kiemmling. Coloradans appear to be unique in their fever for naming places after Gore. He is not similarly honoured in the other states he visited, Wyoming, Montana and North Dakota.

There is also much uncertainty about Gore's relationship with Joseph and Henry Chatillon. The older brother certainly remained with the baronet for less than a year and recalled their association in uncomplimentary terms. Chatillon's principal claim upon posterity was that he had been guide to the writer Francis Parkman on the journey that led to the book *The Oregon Trail* in 1849. He corresponded with Parkman for a number of years afterwards and in his final letter to the Boston author he wrote:

> the last trip I made was with a Lord from England. I was gone
> 11 month and had a hard times [*sic*]. This Lord was a very
> disagreeable 'Jonney Bull' in fact much more than the 'Boeuf de
> la Prairie'. He put on any amount of airs and had 18 Blood
> Hounds to chase the antelope, etc. & play smash in general ...
> Oh, bye the bye I forgot to mention when I went with that
> English Lord I catch 100 Beaver.[13]

(It is interesting that Chatillon should assume an English-speaking
aristocrat to be British. This comes up again and again with Irishmen
of the establishment class in the West. Their accents and manners do
not square with the typical western experience of the Irish and so the
assumption is automatically made that they are British.)

The lack of documentary evidence on how Gore passed the summer
and autumn of 1854 has led to the growth of a number of legends,
which, like all fables, may have more than a grain of truth. For
example, one of the reasons for the naming of the Gore Range in
Colorado arises from the belief that Gore, camped on one side of the
range, became aware that elk were plentiful on the far side. Local myth
has it that he employed a tribe of 800 Indians to cut a road through the
forest so that he could negotiate it with his entourage. Having done so,
he is supposed to have become bored with the game within four days
and returned. He is also said to have spurned the opportunity to enrich
himself with the gold that was later discovered in the area. According
to Henry Chatillon, Jr. some of Gore's men found gold and brought it
to the baronet:

> As soon as he laid eyes on it he said this is gold, but I did not
> come here to seek gold. I don't need it, I am on a pleasure hunt.
> So he called his foreman and told him to break camp immedi-
> ately and move in any direction that Joe Chatillon would dictate
> because this Gold find might cause all his men to leave.[14]

The story is more than likely a gilding of the Gore myth. Any passing
knowledge of the effects of gold fever on a group of forty western men
would suggest that such a discovery would have guaranteed an immediate mass desertion and the premature end of the hunt.

Both legends emanate from the western fixation with Gore's
wealth. He could afford to hire 800 Indians to build a path from
nowhere to nowhere else, *ergo* he did. He could similarly afford to pass

up the chance to enrich himself because he was rich enough already. As Gore's biographer Barry Johnson has shown, this was clearly not the case. Gore was not fabulously wealthy, just comfortably off. To do what he was doing did not require enormous resources, just the willingness to spend the income from his estates passing the spring, summer and autumn in pursuit of bison, elk and antelope and the freezing winter months in the relative discomfort of remote outposts. Whatever the truth of the stories that emanated from Gore's first expeditions, without them he would probably not have been commemorated in the Colorado wilderness in the way that he has been.

By omitting to leave a memoir of any kind behind him, Gore remains something of a *tabula rasa* upon which others have sketched their own character profiles of the man. This, not unexpectedly, has resulted in some very different pencil strokes. For example, was Gore an intrepid hunter who took his chances, *solo*, in the wilderness or did he operate more discreetly, *tout ensemble*?

According to Jim Bridger (as told to Marcy):

> Sir George's habit was to sleep until about ten or eleven o'clock in the morning when he took his bath, ate his breakfast and set out generally along for the day's hunt. Bridger says it was not unusual for him to remain out until ten o'clock at night and he seldom returned to camp without augmenting the catalogue of his exploits.[15]

Clearly a Fenimore Cooper hero! Contrast that icon with the image conveyed by Bostwick (whose account is based on first-hand observation) of a man who

> rarely, if ever, went unattended, his party usually comprising seven men. He never loaded his own gun, but after firing passed it to an attendant, who gave him another ready charged.[16]

More Falstaff than Fenimore Cooper.

The same diverse views apply to his personality. Bridger's Gore (again as mediated through Marcy) was an amiable soul who, after a few glasses of wine over an al fresco dinner, 'was in the habit of reading from some book and eliciting Bridger's comments thereon. His favourite author was Shakespeare which Bridger "reckoned was a leetle too high-falutin for him"'.[17] Bridger did enjoy Gore's recounting of some of the tall tales of Baron Munchausen (ironic given the subsequent embroidering of the baronet's own mythology) and when told the story of the Battle of Waterloo observed that the British must have fought better against Napoleon than they had at New Orleans in the War of 1812.

Stanley Vestal, in his folksy biography of Bridger, claims that the veteran guide and the Irish nobleman

> hit it off from the start. Jim liked the lively, vital Irishman; he was a good horseman, a crack shot and as openhanded as an Indian … Moreover Sir George had sufficient literary taste to appreciate the color and pith of the trapper slang in which Jim habitually expressed himself.[18]

Bostwick's account is less cosy. According to him, Gore was courteous but unsociable. The default impression of the Irish baronet is of a certain *noblesse oblige*, of a rather private, civilised, generous man. His generosity, however, ended if he thought he was being cheated. On one occasion when he had done a deal to acquire beef at a specific price the vendor tried to raise him by fifty per cent. Gore went straight away to an alternative source and bought almost four times the amount of beef that he needed at the original price – just to make a point. He made a similar point to one of the great enterprises of the region towards the end of his stay in the West.

Major Alexander Culbertson ('major' was a courtesy title) was one of the leading lights of the American Fur Company. He was 'about six feet high, of keen eye and a frank, open countenance'.[19] He had married the daughter of a Blackfoot chieftain in 1840 and resented the presence of Gore on his Upper Missouri 'patch'. But he was, first and foremost, a businessman. As the winter of the third and final year of the hunt approached, Gore was in Fort Union in North Dakota (an American Fur Company trading post), preparing for his journey back to St Louis. For that purpose he needed boats. Culbertson, no doubt delighted to see the back of the entire entourage, agreed to sell them to him. He also agreed to purchase all Gore's remaining wagons, goods and animals. Conscious, however, that the Irish baronet was not going to be able to transport the paraphernalia anyway, Culbertson reneged on the deal and dropped his price.

Rather than allow the Fur Company man to get away with this sort of sharp practice, Gore simply burnt the wagons and supplies in front of the fort, standing guard over the flames to ensure that nothing was rescued for profit. He even ordered that the metal from the wagons and carts be thrown into the Missouri River. The cattle and horses that remained from the hunt he gave away to the local Indian tribes around the fort.[20]

His extended hunt, which took him through the four states already mentioned, was not without its problems. One winter camp was raided twice for its horses by braves from the Piegan tribe. The first raid netted twenty-one horses; the second group got no farther than the corral when, according to Bostwick, 'the noise made by them in removing the pickets, roused the men and Sir George cooly fired, wounding Major Culbertson's brother-in-law, Big Plume, who was one of the marauding party, whereupon the Indians fled without securing any horses.'[21]

Gore himself may have encouraged some tallish tales about his encounters with Indians. The *Inverness Courier*, in an obituary in 1879, remarked that 'On one occasion he was attacked by Indians, and almost single-handed he kept them at bay until he was able under cover of night to make his escape. He was, however, obliged to leave all his hunting trophies behind.' No such anecdote exists about him in any American accounts so we must assume that it came to the *Courier*, via some friendly Pegasus, from Gore himself, in Falstaffian mode.

Whatever the truth of his dealings with the Native American popu-lation, there is no doubt that he had an increasingly poisonous rela-tionship with the still-skeletal bureaucracy of the West as his hunt proceeded. The Indian agent for the Upper Missouri in 1856 was Colonel Alfred V. Vaughan (another courtesy title). Bad blood quickly developed between Vaughan and Gore. The 'colonel' was responsible to Alfred Cummings, the Superintendent for Indian Affairs (Central Division) based in St Louis, the man who had issued Gore with the licence or passport to carry out his hunt. In a typical complaint from July 1856, Vaughan wrote to Cumming claiming that Gore had violated the terms of his licence. He alleged that Gore had built a 'fort' in Crow country (which was largely true) and that he was 'carrying on trade and intercourse with the Crow tribe of Inds [*sic*]'. This trade included 'Goods, Powder and Ball'.[22] He then outlined the extent of the slaughter of animals for which Gore had been responsible and described the anger of the Indians. He made no attempt to reconcile the notion of Native American opposition to Gore's activities and 'intercourse' with his camp. Although the letter more or less coincided with the end of the hunt, there is no evidence that it had actually brought that conclusion about. Gore had been in the wilderness for nearly three years and had either come to the end of his tether or of his means.

Although they have to be viewed against the background of personal animosity, Vaughan's complaints have undoubted validity. In his November letter to Cummings, the agent rails against the wanton destruction of the Gore party and its potential effect on the Sioux and Blackfoot. Vaughan's letters were forwarded to Washington, where they came to the attention of Interior Secretary Robert McClelland and Commissioner of Indian Affairs George W. Manypenny. The latter suggested that the 'trophies' collected by Gore might be confiscated and sold to the benefit of the Indians. McClelland demurred, reckoning that the cost of seizing the skins and pelts collected by the hunt might be more than the potential revenue. Instead Cumming was warned not to be so liberal in future in his dispensing of open-ended hunting licences.

Was Gore a ruthless and wanton animal killer who lived up to his name, or a sportsman enjoying unparalleled hunting opportunities? Judged by the standards of the twenty-first century he was certainly the former, especially in light of the virtual destruction of the buffalo herds over the next thirty years. Even by the standards of the times he was profligate in his massacre of bison and his activities were criticised by people whose own reputations would not have been bywords for zoological conservation. Kill figures vary. Vaughan, a clear antagonist, puts the slaughter tally at '105 Bears and some 2,000 Buffalo, Elk and Deer 1,600 … more than they had any use for having killed it purely for sport'.[23] Marcy's figures are slightly more conservative. He goes for forty bears and a total of 2,500 buffalo, elk, deer, antelope as well as other small game.[24] It was still egregious slaughter by any standards.

How did the Native American population react to this entourage cutting such a swathe across their traditional hunting lands? Again, there is a divergence of opinion. In his book *The Plainsmen of the Yellowstone*, Mark Brown writes that 'there is no doubt that Sir George killed wantonly … but it is highly improbable that the Crows complained about it'.[25] Much of the negative attention Gore received is ascribed by Brown to officials of the American Fur Company zealously and jealously guarding their bailiwicks. Vaughan, on the other hand, who is clearly not a disinterested party, claimed that 'The Inds [*sic*] have been loud in their complaints at men passing through their country killing and driving off their game.'[26]

By 1857 Gore was back in the far northern highlands of Britain, adding to his collection of Scottish stags. The estimable Captain Marcy, a westerner who seems to have borne Gore no ill will, describes the grand hunt as a 'constitutional' for the Irish baronet. 'He returned home with a renovated constitution, good health and spirits and a new lease of perhaps of ten years to his life.'[27] Which is more than can be said for his prey or for the Indians whose hunting grounds he invaded. Whether the experience did add to Gore's longevity or not we obviously cannot tell. He died in 1878, having made one return trip to the USA, to the Florida Everglades in 1876, and having spent the rest of his life in the obscurity from which he had emerged to leave his personal mark on the ecological landscape of the Old West.

The Wilde West show

In 1881 Oscar Wilde was merely an apprentice literary phenomenon but one who had still managed to make an impact on British society. His great theatrical and poetic works were ahead of him, but the twenty-eight-year-old Dubliner had a rather slight collection of poems to his credit and had managed the delicate balancing act of becoming famous for being famous. He was perceived as a leader of the 'art for art's sake' Aesthetic movement in Britain. But, as with many of the characters he would create, in the 1880s his real genius was put into his life rather than his art.

His striking appearance (he was tall and sported unfashionably long hair, which he was intent on making fashionable), his calculatedly eccentric behaviour and his natural wit had enabled him to parlay an as yet unrealised talent into considerable social success. This had found expression in the parody of his ideas and persona in the character of Bunthorne in Gilbert and Sullivan's comic operetta *Patience*. It was consideration of the box-office potential of *Patience* in the USA that was to lead to the mutual encounter of Oscar Fingal O'Flaherty Wills Wilde and the American West.

The show had been highly successful in London and that success had been repeated in New York, from where the impresario responsible, Richard D'Oyly Carte, sent Wilde a cablegram in November 1881. One of D'Oyly Carte's other enterprises was the organisation of lecture tours and he saw a compelling synergy in having Wilde/Bunthorne tour the United States, making money for both of them from his lectures while simultaneously being a virtual sandwich-board man for *Patience*.

D'Oyly Carte's promotion of his new protégé involved the use of 'a little bunkum to push him in America'.[28] Americans had no indigenous models for Bunthorne. Even their poets were more muscular than aesthetic. Wilde would be 'sold' as a dandy. He would address his audiences in the costume of an aesthete, which to D'Oyly Carte meant velvet jacket, knee breeches and a sunflower in the writer's buttonhole. He intended Wilde to appeal to both men and women: to the latter as an artist, to the former as a figure of fun. He also had an eye to the increasingly prosperous Irish community that, if it was played to adeptly, might welcome a fellow native who had tweaked the noses of the British establishment by infiltration.

New York was far better prepared for Wilde's arrival than he had expected. The iconoclastic local press, perceiving an icon whose eccentricities merited deflation and fed by the D'Oyly Carte publicity machine, swarmed all over the *SS Arizona* when it dropped anchor in New York harbour on 2 January 1882. Wilde alluded to them as having 'come out of the sea', a description which was no doubt informed by his low opinion of the primeval nature of some of the treatment to which he had been subjected by journalists.

The assembled hacks must have been puzzled by the Wilde who greeted them amiably on board the ship (it had been quarantined overnight). For a start the poet was taller and better built than most of his journalistic audience had expected. One correspondent wrote that 'Instead of having a small delicate hand only fit to caress a lily, his fingers are long and when doubled up, would form a fist that would hit a hard knock.'[29] The New York *World*, intent on detecting *something* of the aesthete about him, decided that he spoke in verse, emphasising every fourth syllable.[30] The reporters' questions moved quickly from the bland (Why was Mr Wilde visiting the USA? What are aesthetics?) to the downright bizarre (At what temperature did he like his bath?).[31] Wilde fielded the queries politely and with complete equanimity, easily winning the first-round scrap with New York's fourth estate on points.

The only glancing blow landed by the press corps related to an innocuous question about his journey. This drew from Wilde the tongue-in-cheek observation that the Atlantic Ocean had been a disappointment. Predictably the result was at least one headline that read, 'Mr. Wilde disappointed with the Atlantic.' This prompted a riposte in a British publication signed by 'THE ATLANTIC OCEAN' that began, 'I am disappointed in Mr. Wilde.' His oft-quoted remark to a New York customs official upon being asked had he anything to declare ('Nothing. Nothing but my genius') was uttered out of earshot of any witnesses.[32] It has more than a whiff of retro-spection about it.

In New York, one of Wilde's first ports of call was, predictably, a performance of *Patience* where he himself became a far greater object of attention than the proceedings onstage. His east-coast tour was a considerable success, despite the extensive newspaper use of quotes from his lectures forcing him to add considerably to his repertoire and attempts by undergraduate clowns to disrupt his talks by aping his costume and persona. D'Oyly Carte's agent, Colonel W.F. Morse, enthusiastically added more lectures to the schedule as Wilde became almost as big a hit as his illustrious precursor, Charles Dickens. The aspirant Irish poet's fame spread to such an extent that he was able to meet with two of the giants of American letters, Walt Whitman and the ailing Henry Wadsworth Longfellow (the latter much against the wishes of his highly protective sisters).

The subjects of Wilde's lectures, 'The English Renaissance', 'The House Beautiful' and 'The Decorative Arts', hardly seemed conducive to the rugged asymetricality of the American frontier but, nonetheless, Colonel Morse was successful in organising talks in some of the prin-cipal cities of the West in March and April of 1882. Furthermore, Wilde was persuaded to make the long and difficult journey, with results that have become a part of the legend of the frontier.

> His hair, parted in the middle, was so long that some Americans thought he was wearing a wig. One observer noted something 'womanly' about his mouth. He usually wore well cut English suits while travelling but for lecturing he donned a costume of

knee breeches, silk stockings, patent leather shoes with bright buckles, shirts with Lord Byron collars and frilly lace cuffs, and a cavalier cloak.[33]

The western historian Dee Brown's description of Oscar and his account of Wilde's twenty-lecture 'mini-tour' reeks of a sense of barely contained but amused incredulity. Although the late George Armstrong Custer sported long hair, Brown makes it clear that Wilde was entering a macho society in which such affectations were exceptional and constituted a statement that would normally invite the mocking attentions of the robust natives. Wilde welcomed derision and returned it with interest.

As he journeyed west Wilde seemed to recover some of his Irishness. St Paul, Minnesota had once been a frontier town. By the time Wilde reached it on St Patrick's Day 1882 it made no such continuing claims but it did boast a significant first- and second-generation Irish population. In addressing such groups Oscar exploited the affection many members of his audience had for his nationalistic mother, who wrote under the pseudonym Speranza. At one meeting she was described by the priest who introduced Wilde as 'one of Ireland's noblest daughters ... who in the troublous [sic] times of 1848 by the works of her pen and her noble example did much to keep the fire of patriotism burning brightly.' Wilde, who often skated over the difference between his native and his adoptive homes, played up to his mother's reputation. 'With the coming of the English,' he thundered, 'art in Ireland came to an end, and it has had no existence for over seven hundred years. I am glad it has not, for art could not live and flourish under a tyrant.'[34] While both theses are open to challenge, the sentiments went down well with his audience.

Oscar's journey to the far West was gruelling and tedious, 'in sleeping-cars stinking of cigar smoke, with ugly and pretentious cities at the end of the line'.[35] Despite his discomfort the poet was conscious of the majesty of the landscape through which he travelled. In his subsequent monograph, *Impressions of America,* he wrote that 'Perhaps the most beautiful part of America is the West, to reach which, however, involves a journey by rail of six days, racing along tied to an ugly tin kettle of a steam engine.' He was not flattered to discover that his reputation had preceded him in a manner guaranteed to cost him money. He wrote:

> I found but poor consolation for this journey in the fact that the
> boys who infest the cars and sell everything that one can eat –
> or should not eat – were selling editions of my poems, vilely
> printed on a kind of grey blotting paper, for the low price of ten
> cents.[36]

Editions of his poems cost up to $8 in New York, so he had good
reason to be peeved. When the young salesmen with whom he remonstrated were told who he was, they brought him some oranges from
their stock as a peace offering.

His first destination on the western leg of his tour was San
Francisco, a city barely thirty years old and singularly lacking in the
social graces (as well as most of the pretensions) that Wilde would have
encountered on the east coast. But he took the city as he found it and
discovered much that pleased him, albeit at times it appeared that he
did so determinedly.

In *Impressions* he wrote that 'San Francisco is a really beautiful city.'
But he reserved most of his approval for Chinatown, which he found
to be

> the most artistic town I have ever come across … In the
> Chinese restaurant, where these navvies meet to have supper in
> the evening, I found them drinking tea out of china cups as
> delicate as the petals of a rose-leaf, whereas at the gaudy hotels
> I was supplied with a delf cup an inch and a half thick.[37]

The 'gaudy hotel' in which he stayed was a San Franciscan landmark,
the Palace, built around a winter garden where an orchestra played
while people took tea, presumably from the very cups that were too
clumsy for Oscar.

While in San Francisco, Wilde demonstrated his ability to consume
large quantities of alcohol without appearing to suffer the consequences. It was a capacity that would stand to him later during his
most authentic brush with the 'Wild West'. Members of an exclusive
'gentleman's society', the Bohemian Club, decided that the city's most
illustrious visitor was 'A Miss Nancy'[38] and invited him to a drinking
challenge. He stayed with them measure for measure before outstripping the entire room and leaving every last Bohemian drunk. So
impressed were the members that they commissioned a portrait of
Wilde for the club's walls.

Oscar was less impressed by his brief stay in Salt Lake City, centre of the Mormon universe and of overt polygamy. With his customary broad brush he described the female members of the Church of Jesus Christ of Latter-Day Saints as ugly and the Tabernacle (the architectural centrepiece of the Mormon faith) as 'like a soup kettle'.[39] Utah was a prelude to Wilde's genuine 'frontier experience', which took him to Colorado. He had been invited there by one of the richest men in the territory, Horace Tabor, who, unsurprisingly, had amassed his huge fortune from mining. Wilde was engaged to lecture in Tabor's two opera houses. One was located in Denver, the other in the Rocky Mountains in the mining 'boom town' of Leadville. Tabor's own story is another of those barely credible tales of the Old West. His impressive full name of Horace Austin Warner Tabor belied his humble background. He was a grocer and occasional postmaster from Vermont who had brought his wife, Augusta, and his family west during the first heat of the Pike's Peak gold rush in the 1850s in Colorado and had made a fortune by 'grubstaking'[40] two miners in his grocery store. They struck it rich and he shared in their good luck.

It was with that money and millions more earned from his Matchless Mine that Tabor built the opera houses in Leadville and Denver where Wilde was to speak. Long before the redoubtable aesthete had ascended the 14,000 feet to one of the highest opera houses in the world, Tabor had divested himself of Augusta and married a young, beautiful, blonde, blue-eyed divorcée named Elizabeth McCourt Doe, known as Baby Doe. A dedicated shopper, Elizabeth in her turn divested Tabor of a goodly percentage of his millions and when the repeal of the Sherman Silver Purchase Act of 1893 led to the collapse of his mines, the couple was left virtually destitute. Ironically, the story of Horace, Augusta and Baby Doe became the subject of an opera by Douglas Moore in 1956 entitled *The Ballad of Baby Doe*.[41]

But it was a Horace Tabor at the height of his wealth and fame who was responsible for bringing Wilde to the true West. Leadville was a mining town with rough and ready manners, hundreds of combative and hard-drinking miners, five banks, three newspapers, seven churches, seven schools, 120 saloons, 118 gambling houses and thirty-five brothels.[42] But it was to the considerably larger and somewhat more cosmopolitan town of Denver that Wilde travelled first. His visit was eagerly anticipated. A reception was planned at the railway station to greet his arrival. Despite the lateness of the train and a cutting April snowstorm, a large crowd greeted him and followed his carriage through the muddy streets of the city to the opera house.

However, it was his visit to Leadville that created the legend of the Wilde West. At first Oscar was understandably reluctant to travel to a town notorious for its tough and often violent inhabitants. But Tabor, and presumably some portion of the magnate's wealth, persuaded him to make the trip. The writer himself, in his subsequent account of the experience, denied any disinclination to make the journey to 'the richest city in the world [where] every man carries a revolver'. 'I was told,' he wrote in *Impressions*, 'that if I went there they would be sure to shoot me or my travelling manager. I wrote and told them that nothing that they could do to my travelling manager would intimidate me.'[43]

Initially the good and rumbustious citizens of Leadville were unimpressed with the famous dandy in their midst. There was no welcoming committee and no curious onlookers in the lobby of his hotel, the Clarendon. Undeterred, Oscar donned his breeches and lectured to the sceptical miners on decorative art. His mood cannot have been improved when he was informed that the act preceding his own had been a lynching. 'Two men had been seized for committing a murder, and in that theatre they had been brought on to the stage at eight o'clock in the evening, and there tried and executed before a crowded audience.' Enough curious members of the lynch mob stayed on to provide a sizeable audience for Wilde. His lecture was interrupted occasionally by ribald comments, but the guns stayed in their holsters. The writer's own account gives something of a flavour of the occasion:

> They are miners – men working in metals, so I lectured to them on the Ethics of Art. I read them passages from the autobiography of Benvenuto Cellini and they seemed much delighted. I was reproved by my hearers for not having brought him with me. I explained that he had been dead for some little time which elicited the enquiry, 'Who shot him?'[44]

Then the fun began as the miners introduced the aesthete to the culture of the West. First came the trawl of the local saloons, during which Wilde made an observation that has become one of the most famous and misquoted in western lore.

> They afterwards took me to a dancing saloon where I saw the only rational method of art criticism I have ever come across. Over the piano was printed a notice:-
>
> PLEASE DO NOT SHOOT THE PIANIST
> HE IS DOING HIS BEST
>
> The mortality among pianists in that place is marvellous.[45]

The line is usually mis-rendered as 'Don't shoot me, I'm only the piano player.' Wilde must have taken his own survival and the absence of any shooting during his talk as a compliment and endorsement.

The saloon crawl was followed by another failed attempt to get the Irishman drunk. By now wearing corduroy trousers and the wide-brimmed hat favoured by the miners, Wilde was brought to Tabor's Matchless Mine and lowered, by bucket ('in which it was impossible to be graceful'), down the mineshaft. There he was greeted by a dozen miners, each with a bottle. 'Having got into the heart of the mountain I had supper, the first course being whisky, the second whisky and the third whisky.' The Leadville miners were no more successful in seeing Wilde in his cups than the Bohemian Club had been. The *Denver Post* reported: 'By invariable Western custom every bottle must make the rounds. Within a few minutes all have had twelve snorters. The miners, without exception are rather dizzy, but Wilde remains cool, steady, and went away showing neither fatigue nor intoxication.' Wilde recorded that 'The amazement of the miners when they saw that art and appetite could go hand in hand knew no bounds.' They cheered him to the echo, calling him a 'bully boy with no glass eye'.[46]

The drinking binge was, however, one of only two diversions laid on by Tabor. The other was the opening blow in the creation of a new shaft to be known as 'The Oscar'. This was done with a silver chisel. Writing back to England, Wilde acknowledged, at his flippant best, 'I had hoped that in their grand simple way they would have offered me shares in "The Oscar" but in their artless untutored fashion they did not.'[47]

Wilde, despite his undoubted misgivings, was as delighted by the miners as they were by him. 'I found these miners very charming and not at all rough,' he wrote. He even began to ape the fashions of his hosts, acquiring a cowboy neckerchief and tucking his trousers into his boots. According to Dee Brown, 'The poet, who had come west to teach frontiersmen the art of proper dress, had wound up adopting their style of clothing.'[48] In his lecture on decorative art in America, he extolled the virtues of western mining couture, hats, cloaks and boots in particular, claiming:

> They wore only what was comfortable and therefore beautiful. As I looked at them I could not help thinking with regret of the time when these picturesque miners should have made their fortunes and would go East to assume again all the abominations of modern fashionable attire.[49]

While he might have admired the well-adapted western costume, Wilde had no illusions about the knowledge or appreciation of the average westerner of art or aesthetics. He wrote in *Impressions*:

> So infinitesimal did I find the knowledge of Art, west of the Rocky Mountains, that an art patron – one who in his day had been a miner – actually sued the railroad company for damages because the plaster cast of Venus de Milo, which he had imported from Paris, had been delivered minus the arms. And, what is more surprising still, he gained his case and the damages.[50]

Throughout his sojourn in the USA, Wilde had been dogged by imitators. Most had adopted his costume and manners in various futile attempts to inflict death by parody. Some had intended to flatter and express their admiration. Eugene Field just did what was expected of him.

Field, editor of the Denver *Tribune*, was a famous prankster. He had allowed Wilde's first visit to Denver to go unchallenged, but when the poet's return offered him an opportunity to perpetrate a hoax on the *nouveaux riches* of Denver, he grabbed it with inky hands. Wilde was to deliver his last western lecture in Denver on 15 April. He was coming from Colorado Springs and managed to miss the train that would have got him to his destination comfortably. He wired ahead to say that he would be delayed but would still make the lecture in time. As luck would have it Colonel Morse's representative in Denver sought Field's advice on what he should do about the reception committee – tell them to go home or say nothing and have them wait for three hours.

Field advised him to say nothing, figuring that few if any members of the reception committee would ever have seen the Irishman at close quarters. He rapidly concocted a plan to fill Wilde's place. Collecting a fur-collared overcoat, a broad-brimmed hat, a long-haired wig, a cravat and a sunflower for his lapel, he drove a buggy to the last stop before Denver and boarded the train that should have numbered the great champion of decorative art among its passengers. A friend of Field's, Joseph G. Brown, later wrote an account of what happened next: 'To the cheering crowd on the platform Field, with bared head, bowed gravely. Then followed a leisurely drive through the principal business streets where he created a sensation.' Field offered the occasional desultory wave but pretended to be ensconced in a book. The carriage drove to the offices of the *Tribune* where, ironically, Wilde was due to give an interview. Only there did Field reveal himself to the more obsequious members of the welcoming committee who had accompanied him all the way.[51] Wilde's reaction to the hoax is not recorded but it was a fitting finale to an eventful trip.

While Wilde had contrived to hobnob with some of the giants of American literature during his visit to the east coast, he narrowly missed an opportunity to meet a legend of the West. On his way back to New York he spent a week or so giving talks in Kansas and Missouri (declining an invitation for a visit from the people of Griggsville by cabling them to change the name of their town and he might consider their request). While passing through St Joseph, Missouri, he learned that the entire town was in mourning for one of their adoptive sons, the outlaw Jesse James, who had just been shot in the back by Bob Ford. In true American fashion someone was already making money out of his death. Wilde wrote to his friend Nellie Sickert:

> his door knocker and dust bin went for fabulous prices, two speculators absolutely came to pistol shots as to who was to have his hearth brush, the unsuccessful one being, however, consoled by being allowed to purchase the water butt, for the income of an English bishop.[52]

The West took to Oscar Wilde and the feelings were reciprocated. He told the San Francisco *Examiner* that 'The further West one comes the more there is to like.' Granted, that is precisely the kind of comment someone trying to sell tickets would make in the circumstances, but he also observed elsewhere that 'Western people are much more genial than those in the East ... I am really appreciated by the cultured classes.'[53] He was quite genuine in his affectionate memories of the Leadville miners and their hospitality. He certainly dined out on his visit and regaled the salons of London with tall tales of his travels. He convinced the French writer Edward de Goncourt that he had seen a man hanged from the scenery uprights while the audience fired their revolvers at him from their seats.

Wilde came and went leaving the West intact. He entertained many and enlightened rather fewer. As Dee Brown put it in his irreverent *Wondrous Times on the Frontier*:

> And so the frontier West bade farewell to Oscar Wilde, who had come there to instruct its denizens in the finer things of life. Whatever the individual Westerner may have thought of the visitor, all would have agreed that his presence brought a goodly amount of jollity to their lives, whether he intended it or not.[54]

Sir Horace Plunkett: aristocratic rancher

The Plunketts of Dunsany had spent more than six centuries living in the shadow of the ancient Hill of Tara, seat of the High Kings of Ireland, before Horace Curzon Plunkett, second son of Lord Dunsany, decided to try his luck in a setting far removed from the rich pastures of County Meath. Plunkett was unlikely to accede to his father's title, barring a tragic accident to his older brother, but he still sacrificed a lot in exchanging the Royal County for Johnson and Converse Counties. While in Ireland, as well as helping to look after his father's estate, situated between Trim and Navan, he was a gregarious individual who rode to hounds three or four times a week, regularly visited the theatre in Dublin and travelled often to London.

He had also made a beginning in the enterprise that would later ensure his place in Irish history, as a great champion of the co-operative movement. When he came down from Oxford in 1878 (with a second in History) he opened a store in the village of Dunsany that sold groceries and offered farmers a market for some of their produce. It was a limited liability company with small farmers and labourers as shareholders rather than a co-operative and Plunkett described it himself as 'a small beginning'.[55]

Why did he leave Ireland? According to his biographer, Trevor West, it was to escape death from tuberculosis, a disease endemic in Ireland at the time and which had taken his mother when he was only four years old. It was not a matter of whether, but of where. He was advised to opt for anywhere with a warm, dry climate. Plunkett chose the American West because he was influenced by the enthusiasm of others who preceded him and by tales of huge fortunes to be made in the region. When he chose Wyoming as his base he was opting for a region that had only become a territory in 1869. Nearly 40 per cent of the population were immigrants and the Irish were the best-represented grouping. So Plunkett would be sharing the territory with many of his countrymen, albeit not men and women of the same social class as himself.

He left for the USA in 1879, arriving in Denver in the autumn of that year before travelling north to Johnson County, Wyoming, more than 200 miles north of the future state capital, Cheyenne. Before the winter of that year he established the EK Ranch in the Powder River valley after buying $135,000 worth of land from the Union Pacific at a dollar an acre. He had ten years to pay the railroad back. His new home was a fertile, well-wooded region in a territory of stark and startling contrasts. Wyoming is well above sea level at its lowest point but rises to between 6,000 and 7,000 feet in parts, much of the higher regions being good grassland. To the west lies what would later become Yellowstone National Park. This landscape includes much of the majestic Grand Teton mountain range, which rises to heights of 10,000 feet and more. Much of the lower-lying parts of the region consist of sagebrush terrain, suitable for the rearing of cattle. The rest was arid 'badlands', suitable for nothing at all unless minerals were located there or the increasingly ubiquitous railways happened to traverse them. Plunkett's EK land was amongst the best in the territory. (Wyoming became a state in 1890.)

Despite the quality of his new establishment, Plunkett had chosen to locate himself in a tough and often hostile environment. To this day the population of Wyoming is small (around half a million) and settlements then were few and far between. The weather, leaving aside the brutal winters, could be violently stormy and freakishly erratic. Conditions in the months from November to March were at least predictable – predictably ghastly. Temperatures of -20 or -30 degrees were a daily reality.

It was a wild, rural landscape in which a man without a horse or a man who owned a horse but lacked the skill to ride it adequately was at a distinct disadvantage. A lifetime spent among the rural Irish aristocracy had refined Plunkett's riding skills but sometimes his sense of direction was found wanting. During one round-up he was directed towards a well-stocked camp but was unable to find it before nightfall. He was forced to camp out on the open range only to discover the following morning, to his considerable chagrin, that the camp was a mere three-quarters of a mile from his temporary and frugal bivouac. To cover his embarrassment he told no one. But when the traces of his overnight camp were found, the story did the rounds and he was subjected to the customary veteran's ribbing of the callow 'greenhorn'.

Plunkett avoided the worst rigours of the Wyoming winter by spending that part of his year in Ireland, returning to Dunsany each October. During the more clement spring, summer and autumn months he dealt with any sense of isolation from society by becoming an active member of the Cheyenne Club. Here the territory's business and agricultural grandees enjoyed their privileges. According to other members, Plunkett could play tennis while simultaneously calling out chess plays to an opponent on the sidelines.[56] He was also a member of the Wyoming Stock Growers Association, an organisation that, shortly after his final return to Ireland, would incur notoriety in the so-called 'Johnson County War'. The Stock Growers Association was meant to look after the interests of its well-heeled members, but what it signally failed to do was protect them against themselves.

In the 1880s most of the land of Wyoming was (and much still is) owned by the federal government. For an initial capital investment in livestock, a rancher could hope to make a significant amount of money allowing his cattle free range on federal land. The idea was to let them breed and fatten on US federal grass, employ a few hands to tend to them all the year round and dozens of itinerant 'cowboys' to gather them together during the twice yearly round-ups and rake in the profits. In the good years this could be between 30 and 50 per cent on the initial outlay. An owner's cattle would be branded to avoid confusion with the herds of other stock growers or ranchers (a practice open to widespread abuse). But the acquisitive nature of the beef ranchers and the frequent need to satisfy the demands of east coast and European investors led to rampant overstocking. One estimate suggested that the entire territory of Wyoming was capable of sustaining, at most, a population of 50,000 head of cattle. In 1884 there were 150,000 beeves grazing the open ranges of the region.

In his ten years in Wyoming, Plunkett faced many hazards. Some came from the weather. Lightning strikes were frequent. Hailstones big enough to kill animals were often recorded, even in spring and autumn. In the spring round-up of 1883 Plunkett nearly lost his horse in a torrential stream. The following day the animal, weakened by the earlier struggle, succumbed to the raging waters of the gloriously named Ten Sleep Creek and Plunkett was forced to swim for his life.

Some hazards came from animals. Snakebites were frequent. The remedy was to suck the poison out and medicate the patient with whiskey. Once when Plunkett came upon a victim he decided not to use the traditional method to extract the rattlesnake venom, as there was no evidence of swelling but much evidence of alcohol. 'I fear the snake less than the whiskey,' he recorded in his diary.

But the biggest threat came from the human population. Although the danger from Native American tribes had more or less disappeared by the time of Plunkett's arrival, rustlers, thieves and fifty-seven other varieties of outlaw abounded in Wyoming. Not long after Plunkett's final departure, Johnson County and the Powder River valley played host to the notorious criminals George Parker and Harry Longabaugh. They were better known in their infamy as the two leaders of the Hole in the Wall Gang, Butch Cassidy and the Sundance Kid.

Just as much of a threat were some of Plunkett's own peer group. Located to the south-west of Plunkett's ranch was that of a couple of aristocratic English brothers, Richard and Moreton Frewen, members of a family with old Irish connections. Around the same age as Plunkett, they had begun their Wyoming enterprise the year prior to his arrival. Initially it thrived but gradually Moreton (who would later become a brother-in-law of Winston Churchill) began to run it into the ground, earning himself the nickname 'Mortal Ruin' in the process.[57] Plunkett struck up a friendship with the two brothers in the early years, but by the late 1880s was writing that 'they have lots of ability but no ballast … Dick is crochety in business and Moreton regardless of the value of money.'[58]

Unfortunately it was other people's money that Moreton Frewen had least regard for and by 1886 his London-based investors in the Powder River Cattle Company wanted him replaced. Plunkett was approached to take over the Frewen ranch and run it along with his own. He agreed, unwisely, in order to protect his own spread from the consequences of any liquidation of the Powder River Company. The result was a 'war to the knife'[59] with the Frewen brothers. Plunkett, on examining the true condition of the Powder River spread, was shocked by what he found but recommended, at first, that the business be continued rather than liquidated. He bent over backwards to be fair to the English brothers, more so than they deserved. In his report he said of the particularly inept Dick Frewen, for example, that 'his zeal somewhat outstripped his discretion'.[60] This sort of understatement did not reconcile either of the Frewens to the Irishman who was now passing judgement on their activities.

The Frewens transmitted their hostility towards Plunkett to their employees as well. However, the Powder River cowboys would have had plenty of reasons of their own to disapprove of the new dispensation. In order to reduce costs, Plunkett was forced to offer the cowboys lower wages for the 1886 round-up. He wrote of the often short-tempered and potentially homicidal employees:

> They were not cordial at all. They have been talking of shooting me all winter, as I have been made the scapegoat of the attempt to reduce wages. I think I shall outlive it. But it is unpleasant being scowled at and talked at by blackguards.[61]

Plunkett expected his many virtues to be reflected in others, particularly those of his own class. But when the combination of reckless adventurism and personal sniping forced him to the conclusion that he was not dealing with men as honourable as he was himself, the Irish aristocrat had no difficulty summoning a streak of ruthlessness to his aid in dealing with his incompetent peers. By early 1887 he had performed an about turn and advocated liquidation of the Powder River Company as soon as was practicable. Moreton Frewen took his struggle across the Atlantic, lambasting the Irishman at a shareholders meeting. He told the general meeting in London in March 1887 that Plunkett had been 'an unfortunate choice' as rescuer of the company, before adding that 'he is altogether too weak a man, in my judgement, for the critical times on which we [have] fallen in this business'.[62]

The times were even more critical than Frewen knew. While the shareholders fought in London, the herds in Wyoming were freezing to death in one of the harshest winters on record in a place where the word 'harsh' and 'winter' are synonymous. When Plunkett returned to Wyoming in May 1887 and the extent of the winter losses (up to 75 per cent of the stock had simply melted away) became apparent to him, he confided to his diary that it was 'a calamity indeed'.[63] The board agreed to cut its losses and liquidate the company. Moreton Frewen blamed Plunkett for abandoning a project that he felt could have been rescued. Plunkett, for his part, had lost all confidence in the Frewens and considered Moreton, in particular, to be an unscrupulous liar. The Powder River Company was wrapped up at a considerable loss to the main shareholders.

There was a postscript to the episode when the two men, coincidentally, met many years later in the home of Shane Leslie, Frewen's nephew (the three Jerome sisters had married Frewen, John Leslie and Randolph Churchill). Given Moreton Frewen's belligerent nature, the occasion might have been marked by some unpleasantness but instead both men chose to remain in 'utter silence'[64] in each other's presence.

The big chill of 1886–7 was the first of three consecutive winters that almost brought the Wyoming cattle business to its knees. By 1889 the game was up for many of the European adventurers who had fetched up in the territory and for their backers at home. Plunkett's departure from the American West was partially dictated by a decline in his and everybody else's fortunes and partly because of his father's failing health and his own increased responsibilities in Dunsany. Prior to his final departure, he prefigured his support for Irish self-reliance and independence by becoming an advocate of statehood in his adopted home. This was a move not generally favoured among his well-heeled peers, who feared increased taxation if Wyoming were to become a state. A referendum on the issue was passed by a three to one majority in November 1889, the winter of Plunkett's departure from Cheyenne. He was given a good send-off by the members of the Cheyenne Club and his own assessment of his decade in the USA was a positive one. He observed that 'I have gained much experience of men and affairs – more valued is my understanding of the vast sprawling energy, the idealism, the crudity and generosity of a country like America.'[65]

One myth that grew up around Plunkett at the time of his death surrounds his supposedly legendary story-telling abilities during his stay in Wyoming. In his obituary, the *Boston Globe* described a story-telling contest between Plunkett and Jim Bridger – should the reader be getting a sense of *déjà vu*, the details make it clear that the story relates to St George Gore, not to Plunkett. To the *Globe*, one Anglo-Irish aristocrat must have been pretty much like any other. By the time Plunkett moved to Wyoming, Bridger had long since left the region – in 1871, at the age of sixty-seven, he had settled on a farm in Missouri and died there in 1881, barely a year after Plunkett's arrival in the USA.

The assessments of Plunkett's time in Wyoming from his biographers are very positive. Margaret Digby pointed out that, though Plunkett was often overworked, lonely and homesick, 'On the other hand he was exercising nearly all his faculties in an environment which gave them full play.'[66] Trevor West believes that 'The challenge of Wyoming lay in the fact that the *a priori* advantages of class and social standing counted for little in the Powder River Valley where he was simply a man among men'.[67] This aspect of his sojourn was reinforced by the *Boston Globe* obituary which pointed out that, while he was 'somebody' in London, 'out on the great Wyoming cattle range he was just "Hod" Plunkett, just as good as anybody else and not one whit better. He held up his end of the "stick".'[68]

Frank Harris: cowboy

James Thomas Harris, better known as Frank Harris, was an Irish-born journalist and writer largely celebrated today for his associations with the likes of Wilde and Shaw rather than for his own prose, with one obvious exception. His authorship, when in his sixties, of the memoir *My Life and Loves* in 1925 guaranteed him the same sort of notoriety as D.H. Lawrence gained from the fictional *Lady Chatterley's Lover* and Casanova earned from his accounts of his own *amours*.

Harris was described by Max Beerbohm as 'the best talker in London' at a time when the likes of Oscar Wilde, Winston Churchill and George Bernard Shaw provided garrulous competition. He had some merit as a writer of literary fiction and much more success as the editor of a number of literary journals. He was a plausible rogue, and reading his work as well as some of what was written about him, one gets the distinct impression of a man who was never quite as astonishing as he believed himself to be. In addition to the controversy he courted with the publication of *My Life and Loves*, he is also best remembered for an excellent but not entirely favourable biography of his erstwhile friend, Oscar Wilde. Wilde had dedicated *An Ideal Husband* to him, citing 'Frank Harris, a slight tribute to his power and distinction as an artist, his chivalry and nobility as a friend'. Harris must have had enough self-awareness to have been conscious of the irony of having a play of that title dedicated to him.

Harris was born (in Galway) on 14 February 1855, son of a naval lieutenant, and spent his early years in Kerry. The family moved to Kingstown (now Dun Laoghaire) near Dublin in 1859, after Harris's mother died, leaving five children behind (in order of age, Vernon, Willie, Annie, Frank and Chrissie). Before he reached his teens he was sent to an English grammar school, a place he despised. He made his escape at the age of fifteen when he won a prize of ten pounds in a maths competition. He fled the grammar school and used the prize money to secure passage on a ship to the USA.

His first work in New York was as a diver, employed in the construction of the Brooklyn Bridge. It was dangerous work and few stuck it for long. Within a short period he had moved to Chicago, where he worked as a night clerk in a hotel called the Freemont House. His sojourn in the West began in the spirit of adventure and (according to his own account) out of a desire to renew an acquaintance with a beautiful Mexican girl whose family had stayed at the Freemont.

In June 1871, when he was barely sixteen years old, three cattlemen, Reece, Dell and Ford, arrived at the hotel. Reece was Welsh, Dell was English and only Ford appears to have been American.

> [They] were going down to the Rio Grande to buy cattle and drive 'em back to market in Kansas City. Cattle, it appeared, could be bought in South Texas for a dollar a head or less and fetched from fifteen to twenty dollars each in Chicago.[69]

Harris was enchanted and with the exuberance and irrationality of youth instantly decided that he wanted to leave Chicago with them and become a cowboy. They agreed to take him along and so his brief career in the Wild West began.

On the journey from Kansas to Eureka in Texas he was introduced to a man who would have a major influence on his western rite of passage, a cowman called simply Bob. Harris described him as 'a little dried up Mexican, hardly five feet three in height, half Spaniard, half Indian'.[70] He put Bob's age at anywhere between thirty and fifty. Had he asked he would probably have been told to mind his own business. Bob was as taciturn in English as he was voluble in Spanish – a language which the young Irishman didn't speak. Bob was an expert horseman and *nonpareil* when it came to his knowledge of steers, their upkeep and their foibles. Over the next six months he warmed to Harris (mainly on the basis that he was 'no Americano') and taught the Irishman much that would prove useful to him as a cowboy.

By Harris's own account (which should be approached with a certain scepticism), he became the hunter of the outfit because of his unerring and totally instinctive sense of direction. He admits to one major limitation as a hunter-gatherer: short sightedness. It is hard to reconcile his claim that he became a 'fair shot almost at once' with his admission that, because of astigmatism, even with the aid of glasses, he could not see very far. Whatever his physical failings, he was certainly well enough armed for the hunt. Before leaving Chicago he had bought a shotgun, a Winchester rifle and a revolver.

His description of his activities on the open prairie between Kansas and Texas have an idyllic quality about them (they were to be lightly fictionalised in his novel *On the Trail*, published in 1930). He enjoyed his solitude. The air was brisk and dry, even on hot mornings, partly because of the altitude (about 2,000 feet above sea level). Harris had plenty of time to ponder the great mysteries of life and credits this period with bestowing upon him the ability to think and reason. He was stimulated to do so by what he describes as an extraordinarily high level of debate around the campfire each evening – 'talk usually turned to bawd or religion or the relations of capital and labour'.[71] Despite his philosophical meanderings, he claims not to have neglected his duties. 'Game was plentiful; hardly an hour would elapse before I had got half a dozen ruffled grouse or a deer.'[72]

After about ten days the small group reached their destination, a modestly proportioned 5,000-acre ranch near Eureka. Ford ('The

Boss') had clearly got his priorities right. According to Harris, accommodation for the horses was vastly superior to that enjoyed by the ranch hands. In Texas in the 1870s a cowman ranked above a steer in monetary value but trailed well behind a good horse.

The group didn't remain in Eureka for long. Within two days they had set about the task of acquiring a herd of cattle to drive northwards. Ten cowboys would gather together 6,000 cattle to be driven to the railhead and beyond. Early on in this process Harris was fortunate not to be killed by one of the many hazards faced on the trail: snakes. While tending the campfire before his day's work he was bitten on the thumb by a small prairie rattlesnake. He immediately bit the poison from the wound and shoved his thumb into the embers of the fire. Because the snake had been so small he assumed it was not sufficiently venomous to cause him any serious problems and thought nothing more of the incident.

Later that day his wound was noticed and he was questioned about it by Reece and Ford. His attempts to shrug it off were dismissed and he was immediately plied with whiskey. Contrary to national stereotype, he was reluctant to drink it. The two older men established, to their obvious concern, that Harris was feeling no pain from his burned thumb and instantly set about ensuring that he did not fall asleep. Grabbing an arm each, they walked him up and down the campsite. When he was almost overwhelmed with fatigue and begged to be allowed to sleep he was told brusquely that if he did so he would never awaken again. Only when he became conscious of an intense pain from his thumb was he allowed to rest. In the course of his time in the West, he would lose two colleagues in similar circumstances.

Harris, however, did not succumb to one of the other perils of the prairie: venereal disease. As the cattle drive began to hit the infamous cow towns, the young hands were given their wages by the trail boss. Harris commented on the collective relief from the sort of cabin fever that even the open prairie can induce. He also witnessed for the first time the alcohol- and testosterone-fuelled orgies for which cowboys were notorious. Clearly their tolerance for alcohol did not match their unbridled enthusiasm for whiskey. Harris maintains that within half an hour of hitting a town those with the money to indulge their appetites would be 'crazy drunk'. This would inevitably lead to the desire for the satisfaction of other appetites. The consequence of their intent to locate 'some girl with whom to spend the night' was usually felt a few weeks later when, one by one, the hands would be forced to lay off because of venereal disease. Harris insists that, on this particular trip, 'all the younger men fell to the same plague'.[73] Their recuperation was often complicated by the painful process of rehabilitation. This caused many to resort to drink, rendering the condition chronic. Harris's youth and his, as yet, relatively underdeveloped libido saved him from a similar fate.

The hierarchy of hazard for the western drover included weather, wildlife (literally and metaphorically), water, women, weapons and wrongdoing. Floods and electrical storms were a constant threat to man and beast. Snakes could cause fatal injury and spook horses or steers into initiating a stampede. Crossing rivers almost inevitably resulted in stock losses and the occasional employee fatality. Randy cowboys were the architects of their own misfortune when it came to their dealings with women. The fact of being almost constantly armed often had its own consequences when disputes, drunken or sober, became ugly. Rustlers (white or Native American) were a regular menace.

In his western sojourn, Harris would meet some of the elements of this hierarchy. His one brief encounter with a Native American was not far from Wichita, a railhead town in Kansas. The drive had been skirting Indian territory for some time without incident. Bob had warned Harris that small bands of Indians, or even single individuals, might try to stampede the cattle in the hope of catching a few strays. Harris recounts one incident in which a lone Indian, with the aid of a flapping white sheet and an 'unearthly yell', tried to stampede the herd. He took a shot at the Indian. Though he missed, the would-be rustler dropped the sheet and fled. Bob and Harris, according to his account, managed to calm the herd, though he doesn't tell us why the shot had no significant effect on the temperamental animals.

A later encounter with Indians was more dramatic and costly. On a subsequent cattle drive during the latter half of his year spent in the West, Harris and four colleagues (including the indefatigable Mexican Bob) found themselves besieged and surrounded by a force of Indians that he claims numbered over 100. Even by Harris's highly developed standards of hyperbole this has to be a monumental exaggeration. Though it was the early 1870s, well before the total military subjugation of the Native American, a raiding party of that magnitude would be extremely rare. What is even more difficult to credit is the notion of such a large force bothering to besiege rather than simply overpower a group of five cowboys, however tough and well armed they might have been. According to Harris, that defensive force was further reduced by 20 per cent after he was dispatched by the others to seek military help in Fort Dodge. Within six days he had returned with a cavalry lieutenant and a force of twenty troopers. His companions were still alive but had only been able to save about a tenth of the herd they were escorting northwards.

Any sympathy for Harris and the Texan drovers would, however, be misplaced. The bulk of the herd had been acquired by means of rustling. Not, perish the thought, from other Texans, but across the Rio Grande from a wealthy Mexican rancher whose stock was considered fair game. In his self-aggrandising account of that particular theft, the casual racism of Harris is extremely distasteful but fairly typical of his class and, unfortunately, of his nationality. The ranch hands of the Mexican stock-owner made an attempt to recapture his cattle and were repulsed by the cowboys. Harris observes in *My Life and Loves* that 'Nobody took the fight seriously; whipping greasers was nothing to brag about'.[74] The very formulation of the sentence is couched in the Texan vernacular. It reads like something overheard by a child and repeated as axiomatic. It is interesting that his contempt for Mexican opponents is not matched by a similar disdain for Native Americans – though any regard he might have had for them was probably based on their formidable combative reputation rather than on respect for their culture or way of life.

One thing that does come across clearly and with little obvious exaggeration or ornamentation in the telling is the often violent nature of western society. This was particularly so in those parts of the West most frequented by cowboys, namely the freewheeling and lawless cow towns at the end of the cattle trails from Texas and New Mexico. Harris makes a telling observation that

> it was the Civil War that had bred those men to violence and the use of the revolver ... that produced the [gunmen] who forced the good humoured westerners to hold life cheaply and to use their guns instead of fists.[75]

Harris would not be the last commentator to make such a claim. There is little doubt that the USA owes much of its fixation with the gun to the aftermath of the 1861–5 civil conflict that left thousands of weapons in the hands of men who had been trained to use them and who were inured to doing so.

Harris records the demise of a young cowboy called Charlie, who liked to have a good time but who had an unfortunate penchant for contracting venereal diseases. While in the grip of syphilis and experiencing periods of wildly irrational behaviour, Charlie found himself in a gambling saloon. He became involved in a dispute with one of his fellow card players. Guns were drawn and shots were fired on both sides. Charlie, along with Harris and a number of other cowboys, fled the saloon, but Charlie had been fatally wounded and died on the trail. In a typical dime-novel conclusion to the anecdote (which serves to diminish its credibility somewhat), Harris has the dying man insisting that the thousand dollars, representing his share of the proceeds of his final cattle drive, is to be sent to his mother in Pleasant Hill, Missouri.

After a year as a cowboy, Harris learned that his older brother Willie had arrived in the USA and had set up in Lawrence, Kansas, a town that had suffered greatly during the Civil War, as a property agent. Willie asked Frank to join him in the enterprise and the younger man decided to abandon real estate for realty.

The narrative offered by Harris of his year in the Wild West is as boastful as are his subsequent claims of sexual athleticism on a grand scale. The fact that his account often reads like the storyline of a pulp novel could well be because much of what he wrote came from his reading or his imagination rather than from his experience. Nonetheless, between the braggadocio and the self-aggrandisement, he does provide an interesting and accurate-enough account of what life was like for the late-nineteenth-century cow-hand. The fact that it is not entirely romanticised lends it considerable credence.

Lord Dunraven: hunter

The seat of the Anglo-Irish Wyndham-Quin family is in the picturesque village of Adare, County Limerick. Today it is close enough to the expanding city of Limerick to fail to qualify for the description 'sleepy' any more. The Wyndham-Quin demesne and castle, once the home of the earls of Dunraven, are now a luxury hotel and a championship golf course. The fourth earl (Windham Thomas Wyndham-Quin) was born there in 1841 and followed the usual routes to Oxford and the army. Later his sense of adventure was satisfied in the leisure pursuits of steeplechasing and sailing and his sense of purpose defined by his work as a war correspondent in Abyssinia and in the Franco-Prussian War of 1870.

In between those two conflicts he squeezed in a wedding in April 1869 and his first visit to the USA. It clearly whetted his appetite and sparked an imagination that had been fuelled by the western adventures of his compatriot Captain Mayne Reid – 'my boyish brain cells were stored to bursting with tales of Red Indians and grizzly bears, caballeros and haciendas, prairies and buffaloes, Texans and Mexicans, cowboys and voyageurs and had not yet discharged or jettisoned their cargo.'[76]

Between 1871 and 1890 he was a regular visitor to North America and acquired 60,000 acres of Colorado land near Denver in what was to become Estes Park. An enthusiastic hunter, he used the area (vast by Irish standards) as a game reserve. He is one of the few Irishmen to have recorded his impressions of the American West. His autobiography, *Past Times and Pastimes*, published four years before his death in 1926, contains a section in which he recounts his 'sporting' triumphs in the West and, incidentally, comments on some of the major events and personalities of the period. It was preceded by a book devoted entirely to his travels in the Continental Divide region, *The Great Divide* (1876).

Two of the first western legends Dunraven encountered were General Phillip Sheridan and William 'Buffalo Bill' Cody. He formed a favourable impression of the diminutive army general ('a delightful man') but complained of his predilection for swearing like one of his troopers in polite company. Sheridan had more on his mind than the sporting activities of an Anglo-Irish peer. The meeting took place a few short years after the Fetterman Massacre and the Red Cloud uprising. Dunraven acknowledges that 'no man who attached any value to his scalp went out hunting or prospecting promiscuously'.[77] He attached himself to cavalry patrols whenever he hunted the prairie.

He also followed up on a letter of introduction from Sheridan to Cody. The latter he described as 'dark, with quick searching eyes, aquiline nose, and delicately cut features, and he wore his hair falling in long ringlets over his shoulders, in true Western style ... he looked like a picture of a cavalier in olden times.'[78] Cody was nothing if not cavalier, especially with the main food supply of the Plains Indians. As an employee of the Kansas Pacific Railway, his job was to supply railroad workers with meat. In the process of fulfilling his contract he killed 4,280 buffaloes in eighteen months.

Dunraven also encountered a colourful companion of Cody's. 'Texas' Jack Omohundro is referred to by Dunraven as a former cowboy. But he was also an ex-Confederate Army scout and an Indian fighter. Later in life he would tour with one of Buffalo Bill's shows and marry the leading lady.[79] At the time the Irish peer met him he had never been anywhere east of the Mississippi (neither had Cody).

A lot of Dunraven's writing consists of tedious hunting narratives. They are about as interesting as someone else's golf stories. He was a keen hunter but he was certainly not as destructive or bloodthirsty as Sir St George Gore. He is eager to emphasise that 'of one crime I have not been guilty, though accused of it. I have never wasted good food, never killed for the mere lust of killing.'[80]

One of the more interesting aspects of his narrative was his visit, in 1874, to the Yellowstone area of north-western Wyoming. Later it would become a national park, but in the early 1870s it was largely unexplored. Dunraven would have been one of the first non-Americans to have travelled there. His account includes one of the earliest descriptions of the Old Faithful geyser, so called because it would faithfully blow every forty-five minutes. Classifying Old Faithful as a male, Dunraven observes of the jet of boiling water that 'He throws it to a height of from 100 to 150 feet for the space of about five minutes during which time he keeps the top of the column almost at one level.'[81]

To underscore the fact that it was difficult to get away from Irishmen in the American West, Dunraven encountered one of his fellow countrymen during a trip to Montana in the autumn of 1874. It was in a tiny settlement called Stirling, not far from Virginia City. The man, who insisted on being known only as Mr Mahogany Bogstick, was unusual in that he was a teetotaller and a non-smoker. According to the Irish peer he was

> partial to petticoats and held that if only England would legislate justly for the Sister Isle, all the Irishmen in the world could

reside comfortably and happily at home with plenty to eat and drink, lots of land to live upon, and not a hand's turn of work to do.[82]

Dunraven does not record whether he engaged the man in political debate. By his own account Dunraven had at least one narrow escape from a grisly and infamous death (though we only have his word for it). Buffalo Bill was not the only mythic westerner with flowing locks whom he met. Colonel George Armstrong Custer appears to have been another acquaintance of the doughty earl. Dunraven insists that Custer invited him on a punitive expedition against the Sioux. The year was 1876. The Irish peer might well have accepted the invitation but it arrived too late. Had he been in a position to do so, he would not have been around to write his autobiography.

Despite avoiding almost certain death at the hands of the Lakota and Cheyenne at the Little Bighorn in June 1876, Dunraven had a soft spot for Native Americans. He recognised that they had been 'evilly treated in the United States' and contrasted their lives there with their management in Canada.

> Starved into submission by the designed extinction of their natural food, the buffalo, they have been secured by treaty in large reservations. Ousted out of their reservation, driven farther and farther, cheated by their agents, treated like vermin by intrusive settlers, they have been forced into chronic hostility. Not so across the border. Fairly treated in Canada, they have given but little trouble; order is kept by a few mounted police.[83]

Dunraven's links to the West were maintained for more than a decade and a half by his ownership of the game reserve in Estes Park in Colorado. When he purchased the property it was remote from civilisation, but as the area became more developed its attractions began to wane and Dunraven spent more time in the 1880s in Newfoundland and Nova Scotia satisfying his hunting instincts than he did in the USA. He died in London in 1926.

REEL
SIX

NOT SO GENTLE TAMERS:
IRISH WOMEN STAKE THEIR CLAIM

The incidence of single Irish women emigrating to the USA in the nineteenth century is far higher than one might assume of a century that looked askance at members of the 'fair sex' (the appellation itself oozes condescension) doing anything even remotely out of the ordinary. But, according to Ide O'Carroll in her book on Irish female emigration, *Models for Movers: Irish Women's Emigration to America*, which covers the post-Famine period, 'Irish women migrating at this time were generally unmarried. Their passage was paid for by female relatives and once established they generally assisted other women to emigrate by sending home passage money.'[1] Fifty-two per cent of Irish

128

migrants in the nineteenth century were women, as compared with 21 per cent of the next largest migratory group, the Italians.[2] German women comprised 41 per cent of that country's total migration, while Greek women were a mere 4 per cent.

Irish women left their homes 'to avoid the consequences of a new economic and social order that offered them only the most dismal prospects'.[3] Their departure had as much to do with the surrender of traditional cottage industries to the Industrial Revolution as it did with the Famine. Most of these female migrants ended up as domestic servants in the great cities of the east coast. Some made good marriages and moved up the socio-economic scale. Others never escaped from the depressing Irish ghettoes in places such as Hell's Kitchen or the Five Points in New York and some were driven into a life of crime and prostitution.

Unlike Irish emigration to the New World, Irish migration to the American West appears to have been overwhelmingly male. A few adventurous Irish women did, however, make the journey. Some did so as part of the westward agricultural migration, generally as the materfamilias of a farming family seeking land in Oregon or California. Some were shrewd businesswomen who saw opportunities for resourcefulness in a 'greenfield' situation, where gender and race were less important than toughness and enterprise when it came to forging a successful business career. Others either were, or became, prostitutes, who saw the western 'boom towns' as a means of achieving a slightly more attractive economic price for their services than that offered by domestic employment. They are not commonly viewed as female entrepreneurs, but many were just that.

In western parlance the women who managed to observe certain societal proprieties have been dubbed 'gentle tamers' by some historians, though many made little claim to either gentleness or gentility. Those whom the arbiters of respectability would have deemed to be of more dubious virtue were archly described as 'soiled doves'.

Initially those women who chose to go into business on their own account would, inevitably, come up against the brick wall of coverture. This was the legal principle whereby on marriage a wife would forfeit ultimate control of her enterprise to her husband. Where the West was concerned, it was federal pragmatism that overcame this egregious gender inequality. The desire to encourage women to settle on the frontier brought modifications to coverture. Changes in the Homestead Act and the introduction of the Married Women's Property Acts in the late 1880s allowed women to protect some of their assets from their spouses' controlling hands.[4]

Some not-very-gentle tamers

The most significant Irish-born businesswoman to thrive in the American West was born in Midleton, County Cork, in October 1845 just as the Great Famine was beginning to bite. Ellen Cashman, familiarly known as Nellie, would give her place of birth as 'Queenstown' whenever asked, and the famous port (now Cobh) was only a few miles away from the parish of Midleton where her birth was registered. She is important enough in the history of the states of Arizona and Alaska to have merited a full-scale biography (by Don Chaput), published in 1995.

By the time she left Ireland with her recently widowed mother and younger sister (both named Frances), Nellie would have been about six or seven, hardly old enough to have carried very many memories of Cork with her to the USA.

The Cashman family settled first in Boston before moving to San Francisco in 1865. At that time the western city was becoming increasingly Irish. It elected its first Irish-born mayor in 1867 (New York got its first in 1880, Boston in 1884). In 1870 Nellie's sister Frances met and married another Irish immigrant, Thomas J. Cunningham, a man who was in the boot business and whose expertise would later become useful to Nellie.

In 1872 Nellie began her association with the mining industry in the town of Pioche, Nevada, where she opened a boarding house. The town was hardly a young girl's dream, but at twenty-seven years of age Nellie was no longer particularly young by western standards. Pioche was a violent town where the saloons (seventy-two) barely outnumbered the brothels (thirty-two) by a factor of two to one. Within a three-year period Pioche saw forty violent deaths, mostly from gunfights. It had a floating population that rarely exceeded 4,000. Many of those were Irish and much of the violence appears to have been caused by miners with very Irish names.

An advertisement in the Pioche *Daily Record* in 1873 draws attention to the Boarding House of Miss N. Cashman, Proprietress, located 'immediately above Connerton's Ice House, Panaca Flat' (John Connerton was purported to own the only ice-cream machine in the West at that time, so Nellie had chosen a prime location).

Whether the violence of the town simply got too much for her or whether she had already developed the nose for an approaching 'bust' for which she would become celebrated, Nellie left Pioche within two years. The town didn't last much longer as a going concern. By 1876 its ore production had declined to about 15 per cent of the 1872 total. But by then Nellie Cashman had established herself elsewhere.

That was in the Cassiar district of British Columbia, a few miles from the Yukon territory. News of a gold strike in the region reached Pioche in 1872 and a number of miners from Nevada would eventually move there. But Nellie got there before them, in 1874. She became known to the Cassiar miners as 'Pioche Nellie'. Once again she opened a boarding house and made the bulk of her money from 'bed, board and booze'.[5] She also began to acquire promising claims and to 'grub-stake' miners in whom she had some confidence. This involved providing them with supplies (and in some cases with investment money) in the hope of a strike. In the event of a bonanza, Nellie shared in the good fortune depending on what sort of deal had been done with the impecunious miners.

Nellie left the Cassiar district in November 1874, before the onset of what would prove to be an unusually harsh winter, but she was not gone for long and the circumstances of her return marked the beginnings of her legend.

She was in Victoria, British Columbia when she got news that the Cassiar region had been cut off by a fierce storm. Many miners had, ill advisedly as it now transpired, hung on in the area far longer than was wise in the hope of making a lucky strike. Hundreds of prospectors, some of them friends of Nellie's, were now cut off and trapped. They quickly exhausted their supply of vegetables and the mining camp was hit by an outbreak of scurvy (brought on by a vitamin C deficiency).

As a member of the 'fair sex' (for 'fair', read the implied 'ineffectual') Nellie could have sat on her hands or even spent hours each day wringing them in anguish. Instead she organised a rescue expedition and led it herself. She hired six men, got together a consignment of vegetables and lime juice and headed for the Cassiar diggings with 1,500 pounds of supplies. Because the snow was fresh and soft, dogs were useless. Each member of the party (including Nellie) had to drag a sled themselves. Progress was slow, sometimes as little as five miles a day, and the party spent most of January and February, the coldest months of the year, on the trail.

Sometime around the end of February the small party reached the Cassiar diggings and delivered their life-saving supplies. The epic trip was reported (and misreported) in dozens of newspaper accounts and earned the thirty-one-year-old Irishwoman the nickname of 'The Angel of the Cassiar'.[6]

Mining camps weren't the only boom towns of the Old West. In places where the construction of the railways coincided with the end of a cattle trail, large amounts of money could be made by those brave enough to risk their capital in the often wild and lawless cow-towns of the West. If the arrival of the railway coincided with the discovery of gold or silver nearby, so much the better. It was to one of the new boom towns of the southwest that Nellie Cashman headed next. She arrived in Tucson, Arizona towards the end of the 1870s. According to her biographer, 'Nellie was basically a "boomer"or a "stampeder". This meant she was attracted to and was early on the scene in new and potentially prosperous communities.'[7] There she met a man who would play a central part in the events that were to make Tombstone, Arizona notorious: newspaper editor John Clum, owner of the *Tucson Citizen*. Clum wrote of his first meeting with Cashman:

> Nellie was the first of her sex to embark solo in a business enter-prise. Her frank manner, her self-reliant spirit, and her emphatic and fascinating Irish brogue impressed me very much, and indicated that she was a woman of strong character and marked individuality.[8]

The strong Irish brogue must have been acquired from years spent in the company of her mother because it would hardly have survived otherwise.

Within a short period she had abandoned Tucson and headed for what she knew best, a burgeoning mining town. In this case it was Tombstone, seventy-five miles to the southeast, which had just had a silver strike. John Clum followed soon afterwards, establishing the *Tombstone Epitaph* in the town in 1880. Clum may have had an overdeveloped sense of irony, but his choice of title couldn't have been more appropriate.

Cashman and Clum weren't the only notable new arrivals in Tombstone. The notorious Earp family had also begun to collect in the town. By no means the sainted lawmen of myth (Wyatt, Virgil, Morgan, Warren and James were known in Tombstone as gamblers and pimps as much as they were for their talents as US marshals or deputies), the Earps allied themselves with members of one of the two political factions that dominated the town.

Tombstone was prey to the same post-Civil War tensions as many other western boom towns. The 'Merchant' faction was benefiting from mining and commercial riches. Its members were predominantly urban (based in Tombstone itself), Republican (the party of Lincoln and the anti-slavery faction) and often eastern in origin (the Earps were from Illinois), while the 'Cowboy' faction was rural (living in Tombstone's outlying districts), Democrat and Texan (with all that implied). Each side had its own champions – the Earps in the case of the Merchant faction; the Clantons and McLaurys in the case of the Cowboys. They also had their own propagandists, Clum's *Epitaph* speaking for the Merchants while the rival newspaper the *Nugget* represented the views of the Cowboys.

Nellie Cashman, based in various businesses within the city limits of Tombstone and a friend of *Epitaph* editor John Clum, might have been expected to ally herself solidly with the Merchant faction, but, conscious of not alienating anyone needlessly, she made certain to advertise her Cash Store, her Boot and Shoe Store and later her hotel, boarding house and restaurant in both local papers.

Like Pioche and the Cassiar district, Tombstone had a large Irish-born population (in addition to the first-generation Irish, who would have been classified as American). The 1881 Cochise County census (Tombstone was the county seat) shows a population of 5,300 in Tombstone, of whom 2,880 were American while 559 had been born in Ireland (the largest foreign-born contingent – next were 423 Mexicans and 300 Germans).

This meant that there were many Roman Catholics in the town and it was in Tombstone that Nellie Cashman became involved in one of the activities that was to shape her life and become the basis for her reputation. She led a campaign to build a Roman Catholic church and a county hospital in the town. It was a highly successful campaign, due in no small part to Cashman's incredible energy. Not only did she run a number of businesses (some with her sister Frances, who had arrived in Tombstone, with five young children, after the death of her husband), she became a highly persuasive fundraiser and still found time to champion the cause of the Irish Land League in Tombstone. (She collected $200 for the Land League in 1881 – Tucson, in the same year, despite having twice the Irish population, contributed nothing.)

On 26 October 1881 came the infamous blood-letting at the OK Corral. Three members of the Clanton–McLaury faction were killed by the Earps (with the assistance of Doc Holliday) in the most famous street gunfight in western history. The Earps were not universally applauded for their actions even within the city limits of Tombstone (the Irish American Johnny Behan, who had lost his lover to Wyatt Earp, attempted unsuccessfully to arrest them). Cashman's friend John Clum, mayor of the town as well as editor of the partisan *Epitaph*, sided with the Earps in the murderous struggle that followed, but Nellie had other things on her mind. Frances Cunningham became ill in December 1881 and Nellie was forced to sell out their joint business interests while she looked after five children under the age of ten.

After Frances recovered her health, Nellie went back into the restaurant business again, opening the grandiosely named American Hotel on Fremont Street, only to suffer a further setback when one of Tombstone's periodic fires, on 25 May 1882, destroyed much of the town's business district. Both Nellie and Frances suffered minor personal injuries protecting their hotel. One report claimed that 'the plucky ladies stationed several of their friends with buckets and kept the building thoroughly saturated with water, thereby preventing the flames from communicating'[9]. Financial disaster was averted. The American had only been in business a month at the time of the fire. The following year Nellie's sister gave up in her battle with tuberculosis. Frances Cunningham died on 3 July 1883. Nellie had already made arrangements for the five children for whom she was now legal guardian. Places were located for each of the young Cunninghams in Catholic boarding schools and their aunt set about finding the means to support them.

Her first venture almost ended in disaster. Attracted by rumours of a gold rush in the Baja California region of Mexico, Nellie and a group of Tombstone miners set off to travel the 1,000 miles from Arizona to the Mission Santa Gertrudis. Because of her experience elsewhere, Nellie appears to have been in effective charge of the operation. Legend has it that the miners were ill equipped for the heat of the Baja (far hotter even than the Arizona desert) and quickly began to run out of water. Nellie is supposed to have volunteered to find the mission, locate water and return to the rest of the group. All, according to anecdote, was accomplished successfully, enhancing the legend of the 'plucky Irishwoman'.

The truth, according to her biographer Don Chaput, is probably more mundane. Nellie appears to have made one crucial leadership decision when she insisted that she would lead only a small party of Arizona miners to the reported location of the gold. If a strike had indeed been made and if conditions allowed, then the rest of the group would follow. It was, in fact, the reserve group that rescued Nellie and her advance party. By then dozens of other returning miners had brought the bad news that the significance of the find had been greatly exaggerated. If there had been gold, then it was already gone.

The Arizona miners returned to Tombstone empty handed, but the legend of Nellie Cashman continued to grow. The *San Diego Union* of 16 June 1883, writing about the abortive Baja gold fever, singled the redoubtable Irishwoman out for praise:

> In all the vicissitudes of life she has maintained the highest self respect, but is as ambitious in her notions as Joan of Arc. In Arizona she could raise a company at any time who would follow her to the death, either in search of gold or Apaches.[10]

The flowery article glossed over the fact that she had very nearly led just such a company to their deaths.

For the next few years Cashman, confidence dented by the narrowly averted disaster in the Baja, contented herself with running a boarding house in Tombstone and making significant amounts of money on the side by buying and selling prospecting claims (one of which she named the Parnell Mine, in honour of one of the motive forces behind her beloved Irish Land League, the great Charles Stewart Parnell).

Two incidents in 1884 have been cited as further demonstrations of Nellie's entitlement to western canonisation. In one she is said to have objected strenuously to the erection of a grandstand in Tombstone designed to give local voyeurs a more comfortable vantage point for witnessing the hanging of five convicted murderers. Her sympathy is supposed to have been aroused by the fact that two of the men waiting to be executed were Irish: Daniel 'Mick' Kelly and William 'Billy' Delaney. Taking the law into her own hands, she gathered together a group of like-minded individuals on the eve of the communal execution and destroyed the grandstand. Later she made sure that the bodies of the five men (three of whom she is said to have converted to Catholicism) were not handed over to the nearest medical school for the use of pathology students. Less florid accounts of the affair suggest that local miners tore the bleachers apart when they discovered they were expected to pay a dollar and a half to get a favourable view of the executions.

She is also said to have thwarted a murder attempt by some of the miners whom she normally championed. Whether as a simple (if courageous) act of humanity or as a way of aligning herself with 'capital' against 'labour', she managed to conceal the superintendent of the Grand Central Mining Company in her buggy and convey him through the streets of Tombstone to the nearest railway station (Benson) and safety. E.B. Gage had aroused the animosity of the town's miners by enforcing a fifty-cent-a-day wage cut after a fall in the price of silver. This had led to threats of kidnapping and lynching against him.[11] This story has the imprimatur of John Clum, but contemporary accounts contain no reference to the involvement of Gage in what was a brief, but nasty, labour dispute. Still less do they talk of any 'rescue' by Nellie Cashman. Nevertheless, both stories have added to the angelic aura surrounding Cashman.

By 1886 Nellie was getting restless again. Her nephews and nieces had either been started in business or otherwise provided for, so her ties to Arizona were loosening. A trip to New Mexico in 1887 brought her no joy and the following year saw her back in Tombstone. For much of the next decade she followed the rushes and the booms around the newly established mining camps of Arizona before she swapped the arid deserts of the southwest for the ice and tundra of the northwest.

In 1896 the Yukon bonanza began in earnest in the vicinity of the newly established town of Dawson at the junction of the Yukon and Klondike rivers. By 1897 Nellie Cashman was already making plans to join the new rush northwards – Arizona newspapers were carrying the report that she was preparing 'to organise a company for gold mining in Alaska, where she has visited three times. Her many friends in Arizona will wish her success, for during her twenty years' residence in the Territory she has made several fortunes, all of which have gone for charity.'[12]

Nellie may have been trying to replicate her Baja expedition of 1883, this time in a geographical area of which she had more knowledge and with a climate that, although grim and hostile, was more conducive to prospecting. If that was indeed the case, she failed to interest enough Arizonan miners in abandoning the heat of the southwest for the chill of Alaska. In February 1898 she made the trip alone. At fifty-four years of age she was about to become one of the few women to join the new Alaskan goldrush. Her journey to Dawson was an odyssey in itself – she was a lone woman hauling the statutory 900 pounds of provisions (verified by members of the Royal Canadian Mounted Police or else the prospector was to be turned back) through some of the least hospitable terrain on the planet. Her journey began at the base of the famous Chilkoot Pass. From there a trail of prospectors would set out each day, snaking upwards on a hike that barely half managed to complete. Having negotiated that obstacle, Nellie then faced a hazardous journey by barge along the melting waters of the Yukon River. She finally reached Dawson in April 1898. A few months later her path crossed once again with that of her old friend from Tombstone, John Clum. By then she was clearly doing well (she was already involved in church charity work). Clum described her as 'robust, active, prosperous and popular'.[13]

For the next six years it was 'business as usual' for Nellie Cashman. She spread herself between mining and the restaurant business. In the past such diversification had stood her in good stead in such a highly precarious economy. She was an oddity in a society that was overwhelmingly male and where the preponderance of females were prostitutes. Nellie was approaching sixty, living in a hostile environment but still prepared to buy claims and work them herself. One such claim (according to Clum) produced up to $100,000. Nellie, however, insisted that she had reinvested the entire sum in purchasing other less-rewarding diggings. It is also likely that she gave a large portion of the sum away to Roman Catholic charities.

In 1904 she shifted her attention from Dawson to a new strike in Fairbanks, Alaska. By now she was a tough, resourceful and personally wealthy sexagenarian. She stayed for a winter, made a profit of $6,000 and her departure, in 1905, was a further object lesson in good timing. Within less than a year the business centre of Fairbanks had been burned to the ground.

Most of the final years of Cashman's life were spent on or near the Arctic Circle in the Koyukuk River region. Once again she emerged with a profit from what was, at best, a modest 'boom' with her combination of business skills and physical tenacity. Although her claims in the Nolan Creek area were far from being the most lucrative she had ever worked, she appears to have been content to settle in this remote region. Her newly acquired sedentary ways may have had something to do with the slow winding down of the 'gold fever' of the latter half of the nineteenth century. There were fewer and fewer new 'boom towns' in which a woman could establish a restaurant while working as many claims as she could afford. Perhaps she was simply running out of energy. After all, she was getting on for seventy by the time of the outbreak of World War I.

Her survival in this tough man's world was due to her own strength of character and to the respect she commanded among the miners alongside whom she worked. She, in her turn, reciprocated that regard. In one interview she observed:

> I have mushed with men, slept out in the open, swashed it with them and been with them constantly, and I have never once been offered an insult. You won't find that class of men among the sourdoughs of Alaska.[14]

There was only one hint of a heterosexual romance in Nellie's life, but neither were there any suggestions of homosexual relationships. A photograph of her taken in 1921 (when she was seventy-six years old) reveals a very spry woman who has adopted an almost aggressively masculine appearance (slicked back hair and what looks like a jacket and tie), but this preference for masculine attire and appearance might well have arisen over the years as a protection against identification as a prostitute.

In 1918, on hearing that the USA had entered the Great War, she managed to persuade more than fifty of her beloved sourdoughs to travel (with her, of course) 700 miles to enlist in the US Armed Forces. By the time they got to a recruitment centre, however, the Armistice had been declared and their services were not required. At the age of seventy, on one of her frequent returns to civilisation, she managed to mush a dog team 700 miles in seventeen days from Koyukuk to Seward, Alaska. It is a record many of today's highly competitive Iditarod drivers would be proud of.

In 1924 she was taken ill with pneumonia and was transferred from Nolan Creek to Fairbanks. She survived the journey and recovered from the illness, but died the following year in a hospital in Victoria, British Columbia. Ironically, her money and fundraising had helped build the hospital.

To her biographer, she was a woman with the quintessential 'stampeder' mentality. She needed the buzz and the invigoration of a potential bonanza. But the excitement of prospecting rather than the desire to accumulate vast wealth was what appeared to drive her.

Just as Thomas Fitzpatrick, thanks to his courage, tenacity, intelligence and longevity, is the single most important Irishman to have operated in the American West, Nellie Cashman is head and shoulders above her Irish female contemporaries.

Belinda Mulrooney was a talented businesswoman from her teens to her eighties.[15] She was born in Carns in County Sligo on 16 May 1872 and christened Bridget before her name was changed to Belinda Agnes Mulrooney. Her father left for the USA shortly after her birth and her mother followed a year later. She was left in the care of her grandmother until she was a teenager. In 1885 she joined her family in Archibald, Pennsylvania, a mining community that was not to her taste. Unhampered by any sentimental family ties, she left the town at the age of seventeen and settled in Chicago. There, at the age of twenty-one, she made a small fortune ($8,000) in the restaurant business during the 1893 Chicago Exposition.

That fund brought her to San Francisco the following year for the Midwinter Fair. She invested the money in real estate and lost it all when her property was burned to the ground, probably by a greedy adjacent landlord seeking an insurance payout. She was barely twenty and had already lost her first fortune.

Belinda was then forced to seek work and gravitated towards the *City of Topeka* steamship. It sailed along the American western coast from San Francisco to Alaska. She supplemented her income as a stewardess by peddling illegal whiskey. She took advantage of the extreme cold on the route and often wore a long fur coat with a canvas lining. Stitched into the lining were twenty-four pockets, each capable of holding a half-pint bottle. Somehow she managed to move around without clinking.

Her days in the marine life ended with the discovery of gold in the Klondike in 1897 at a river that, logically, became known as Bonanza Creek. It was more than 400 miles northwest of the Alaskan town of Juneau and almost inaccessible to all but the most doughty.

The already formidable Mulrooney decided to join the stampede to the Klondike, but hedged her bets by bringing something marketable with her. She purchased, among other items, a consignment of hot-water bottles, figuring that miners who had already struck it rich by the time she got there would be happy to pay over the odds for the luxury of a little warmth in the tent towns of the Klondike.

With help from Indian guides and co-operative fellow travellers, she managed to get her goods intact through the treacherous Chilkoot Pass and down the Yukon River to Dawson, a boom town of tents, shanties and some of the richest people in the American Northwest. There she managed to sell her goods to freezing miners (trading in the local currency – gold dust) at a 600 per cent mark-up. She used that money to open a diner and build cabin accommodation for the miners. Later she built a very successful roadhouse hotel that she used to make money in a variety of interesting ways. Working the bar herself, she listened to the miners' gossip and made some shrewd investments on foot of the information she gleaned. By the winter of 1897 she owned a number of profitable mines.

With the reality of rapidly acquired wealth all around her, Mulrooney decided that there would be custom for an upmarket hotel in Dawson, so she built the twenty-two-room Fairview Hotel on Front Street. It boasted steam-heated rooms, electric lights, steam baths, a dining room with linen tablecloths, sterling silver knives and bone china. The lobby was decked out with cut-glass chandeliers and a full-time orchestra. The newly rich miners were prepared to pay handsomely for these unaccustomed luxuries.

Mulrooney could be an implacable opponent if crossed. One business partner who cheated her and left her with hundreds of useless rubber boots from a salvage operation had little time to enjoy his triumph. Severe flooding a few months later forced him to buy the boots back from her for his miners. The asking price was $100 dollars a pair – Nike prices in nineteenth-century Yukon. He had no option but to pay up. Once a teamster who had been engaged to transport fittings for the Fairview Hotel by mule pack dumped the lot when he got a better offer (to move supplies of whiskey). In retaliation Mulrooney hired a set of heavies, led them to the mule train and watched as they assaulted the mule drivers, deposited the whiskey by the side of the trail and replaced the Fairview fittings.

It might well be wondered, given both their presences in the Klondike at the turn of the century, whether or not Mulrooney ever encountered her fellow countrywoman Nellie Cashman. In fact the two did meet – head on.

In the summer of 1898 Cashman (along with her nephew Tom Cunningham) had bought a claim on the elegantly named Little Skookum Creek. There was a subsequent dispute over the nature of the claim, a surveyor was called in and the local mining inspector, a man named Norwood, was called upon to adjudicate.

On the basis of a rumour that Norwood was romantically involved with Belinda Mulrooney, Cashman approached Mulrooney and offered her a share in the claim in return for the exercise of some influence on Norwood. Mulrooney, although it appears that she may not have been having an affair with the mining inspector at all, was glad to accept the offer. Nellie then, ill advisedly, boasted to Norwood that his 'friend in Dawson' had been 'looked after'. It was a blatant attempt to bribe Norwood into making a decision on the claim favourable to Cashman and, as such, it was reported by the inspector to the local land commissioner, William Ogilvie. Nellie was dragged before a highly embarrassing inquiry and required to attest that she had no evidence whatever of any potential conflict of interest on the part of Norwood. She was forced to concede that Mulrooney had been 'putting a job up on me' when she had accepted the partnership offer. As Cashman's biographer puts it, 'Nellie Cashman may have been a known presence in the Yukon, but Belinda Mulrooney was one of the giants.'[16]

In 1899, by now dubbed the 'Queen of the Klondike', Mulrooney was becoming increasingly interested in one Charles Eugene Carbonneau, who claimed to be a French count. He stood out in the region because of his aristocratic manner and his highly developed sense of European style. They had met in 1898 when Carbonneau had arrived in Dawson to purchase stakes in mines at the behest of an Anglo-French syndicate. Their first encounter didn't impress Mulrooney – it was a dispute over the price of wine in her hotel. However, she remembered him as having eyes that 'were large with a sort of sleepy, gentle look some Frenchmen have. A dashing sort of chap in his good clothes'.[17] The two appeared to be opposites. The soft, overweight Frenchman provided a physical contrast to most of the muscular, chiselled miners of the Klondike. He was also something of a snobbish dandy. Mulrooney was no respecter of titles and provided her own physical contrast to the Frenchman: she was, in the words of one contemporary, 'short, dark, angular, masculine, could swear like a trooper on occasion and was, generally speaking "hard boiled".'[18]

Perhaps it was the attraction of opposites but, despite certain misgivings on the part of Mulrooney, the two married in 1900. They honeymooned in splendour in Paris but it was not long before Belinda's reservations about her new husband were borne out. The French 'count' was, in fact, a con man whose scams and fraudulent enterprises would cost Mulrooney a small fortune. His activities, in which the Irishwoman was implicated by default, involved Mulrooney in a series of costly legal battles. Their marriage had effectively ended long before she divorced him in 1906. Carbonneau himself continued his fraudulent activities in the USA and Europe until his death in 1919. Partly because of her association with him and partly because her own talents did not include the ability to nurture and sustain an enterprise in the long term, Mulrooney's fortunes declined. She acquired an unfortunate and undeserved reputation for dubious business practices. By the 1940s she had curtailed her activities to the acquisition of a small property portfolio.

Belinda Mulrooney survived her shady husband by almost fifty years. She eventually settled in Seattle and died there in 1967 at the age of ninety-five, having signed over her remaining property to the nursing home in which she died. Ironically, her death certificate listed her occupation as 'housewife', the one occupation she had managed to scrupulously avoid in a long and fascinating life that alternated between success and failure.

Her story, not unlike that of the redoubtable Nellie Cashman, is not unique amongst western women but is still an unusual one of a businesswoman surviving and thriving in a tough, inhospitable man's world.[19]

Some thoroughly soiled doves

Earning a living as a woman in the USA was not easy in the nineteenth century; earning your keep as a prostitute was more difficult again. Given that America was built on puritanical foundations, prostitution (while socially and economically significant) tended to be a less than visible activity, largely confined to certain working-class areas of the nation's cities. Given that female actresses were not permitted to work in the theatre until the mid-1800s,[19] female entertainers were often seen as prostitutes by another name.

The movement of population into the American West was overwhelmingly male in its initial incarnation. In 1849, the year after gold was discovered in California, there were two women for every 100 men on the American frontier. Men are recorded as having travelled miles just to *see* a woman. Until the wagon trains moved entire families to Oregon and California, many of the women who established themselves on the frontier were there to supply services to the miners and cowboys. Some, like Nellie Cashman and Belinda Mulrooney, ran boarding houses or sold legitimate goods, often at a handsome profit. Others sold sexual favours, often at an equally handsome profit. Both discovered the great axiom of the mining boom culture – by and large the profits accrue to he (or she) who supplies goods and services, not to he who works the seam. 'Greater rewards lay in mining the miners,'[20] as historian Patricia Limerick has put it succinctly.

As in many other instances where the West was concerned, the rules of conformity and morality were rewritten in the mining towns. The red-light districts (the term is said to originate from the miners' habit of leaving their lanterns outside brothels while they were inside) were very visible and, in fact, became the social centres of many western towns. The diabolical trinity of alcohol, gambling and sex provided the electricity that lit up these red-light districts and offered miners a bewildering array of opportunities to part with their hard-earned profits or wages.

It did not take long for the rules to be rewritten by the so-called 'Gentle Tamers' who began to arrive in greater numbers towards the

latter half of the nineteenth century and who were quick to assert themselves. The creation of a sizeable western middle class, dominated by the
morality of the 'respectable', ensured that the wage earners of sin were
either closed down or moved out of the eye-line of the new arrivals.

But up to that point the 'Fallen Woman' or the Soiled Dove had
held her own. Interestingly, many (according to local censuses) were
single mothers. This begs the question as to how many of the inhabitants of the reputable West that was created out of the Babylon of the
1840s and 1850s were the illegitimate progeny of prostitutes. If it is a
significant figure, it would be a form of poetic justice for the many
Soiled Doves who became social outcasts. As one amusing quatrain
puts it:

> The miners came in '49
> The whores in '51
> And when they got together
> They produced the native son.

There was a fairly direct correlation between the prosperity of any
mining town and the number of its prostitutes. In fact, when tracing
the rise and fall of boom towns such as Tombstone, Arizona or Bodie,
California, historians could probably ignore the annual ore-production
figures and simply refer to the census of local prostitutes. One
completely unscientific survey compiled in an Alaskan mining region
showed that in 1915, when gold production was valued at $290,000 per
annum and there were 300 miners, there were fourteen 'working girls'
at hand to supply the sexual needs of the male population. By 1920,
production was down to a mere $90,000, there were only 119 miners
left and all the prostitutes had gone.[21]

We must assume that a significant percentage of western prostitutes
were Irish. In her book *Erin's Daughters in America*, Hasia Diner
suggests that sexual immorality was not a prominent feature of Irish
behaviour in the New World, amongst either men or women. 'Bridget
might have been dirty and disorganized, ignorant and tempestuous,
slightly dishonest and strikingly inebriated, but she was always
chaste.'[22] Yet a survey carried out in New York in 1859 found that of
the women working in prostitution, 60 per cent were foreign born and
half of those were Irish. On the other hand, just over 1 per cent of
Irish-born women arrested in Chicago between 1905 and 1908 were
charged with prostitution.

There were, undoubtedly, many Irish prostitutes in the American West. Some, such as 'Bridget Fury', 'Irish Mary', 'Irish Queen', 'Molly b'Damn' and 'Chicago Joe', acquired some measure of fame, wealth or notoriety. The vast majority were anonymous at the time and are now long forgotten. For every story of a successful madam, there are hundreds who eked out a living and died in obscurity. As one historian has put it, 'profiles of the prostitutes reveal that their lives were invariably tragic, often violent, and occasionally cut short by suicide or … murder'.[23] They entered the oldest profession for a variety of reasons. Many had been eastern prostitutes, driven into 'the game' by poverty. They would have journeyed west in the hope of capitalising on the get-rich-quick mentality that pervaded the mining towns in particular. Some of the more adventurous spirits would have had hopes of striking it rich themselves through the overwhelmingly male activity of prospecting. When reality finally bit, as it did for almost all such adventurers, they would have fallen back on one of the few marketable commodities they had left: their own bodies.

Some were women abandoned by their husbands who did not see any alternative means of survival. All were victims of the reality that any well-paid work in western towns went to members of the male population. In a largely pre-industrial society with little or no factory work available, the two alternatives for most women were badly paid domestic employment or prostitution. To many the latter option seemed far more attractive. One study has shown that a 'fancy lady' in Helena, Montana could earn a monthly income of $233. A miner averaged $100 a month.[24] However, clearly, not that many Helena prostitutes were 'fancy ladies' because only a small minority made that kind of money.

Some worked in 'canvas shacks' or cribs, some in saloons; the more fortunate worked in brothels for madams. They faced the risks that have always been a part of their profession, lack of status and dignity being the least of their worries, death and disease of more concern. Many acquired reputations for their kindness and charity, helping to humanise some of the wilder towns in which they settled.

Double standards existed in the treatment of prostitutes in the West. While some were grudgingly respected in their communities (though having to work hard to achieve that status), most were ostracised and treated differently to 'respectable' women or 'ladies'. The

California mining town of Bodie offers an interesting case study. It is still preserved today in what the National Parks Service calls a state of 'arrested decay', looking much as it did when it was finally abandoned in the 1930s. In the nineteenth century, despite its remoteness in the Sierra Nevada, it boasted a population of up to 10,000. At least 20 per cent of that population would have been native-born Irish – the town had chapters of the Ancient Order of Hibernians and the Irish Land League.

Analysis of crime and social statistics for the town is very revealing. It shows, for example, that prostitutes were overwhelmingly the main victims of male-on-female crime. Men who attacked or beat prostitutes would generally be arrested if caught but would find judges taking a far more lenient attitude than if they had assaulted 'ladies'. Newspapers would often publish humorous accounts of attacks on prostitutes, as if they should not be taken too seriously. If they died, either from violent or natural causes, the same double standards applied to their interments. Prostitutes were not even allowed on Boot Hill – they were buried outside the confines of the town graveyard. Even in death they were not to lie alongside 'respectable' women or their regular customers.

However, the biggest killer of prostitutes in Bodie was not homicide but suicide. Most prostitutes who died violent deaths in the town did so by their own hands. During its boom years in the late 1870s and early 1880s, the suicide rate in Bodie was a statistically astronomical twenty-four per 100,000. Rates in eastern cities at a similar time would have been around two per 100,000. Women made up 10 per cent of the Bodie population. Though far less than half the female population, prostitutes accounted for half the suicides. In Bodie a woman was six or seven times more likely to kill herself than a man. (This statistic was neatly reversed in east-coast cities.) There was also a very high rate of failed suicide attempts amongst women.[25]

What we don't know about Bodie is the percentage of prostitutes who were Irish. Studies done on another western mining town, Butte, Montana, are illuminating in that regard. It was as Irish as Bodie, but it developed into a more stable and permanent urban settlement than did the California boom town. A similar percentage of the population of Butte was Irish born or first-generation Irish. It was a very 'Irish' town. In the early 1900s a census revealed a sizeable red-light district boasting 300 prostitutes.[26] Of those, only eight claimed to be Irish or of Irish parentage. This may have had something to do with the relative wealth of the Butte Irish and the stabilising influence of such a large Irish community on the behaviour of elements of its female population that might otherwise have drifted into prostitution. It may also mean that in the American West you were more likely to find Irish prostitutes removed from centres of Irish population such as San Francisco, Denver and Butte (and possibly Bodie as well).

Lola Montez is the object of as many myths and inventions as the history of the West itself. At this stage it is virtually impossible to distinguish fact from fiction, partly because her life was so extraordinary. She was responsible for many of the fabrications herself in her thoroughly unreliable autobiography. (Among her many claims was that she was the illegitimate daughter of Lord Byron – a lie which the tragic poet was not around to contradict.) She spent only a short time in the American West, but then she led only a very short life. As the late Dee Brown put it, 'No western stage performer ever equalled the glamorous Lola Montez in creating an aura of seductive mystery and exquisite scandal around her personality.'[27]

The first dispute surrounds the time and place of her birth. Most accounts suggest that she was born in Limerick in 1818. However, authoritative sources have it that the date of her birth was, in fact, 1821 (she claimed to be younger) and that she was actually born in Grange, County Sligo.

Then there is the question of her name and the nationality of her mother. She claimed that she had been born Maria Dolores Eliza Rosanna Gilbert, daughter of a Spanish mother and a British Army soldier. In fact, she added the Maria Dolores later to make her seem more exotic and her mother was not Spanish but the illegitimate daughter of Charles Oliver, a member of Parliament and of an old, established Irish family.

Nominally a dancer or 'danseuse' (her dancing skills were, apparently, negligible), she was, in fact, 'one of the most sought after courtesans of her era'.[28] One observer described her thus: 'She is of medium size, slight figure, gracefully formed, face rather thin, with large flashing black eyes and thick glossy black hair.'[29] (Dee Brown claims her eyes were blue.) Through a combination of good looks, plausibility and the supreme self-confidence and charm of the inveterate mounte-bank, she managed to inveigle her way into the upper reaches of European and American society. Her infamous economy with the truth proved to be a valuable asset. She reinvented herself more often than an endangered chameleon and was pleased to be whoever she wanted to be as the situation required.

Among her celebrated European conquests were King Ludwig of Bavaria, Tsar Nicholas I of Russia and the creator of the *Three Musketeers*, Alexandre Dumas. They, and many others, were in thrall to her unique selling point as a performer – the Tarantula Dance (also known as the Spider Dance). This had been premiered in Her Majesty's Theatre in London. In essence it involved the 'discovery' in the course of a dancing routine of a large furry spider in her clothes (it was made of rubber, cork and whalebone). Her frenzied attempts to remove the spider would, of course, necessitate the removal of much of her clothing as well. One writer described it as 'a bouncing and navel-exploiting exhibition that had all the belly fetishists of the Continent fighting for her favours'.[30]

Sometime in the 1850s she appears to have decamped to the USA and eventually arrived in the burgeoning city of San Francisco. Like many California towns grown rich on the proceeds of the gold rush, the Bay City had sprouted theatres and variety palaces by the score. It was Lola's new Rheingold and she was, however briefly, one of its Valkyries. She sought to create a sensation and didn't have to try very hard. Whenever she ventured out she was accompanied by two grey-hounds. A parrot adorned her shoulder. She made good copy.

She quickly snared the publisher of the *San Francisco Whig* (or the assistant editor of the *San Francisco Courier*, depending on whose account you believe), a former forty-niner by the name of Patrick Hull. The attraction, she claimed, was based on his ability to tell a funny story. It was a tenuous basis for a relationship and, predictably, it was a union that was not blessed with any longevity. Lola's sojourn in San Francisco ended when she began to lose audiences to another great burlesque diva, Caroline Chapman, who, as part of her own act, sent up the Spider Dance and undermined Lola's credibility.

In 1854 Lola undertook a tour of the music and concert halls of the mining towns of the Golden State. But the rough-hewn element of the boom towns was not as susceptible to her charms as the more sophisticated denizens of San Francisco. Her act 'wasn't warmly received. In fact, the miners booed her off the stage,'[31] according to one account. A newspaperman who gave her a bad review was threatened with a horsewhipping while a second was challenged to a duel.

In the past Lola had demonstrated that such threats of physical violence were not all aggressive bluster. She had displayed an ample penchant for muscularity. She rarely travelled without a whip (it was a prop in her act) and it did not take much to provoke her into using it. If the whip was not at hand she would employ anything vaguely resembling a blunt instrument. According to one San Francisco newspaper, en route from New Orleans to California 'she gave us a taste of her quality by trying to whip a theatrical manager and by breaking the nose of her agent with a heavy brass candlestick'.[32] In New Orleans she had stood trial for an assault on an unfortunate prompter who had asked her to leave his backstage prompt box at the Placide's Varieties Theatre. He had been kicked for his impertinence.

After her unsuccessful tour Lola briefly abandoned the stage and settled down near the mining town of Grass Valley. Accounts diverge at this point as to the state of her marriage. Historian Dee Brown claims that Patrick Hull had vanished from the scene shortly after the disastrous tour of the mining towns (thrown down the stairs of a hotel with his baggage pitched out the window after him). Other accounts suggest that the connubial bliss of Mr and Mrs Hull survived the removal to Grass Valley and that Lola was kept by her new husband in the style to which she had become accustomed in Europe. She lived on imported food and the finest wines. One story about her that gained local currency was that she habitually bathed in champagne and dried her much admired body with rose petals. She is also said to have shared her life with a pet bear in addition to the adoring Mr Hull.

As with all Lola Montez stories and 'facts', the reader pays their money and makes their choice. However, by the end of the Grass Valley sojourn the affable raconteur, Mr Hull, was out of the picture and Lola, who was alleged to have engaged in numerous extra-marital liaisons while in Grass Valley, was on her way to Australia.

Lola's departure from Grass Valley and from California was regretted by many. The San Francisco *Golden Era* of 3 June 1855 said of her that 'a kind nature and many courtesies and charities have made her a favorite with those who knew her well enough to reconcile not a few eccentricities and erratic inclinations'. Those sentiments were echoed by the local Grass Valley *Telegraph* on 6 June:

> That she has her faults, none can deny. She is far from being a proper exemplar, to be held up as a pattern for others, yet that she has many good qualities and possesses in an eminent degree the generosities and sympathies of her sex, can be well attested by many in Grass Valley who have been recipients of her kindness.

On 17 January 1861, the once-celebrated courtesan whose beauty and vivacity had turned the crowned heads of Europe was so far down on her luck that she died in a dilapidated boarding house in the notorious Hell's Kitchen area of New York City. Some sources suggest that she was actually well provided for at the end of her life and that accounts of her sad decline had more to do with the need of some writers to moralise and draw attention to the fruits of a misspent life. She had suffered a stroke in June 1860 that had partially paralysed her. By December she was sufficiently recovered to venture out for a walk. But the cold New York winter weather and her own weak lungs brought on pneumonia to which she succumbed a month later.

She was forty years old (or thirty-eight, or forty-two).

Mary Welch was born in 1844 and emigrated from Ireland at the age of fourteen, arriving in New York, as did thousands of her compatriots, with little more than the clothes on her back. It is more than likely that she sought and secured work as a domestic servant, but at some point Mary Welch became Josephine Airey. This is likely to have coincided with a career change, as she discovered that she could make considerably more money as a prostitute than as a maid. The metamorphosis from simple Mary Welch to the more exotic Josephine Airey may have come about because she did not want to bring shame on her family name or simply because the new name was more marketable in the bars and brothels of New York and then Chicago, to which she transferred in the 1860s.

In 1867 she made the last and most significant move of her life when she boarded a train for the mining town of Helena, Montana. By then she had accumulated a considerable nest egg as well as an excellent grasp of business and a thorough knowledge of life.

Her first move when she arrived in Helena was to acquire property. It was a modest acquisition, and for 'modest' read 'squalid'. Its lack of pretentiousness didn't impinge on its profitability, though, and within three years Mary/Josephine needed to expand. In order to do so she borrowed money, mortgaging everything she owned, including three dozen pairs of underclothes. She could have followed the example of the likes of Nellie Cashman and established a totally legitimate boarding house, but Josephine's background was in the more lucrative calling of prostitution. She was not ready to go 'legit' before she had secured her future prosperity.

In 1874 the misfortune of others became a stroke of good luck for Josephine. A huge fire swept through the wooden settlement that was Helena. It razed shanties, bordellos, saloons and respectable dwellings alike to the ground. Unable to rebuild, many victims of the fire were forced to sell out. Josephine had the necessary capital by now and was able to put together a large property portfolio at knockdown prices.

In 1878, at the age of thirty-four, the proud possessor of the nickname 'Chicago Joe' and a powerful businesswoman in her own right, Josephine tied the knot with James T. Hensley. Known as 'Black Hawk', he was a fellow entrepreneur and the marital alliance extended to joint business interests. Between them they built the Red Light Saloon and a dance hall (fireproof – the lessons of 1874 had been well learned). Josephine, however, continued to put prosperity before middle-class respectability by operating a brothel in the Red Light.

In 1886 the city fathers of the prosperous and growing Helena decided that it was time to clean up the town. Such fits of righteousness were part of a pattern in the West. Immorality and licentiousness were tolerated during the 'boomer' period of development of most western towns. Then the merchant class became established and seized political power. The good burghers (or their even better wives) would become 'improvers'. They would decide that their town could survive economically without many of the bordellos and low dives that had, heretofore, extracted much of the cash from the pockets of miners and cowboys. In addition, the newly established railroads were bringing entire families westwards. It was felt unbecoming that children should be exposed to the activities of common prostitutes.

Accordingly the city of Helena outlawed prostitution and declared 'hurdy gurdy' houses immoral. The expression 'hurdy gurdy' had become the standard euphemism for some of the more rudimentary brothels because a few, in a vague stab at providing musical entertainment, had installed these basic and easily transportable wheezy mechanical hand organs. Unfortunately for the city fathers, in compiling their new legislation they had been somewhat loose in their terminology. They actually used the expression 'hurdy gurdy house' to describe the town's brothels. The resourceful Josephine Airey hired a lawyer who went to court with a dictionary that clearly defined what a 'hurdy gurdy' was. He then argued that as the Red Light Saloon employed a three-piece band (piano, violin and horn) to provide its music, it was therefore exempt from the legislation. She won her case and the Red Light stayed in business. The legislators of Helena were obliged to reword their laws but were unable to retry 'Chicago Joe'.

Encouraged by this success, Josephine now moved further up the entertainment ladder with an elegantly appointed and beautifully furnished variety theatre, the Coliseum. She looked to the east coast to provide fresh performers for both the public and the private side of her new venture. This influx of new talent quickly established the Coliseum as the most popular venue in Helena and the countryside around. For her more valued customers, an innovation was introduced which anticipated the football-stadium corporate box by more than half a century. Private curtained booths were available for the well heeled with an electric bell button in each designed to summon a 'box girl' with beer at $1 a bottle and champagne at $5 a pint. The city fathers expressed their reservations at the notion of women being summoned to these private lairs but were unwilling to go back to law with the redoubtable Ms Airey.

'Chicago Joe' was very much the hands-on entrepreneur. She was to be seen in the Coliseum on a nightly basis. Her obituary in the Helena *Daily Independent* gives some idea of the gaudy but impressively ostentatious figure she cut:

> She wore a flowing robe of heavy velvet, generally green or purple, with a pink-lined Elizabethan collar of enormous size, a wide golden, jewel-studded girdle around the immense expanse where her waist once was and jewels on every part of her dress where it was possible to place them. Thus attired and carefully painted and powdered she presented an imposing appearance as she swept along.[33]

By the age of forty-four, respectable or not, 'Chicago Joe' was paying city taxes on property worth over $200,000 (millions in twenty-first-century terms). She was also ensuring the continued existence of her business by making generous and very public contributions to local charities while simultaneously making those even more vital covert donations to local political power brokers.

However, though it was a substantial town by the 1890s, not even Helena was immune to the 'boom and bust' cycles that dogged the western economy. The harsh winters of the late 1880s had almost wiped out the cattle industry in Montana and Wyoming and the mining industry depended on high prices for gold, silver and copper. A fiscal crisis in 1893 led to panic and a downward trade cycle. Josephine had already been experiencing the fickle nature of public taste in her efforts to keep the Coliseum ahead of the game, but the collapse of the local economy led to an inevitable retrenchment. The entertainment industry, in all its forms, was hit hard. James T. Hensley and 'Chicago Joe' lost all their businesses except the Red Light Saloon and were forced to sell their house and live 'above the shop'.

In October 1899, at the age of fifty-five, Mary Welch, aka Josephine Airey, aka 'Chicago Joe' Hensley, died of pneumonia. The Helena *Daily Independent*, while avoiding any reference to the real basis of her wealth, acknowledged the power of her personality, her personal generosity and her impact on the society in which she lived. Her obituary noted:

> 'Chicago Joe' had her faults, but she was a woman of generous impulses, and she assisted many unfortunate women who came to her for help. In former days she contributed liberally to every public enterprise … her life was a checkered one. She suffered numerous losses from friends who sought her assistance and who generally failed to return the money she loaned.[34]

'Chicago Joe' might never have been accepted into the Helena Chamber of Commerce, but her charitable contributions, though not of the order of Nellie Cashman's, ensured that when she died she did so in the bosom of the Church of her birth. Her funeral took place in the Roman Catholic cathedral of Helena and she is buried in the local Catholic cemetery.

*

If 'Chicago Joe' Hensley is the archetypal madam (tough, resourceful entrepreneur operating in one of the few businesses open to a woman on the frontier) and Lola Montez the 'femme fatale' (amoral, scheming, grasping woman of dubious morality), then Molly Burdan[35] was the stereotypical 'whore with the heart of gold'. She was born Maggie Hall in Dublin on 26 December 1853 to a middle-class English Protestant father and an Irish Catholic mother. She received a good education and grew up to be a confident and attractive woman of above-average height for the time with blonde hair and blue eyes.

In 1874, against the wishes of her parents, she headed for New York. She quickly discovered that not even her excellent education, good looks and self-confidence were a guarantee of securing a decent job. She ended up working in a bar, like many of her fellow country-women who didn't boast her advantages. There she met the man who would become her husband, a well-to-do individual named Burdan. At first the marriage was kept a secret from his family for fear of his losing the allowance that permitted him to have a lifestyle that would other-wise have been well beyond his means.

But it was this very dissolute existence that would set Maggie Burdan (now called Molly on the insistence of her husband, who disliked her birth name) on the path she would follow for the rest of her working life. Burdan's parents, hearing of his covert marriage to an Irish immigrant, cut off his allowance. Desperate for money and disin-clined to work himself, Burdan saw the potential in his young, strik-ingly beautiful wife. It began with requests to facilitate some of his 'friends', to which Molly reluctantly acceded, but within a short period Burdan was effectively pimping his wife.

By the age of twenty-four Molly Burdan had clearly decided that if she was going to work as a prostitute she was not going to hand her income over to her deadbeat husband. She left New York to continue her chosen profession in the lucrative West, where the ratio of men to women was often upwards of fifty to one.

Her youth and beauty meant that she was much sought after in the mining and cow towns of the West and she quickly accumulated considerable wealth. She acquired this by adopting the same unsenti-mental approach to her work as she had done to her superfluous husband. She followed the money. Her strategy was to remain in a town for as long as the wealth being produced persuaded her to do so.

Once the money was sucked out of a mining town she would move on, following her own unique cycle of 'boom and bust'.

That was the mentality that brought her to a promising gold strike in the Cour d'Alenes district of northern Idaho in 1884. The journey to Murray, Idaho provides us with three of the stories, one probably apocryphal, that contribute to the legend of Molly b'Damn. Supposedly also on the train that took her to Idaho was Martha Jane Cannary, better known to history as Calamity Jane. Legend has it that the two met in Dakota Territory and that Jane, impressed by the beauty and resourcefulness of Molly, decided that the competition in Murray would be too stiff so decided to remain in Deadwood. It's probably just too good a story to be true (just as it is too good not to print) but, given that within a matter of months Calamity Jane would be married to one Charles Burke, she might have had other reasons to remain in the Dakota Territory.

What is undoubtedly true is that Molly left the steam train in Montana and joined a pack train bound for Murray. Those with money to pay for horses did so; anyone who didn't walked and dragged their belongings behind them. Within hours the pack train was bogged down in a snow blizzard. Noticing a mother and child falling behind the other travellers, Molly took both on her own horse. Realising that her new charges were not dressed appropriately for survival in freezing conditions, Molly sought shelter with them, telling the pack train to continue on to Murray. All three spent a long night in the open, exposed to the merciless Idaho winter. The following day, the blizzard having eased, they continued their journey on horseback.

Their arrival in Murray caused a minor sensation. Few had expected them to survive. The legend of Molly b'Damn was complete when a fellow Irishman, named Phillip O'Rourke, sought the name of the beautiful Angel of Mercy who had selflessly and courageously rescued two fellow travellers. The tired and probably indistinct Dubliner replied 'Molly Burdan', which was misinterpreted by O'Rourke as 'Molly b'Damn'. The name had stuck before the former Maggie Hall had had time to correct it.

Thus began an association between Murray and Madam that was to continue until Molly's premature death at the age of thirty-five. She quickly acquired premises of her own and became a highly successful brothel keeper. Despite the nature of her business, Molly was well respected, though more for her many recorded acts of charity than for her expertise as a madam. Given that her brothel depended on healthy, sexually active prospectors for its considerable profits, her work among sick and ailing miners might be seen merely as sound business sense, but her charitable activities were more to do with altruism than the profit motive.

On the professional side of things her speciality was exotic bathing. She was to the bath-tub what Lola Montez was to arachnids. Regularly she would advertise what she described as her 'big cleanup bath'. This would take place in a tub behind her establishment. It would be filled with water while a group of expectant miners looked on. They would be encouraged to deposit some of their gold in the bottom of the tub. When she was satisfied that there were no free-loaders Molly would peel off and begin to bathe, thus cementing in the mind of the prospectors an all-important connection between sexual desire and hygiene.

In 1886 a crisis hit Murray, Idaho. An outbreak of smallpox crip-pled the town. The numbers of infected multiplied quickly and dozens died. With only the most basic medical facilities available (one doctor and no hospital), people opted to hide away from the infection. Murray quickly took on the aspect of a populated ghost town. But hiding from the disease did not prevent its spread. Molly and her girls were among the few who took direct action. She summoned a town meeting and berated the local authorities for their sins of omission. She admonished them by pointing out that 'You don't lick anything by running away from it, or hiding your heads under your pillows'.[36] Aided by Phillip O'Rourke, the Irish madam took control of the town's anti-smallpox procedures, clearing out the hotels and establishing them as hospitals. With prostitutes acting as nurses, the local doctor began to slow down the progress of the disease before finally arresting it altogether.

Ironically, Molly subsequently paid insufficient attention to her own state of health. In late 1887 she began to decline physically. She was subject to frequent coughing fits and fevers. Within a month she was bedridden and had been diagnosed as a consumptive. Within six weeks the then fatal disease had killed her. She died on 17 January 1888. Her funeral was, reportedly, attended by thousands. It was presided over by a Methodist minister. In his eulogy he described the young Irishwoman as

generous to a fault with her world's goods, and with her bodily
strength, she was one in whom no sacrifice was too great. She
was a ministering angel to the sick and suffering when exposure
or illness laid men low. Neither snow nor heat kept her from an
unfortunate's bedside and these kind acts have been recorded in
the Book of Books to her credit, overbalancing the debt side.[37]

However, such a tolerant judgement was clearly not shared by all the
clergy of Murray. The local Roman Catholic priest resolutely refused
absolution to a 'notorious brothel keeper'.

She was buried, at her own request, as Maggie Hall and her name
is still commemorated today in the town of Murray in an annual two-
day festival every August.

If Mary Gleeson[38] had been a prize-fighter (and she regularly acted like
one), she would have been a heavyweight. Weighing in at 200 pounds
for a considerable part of her adult life, this five foot, four inches Irish-
born madam made a fortune out of the skin trade in Missoula, Montana
between her arrival there in 1888 and her death in 1914.

Gleeson was born in Ireland in 1845 and little or nothing is known
of her early years. After spending time in New York, San Francisco and
St Louis, she arrived in Missoula with a decent fortune and a malleable
husband, John Edgar Gleim.

On 19 May 1889 the following advertisement appeared in the
Missoula *Gazette*:

> Mrs M Gleim begs to inform the public that she has returned
> from Chicago with two car loads of the newest and latest styles
> in furniture. Having more than she requires for her new lodging
> house she will sell bedroom sets at cost price. Don't forget to call
> at the big new red house on Main Street. No reasonable offer
> will be refused.

The ad was coy but effective. 'Mother' Gleim might just as well
have hung a sign outside the house loudly proclaiming 'Brothel Open
for Business'. She quickly set about adding to her property portfolio
and within a year had acquired eight buildings on West Front Street –
the Missoula red-light district.

Gleim's notoriety comes less from the business that brought her a
large fortune than from her violent and erratic personal behaviour. For

example, in January 1892 she was charged with assaulting two Roman Catholic priests. Her defence included the claim that she had spoken to the clerics in Latin and had been frustrated by their inability to reply in the vernacular language of their own Church. She was found guilty and fined $50. Two weeks later she was back in court for breaking a bottle over a fellow citizen's head. Some intemperate ranting about the legal profession earned her two counts of contempt of court on that occasion.

She seems to have spent more time in the Missoula courthouse than in any of her West Front Street establishments, picking up fines for assault, contempt and perjury as she went. But in 1894 she went too far when she was accused of the attempted murder of a business rival, C.P. Burns. He had already felt her wrath when, after testifying against her in a property dispute, she whipped him in the street. Then, in the early hours of 12 February 1894, Burns's home was levelled by an explosion that the occupant, by some miracle, survived. Two men were arrested and Gleim was accused of having conspired with them to kill Burns. She was taken into custody but later bailed on the grounds that her 'considerable girth' made it difficult for her to flee the jurisdiction without detection.

When some of her own prostitutes testified that they had overheard Gleim plotting with the two men who had caused the explosion and when one of her co-accused turned state's evidence against her, the result of Gleim's trial was a foregone conclusion. Not even the expensive legal team she had assembled could do much against actual evidence. Mary Gleeson Gleim was sentenced to jail for fourteen years. What her expensive lawyers, however, did win for her was a retrial on the basis of technical argument in the Montana Supreme Court. When the new trial began it was discovered, astonishingly, that most of the prosecution witnesses were no longer in Missoula.

While awaiting her retrial Gleim entertained herself by assaulting one of her West Front Street tenants and almost beating her to death (that cost her $550 in fines and costs). Then, in an example of the kind of good fortune that always favours the virtuous, the State of Montana case against her finally collapsed when C.P. Burns obliged her by dying of a heart attack. The attempted murder case against her was dropped in May 1896.

Relieved at such a let-off, did she mend her ways in the future? Not in the slightest. In February 1897, she was accused of entering the house of one C.A. Clayton, along with two men, and bludgeoning him on the head, face and shoulders. She pleaded self-defence. She was found 'not guilty' by her Missoula jury.

Gleim died of influenza in 1914. She left nearly $150,000 in her will. Legend has it (which almost certainly means its untrue) she left instructions that her tombstone face the railroad 'so her boys could wave goodbye to her'. From this we must assume that, despite her record for personal violence, she had a good grasp of customer relations.

REEL SEVEN

Heroes and Villains:
The Irish Good, Bad and Distinctly Ugly

John George Adair: proxy cattleman

John George Adair, born in the 1820s, is rather more fondly remembered in the USA than he is in the country of his birth. The son of a gentleman farmer from Laois, he once stood as a Tenant Rights candidate in a parliamentary election and was described by the Young Ireland mouthpiece the *Nation* as 'a cultured young squire'.[1] By the 1860s he had travelled about as far from the Tenant Rights cause as it was possible to do. One account of his life has him buying up bankrupted post-Famine estates and evicting tenants wholesale. He was certainly responsible for one of the most notorious mass evictions in Irish history.

In 1857 he had begun to acquire land (around 30,000 acres) in the Glenveagh/Derryveagh area of Donegal. Later, in 1867, he would build the magnificent Glenveagh House on the site. Exactly what prompted him to clear the estate is disputed. It may have been the murder of his steward, James Murray, in 1861[2] or it may have been an incident during which he was surrounded and intimidated by tenants while he exercised his hunting rights over their land. Whatever the cause, the outcome was a bitter and vindictive campaign in the course of which 244 men, women and children from forty-seven families were thrown out of their holdings and left to shift for themselves. Such was the outcry at the time that a charitable organisation, the Donegal Relief Committee, was formed that paid for the passage of most of the evictees to Australia, where they were given plots of land to work.

In retrospect it seems bizarre that Adair had originally been intended for a diplomatic career. But he quickly tired of that avocation and turned instead to the financial world. He established himself in New York in the mid-1860s, married well – to Cornelia Wadsworth Ritchie of blue-blooded Connecticut stock – and began making a fortune that would enable him to divide his time between the USA (he moved his operations to Denver) and his Donegal estate.

Adair's direct contact with the American West was limited but significant. The effect of one financial investment was to associate him with the greatest cattleman in western history, Charles Goodnight. In the 1860s Goodnight, along with his partner Oliver Loving, had brought his herd from the agriculturally depressed Texas as far north as Wyoming in search of a decent market price for cattle. In doing so they created what became known as the Goodnight–Loving Trail. Loving had died as a result of an Indian attack in New Mexico in 1867. At one point in his long life (he lived into his nineties), Goodnight owned upwards of twenty million acres of Texas land and vast herds of beef. In the process of acquiring this wealth, Goodnight had frequent need of capital. In March 1876 he borrowed $30,000 from one of Adair's agents.

The Irishman's interest in the West seems to have begun with a trip to Kansas in 1874 that almost had a tragic ending. Adair and Cornelia both enjoyed hunting and while on the prairie Adair did what far too many of his ilk were doing and went on a buffalo hunt. Activities such as these were severely depleting buffalo numbers, leading to the virtual extinction of the breed and to straitened times for the Plains Indians whose entire way of life was based on their own untrammelled pursuit of the beast. Adair's attempt at buffalo hunting was inept. He managed, in the course of a hunt (as did George Armstrong Custer at around the same time), to shoot his horse in the head and almost kill himself in the process.

The agricultural depression of the early 1870s was beginning to lift when Adair decided it was time to get into the cattle business. He was introduced to Goodnight and the two men entered into a financial arrangement that was far more advantageous to the Irishman than the Texas cattleman. The partnership deal was for five years, from June 1877, and involved the injection of capital by Adair while Goodnight would manage a ranch, based at Palo Duro, for an annual salary of $2,500. Adair's original investment, with 10 per cent interest, was to be paid back in full at the end of the five years, with the spoils resulting from the enterprise to be divided, one-third to Goodnight and two-thirds to Adair. The Palo Duro spread was also to bear the initials of the Irishman: it was to be called the JA Ranch.

Adair had driven a hard bargain but Goodnight did not seem too perturbed. 'It was mighty high interest,' he acknowledged, 'I did not mind it, because I knew I had a fortune made.'[3] Although Adair was, by and large, a 'sleeping' partner, he had clearly made this particular investment as something of an indulgence, an attempt to ingest, vicariously, some of the romance and adventure of the West. He and his wife insisted on accompanying Goodnight on the trip from Colorado to Texas with the cattle that would form the basis of the new herd. In the course of the journey the Adairs reported to their host that they had spotted a party of Indians through their field glass. Upon examination, an exasperated Goodnight discovered that what they had in fact seen was a US cavalry troop.

Adair became the butt of some cowboy practical jokes when the party reached Palo Duro. On one occasion, when he peremptorily ordered that a mount be saddled for him by a group of cowboys who were breaking some wild horses, the hands picked out the meanest and most untameable beast. As luck would have it, when Adair mounted him the horse shrugged off the habits of a lifetime and behaved like a meek dressage champion.

After two weeks of qualified 'roughing it', the Adairs were ready to return to Denver and one can imagine that Goodnight was happy to be seeing them leave. But the circumstances in which they finally departed were unfortunate. Although they did not affect the business relationship between Goodnight and Adair, events took place that caused a personal rift between the two men. Adair became a conduit for the anger of James T. Hughes, an English rancher based in the Texas panhandle, and Leigh Dyer, the brother of Goodnight's wife, Molly.

Hughes was the son of Thomas Hughes, author of *Tom Brown's Schooldays* (creator not only of Tom Brown but of the Rugby school bully Flashman, further fictionalised in a series of novels by George MacDonald Fraser). He and Dyer had fallen out and Hughes alleged to Adair that Dyer was stealing cattle from Goodnight and, by extension, from Adair himself. When the Irishman brought this accusation to his partner, Goodnight demanded to know who was the source of what he considered to be a malicious lie. Adair refused to tell him and Goodnight responded by snarling, 'We Southerners expect a man who makes any such statement to cite his authority, and if he refuses, we figure he's a damned liar on his own account.'

In the 1920s, now in his nineties, Goodnight would recall the incident with remorse. But his regret came not from any sense of self-recrimination at having called his business partner a liar. He was annoyed that he hadn't taken more drastic action. He told his biographer, J. Evitts Haley:

> He was an overbearing old son of a gun and would have been beat up several times if it hadn't been for me. I don't see why I took it. I ought to have challenged him to fight and if he wouldn't, I should have pulled him off his horse and beaten him up.[4]

What he would have done to the son of the creator of Tom Brown had he been apprised of the source of the accusation doesn't bear thinking about.

Despite the rancour and animosity that existed between the two men arising out of that incident, the Irishman refused to let personalities get in the way of a good business deal. In 1882, when the first JA Ranch contract expired, Adair signed up for another five years. The first deal had proved to be as sweet as Goodnight thought it would. After the repayment of all Adair's initial outlay (plus 10 per cent interest) there was a clear profit of just over half a million dollars.

Extraordinarily, Goodnight didn't secure greatly improved terms and conditions second time around. He did manage to extract from Adair a much larger annual salary for managing the JA ($7,500 – three times what he had been getting), but this time Adair's investment was secured by a mortgage on the entire Palo Duro property.

In 1885 Adair paid another visit to the ranch that bore his initials. He brought with him a 'gentleman's personal gentleman'. When asked by Goodnight what his function was, the valet responded that he was to be there to be cursed at whenever Adair would stub his toe. The Irishman remained at the ranch for a few weeks before beginning his return journey to Denver. He only made it as far as St Louis, where he died on 14 May 1885. Thereafter, Goodnight continued the partnership with Adair's wife, Cornelia. She continued to divide her time between the USA and Ireland.

Whether or not John George Adair felt spiritually enriched by his sojourns in the American West, he certainly ended up financially enriched. The hard work and dedication of Charles Goodnight made him a considerable fortune, despite their mutual antipathy. The two men had little in common. One was a man of action who worked incessantly even into his nineties. The other was a man of business who could afford to simulate romance and adventure when it suited him. The irony is that one of the most famous western brands, the JA, bore the initials of the dilettante rather than the cattleman.

Jim Kirker: scalphunter

In the mid-1840s the impoverished Choctaw Indians famously scraped about $200 together and sent it to Ireland for famine relief. It was an act of great charity, given their means. In return the history of Irish dealings with the Native American has, with honourable exceptions, been one of active and often enthusiastic participation in their brutal suppression. A few years before the Choctaw gesture, an Irish fur trapper made a gesture of his own. As the price of beaver declined, he sought out a useful alternative: Apaches. Like a character out of Cormac McCarthy's *Blood Meridian* or the Hollywood movie *The Scalphunters*, James Kirker led a paramilitary force in Mexico and New Mexico that killed and scalped up to 500 Apache Indian warriors at a dividend of up to $200 a scalp, the same as the entire Choctaw nation had been able to afford to send to Ireland. Ironically, Kirker had once earned the title of War Chief of the Apache nation.

The eventful life of James Kirker began in the small village of Kilcross in County Antrim, a few miles north of Belfast, in 1793. The young Presbyterian would have had some experience of the 1798 Rising, where his co-religionists rose against the British administration. He came from a prosperous family of tradesmen who could afford to send him to the USA in 1810 at the age of sixteen. This was done to avoid having him become a statistic of the Napoleonic Wars. Instead, the second son of Rose and Gilbert Kirker almost became a statistic of wars in the New World, some of his own devising. But he would survive to become Don Santiago Querque.

Jim Kirker landed in New York in June 1810 and went to work with a merchant of Irish Catholic stock named Peter Dunigan. That employment was short lived because within two years the boy who had come to the USA to avoid military service on behalf of the British would play his part in antagonising them in the War of 1812. He joined the crew of an irregular US naval vessel or privateer called *The Black Joke*.

In 1812 the USA did not have anything resembling a decent navy so the naval war was, in effect, franchised out. Private vessels (privateers) were engaged to harass British shipping on the high seas on the understanding that the US government would share in the proceeds of the looting of those ships. The vessel on which Kirker sailed was one of at least three called *The Black Joke* in the American fleet. The name derived from a bawdy popular song that included the line 'her black joke and belly so white'.[5] The black joke in question was a euphemism for female pubic hair.

Some of his experiences on board the good ship *Black Joke* would doubtless have inured Kirker to the bloodshed of his subsequent career. In addition to the normal casualties of war, the massacre of prisoners was not uncommon in this unorthodox naval conflict. It is hardly coincidental that, in his future activities, Kirker would not be noted for a highly developed sense of clemency.

At the war's end Kirker abandoned his profitable life on the ocean wave (peacetime piracy being frowned upon) and returned to New York. There he discovered that his former employer had died, leaving a pregnant twenty-year-old wife. He married a very healthy grocery business and the Irish-born Catharine Dunigan the following year. For the next four years Kirker seemed content to lead the life of a prosperous New York merchant. Then, in 1817, some more members of the Kirker clan arrived from Northern Ireland, including his cousin David, and suddenly he was on his way to St Louis. He promised his wife that it would only be a short trip. In 1831 Catharine had herself legally declared a widow. Her husband's short trip had lasted more than a dozen years.

The St Louis to which Kirker migrated was a very Irish city. It had a population of 3,000 at that time, many of whom were foreign born. Of the non-Americans, two-thirds were Irish. On his way to the Missouri, Kirker would have passed through the state of Ohio where another cousin, an earlier arrival in the USA, Thomas Kirker, had just served a term as governor.

At some point in the years that followed, Kirker became involved in the fur business. He claimed to have been part of the Ashley–Henry enterprise, but his name does not appear in any account of those first concerted attempts to organise the trade. He was certainly one of a group of entrepreneurs who shifted his attention to the Santa Fe Trail between St Louis and New Mexico. The more prosperous citizens of what was then a province of Mexico required US-manufactured goods. Kirker joined a 100-strong wagon train bent on meeting that need, at a hefty profit, of course. Each of the merchants who returned to St Louis did so as merchant princes – having realised a profit of roughly $15,000 each. Kirker, however, was not amongst them. He chose to remain in the southwest.

He returned to winter beaver trapping, illegally, in New Mexico. But he did so with the security of employment at the Santa Rita copper mines in the summer. Empty mineshafts also gave him a convenient place to store his illicit traps and to cache his beaver furs. The Irishman didn't make huge amounts of money from this illegal trade, so he did it in tandem with an activity for which he seemed to have a particular talent. The produce of the Santa Rita mines needed to be hauled to civilisation across territory that was the playground of the Apache Indians. None of Kirker's predecessors had made a very good job of protecting the ore in the past. Kirker was convinced that he could do better.

His opponents were a race of tough, resourceful and aggressive Native Americans who had originated in Canada and migrated to the Mexico/Arizona/New Mexico region. They had a lot in common with the mighty Lakota/Sioux race. They had come a long way from their original home and were resented by the tribes they had displaced. The name by which they went was also similar to the name by which the Lakota were known. The word 'sioux' meant 'enemy' to the tribes of the Great Plains. 'Apache' means the same thing in the language of the southwestern desert inhabitants, the Zuni.

The Apache warrior was hardy and resilient, able to travel by horse up to seventy miles a day if required. As a military force they were well organised tactically (they would produce two of the great Indian military leaders in Cochise and Geronimo). They never attacked in a single group, always dividing their forces and scattering into many more groups if threatened with defeat. In their relations with Mexican and New Mexican farmers, they operated what can only be called a system of crop rotation. Except that they didn't grow the crops themselves. They stole from Mexican farmers, leaving them just enough so that they didn't completely abandon their farms and deprive the Apache of their principal source of food.

In his dealings with the Apache, Kirker demonstrated considerable subtlety. Instead of opting to fight them, he chose to befriend one of their most influential chiefs, the Mission-educated Juan Jose Compa. In order to protect his copper convoys, Kirker became a 'fence' for the cattle the Apache rustled from their Mexican neighbours. The policy seemed to work. In 1831 he was prosperous and expansive enough to take on a second wife (though there is no evidence to suggest that she was ever told she was Mrs Kirker No. 2). Rita Garcia from Chihuahua was described in a contemporary account as 'a handsome and fine woman'. Kirker, now becoming known locally as Don Santiago Querque, at around this time became an adopted War Chief of the Apache. Things couldn't have been going better. Which, of course, meant that they quickly went to hell.

Largely because of his alliance with the Apache, a warrant was issued for Kirker's arrest. He was enthusiastically pursued by Albino Perez, governor of the New Mexico Territory, for the $800 reward offered. When he found there was a price on his head, Kirker fled to Bent's Fort in Colorado. While in a brief exile there he met someone who would become one of his most loyal allies in the years ahead, a half-breed Shawnee Indian called Spybuck. There Kirker remained until he profited from the volatility of Mexican politics. Perez was beheaded by a mob convinced by his political enemies that he was going to impose crippling taxation. One of the proposed policies, according to the rumour mill, was a tax on sexual intercourse. The man who took over from Perez, Manuel Armijo, invited Kirker back to New Mexico.

A few months prior to the assassination of Perez, another killing had taken place that was to lead Kirker's life in a new and homicidal direction. Juan Jose Compa, his Apache ally, had been murdered. The Apaches were on the rampage again, this time killing people in the streets of Chihuahua itself. In a move worthy of the plot of *The Magnificent Seven*, the new governor of Chihuahua, lacking any confidence in the will and the ability of the Mexican Army to combat the Indians, raised private money to fund a mercenary protective force. The oddly named Sociedad de Guerra Contra Los Barbaros (Society for the War against Hostiles) was formed and James Kirker was invited to lead a band of Indian fighters. These 'Scalp Hunters', with Spybuck as Lord High Executioner to Kirker's Mikado, were fifty strong when the group was established in September 1839. They were mostly recruited from the USA. They included a number of Shawnee Indians and earned sums that seem astonishing today: $100 was to be paid over for the scalp of an Apache warrior, $50 for an Apache woman and $25 for a child.

On one expedition the Scalp Hunters slaughtered dozens of men, women and children of a group led by Cochise. The great Apache chieftain was able to escape. Such was the ferocity of the bloodthirsty campaign of the Irishman and his private army that it further upped the violent ante that prevailed in New Mexico. The Apache attacks on Mexican settlements became more merciless. Unhappy at one point when the Chihuahua exchequer was unable to cover the cost of his scalps, Kirker disbanded his group and the war continued without him. But after a retirement of two years he was enticed back when the government increased the reward on a warrior scalp to $200.

Over a six-year period – for just over half of which his band was active – Kirker is reckoned to have killed up to 500 Apache Indians with the loss, or so he claimed, of only three of his own men. Nowadays it would be called genocide or, at the very least, ethnic cleansing. But in the 1840s Kirker was a hero – never beloved of

Mexican politicians, but celebrated by a grateful populace. His reign of terror came to an end with the beginning of the Mexican–American War in 1846, when he was forced to make a choice between his two adopted countries. He went with the likely winner and his judgement proved correct. Kirker became a scout and guide for Colonel William Alexander Doniphan, second in command to Colonel Stephen W. Kearny, leader of the force being shepherded into action in New Mexico by Thomas Fitzpatrick. Doniphan's successful capture of Chihuahua meant that Kirker could be reunited with the family he had been forced to leave behind when he opted to assist the US Army in the war. In his absence the Mexican government had put a price on his head of $10,000, a far cry from the paltry $800 made available for his scalp a few years before.

Unusually for a man of that time, Kirker once returned to Ireland. Not many Irish emigrants could afford to make a return journey across the Atlantic to visit family. Kirker is reckoned to have made the trip, in 1849, to secure an inheritance. He spent a very short time in Antrim before returning to New Mexico. By the early 1850s he, and his ever-faithful band of Shawnees, was in California, which had become a State of the Union in 1850.

Kirker settled in Contra Costa County, near San Francisco. He lived there for less than three years, dying of natural causes in late 1852. It would appear that his death was due in no small part to excessive drinking. The marker left over his grave by the Shawnees has disintegrated, leaving only a small remnant of his gravestone jutting out of the ground near Kirker Pass. Given the life he led and the vocation for which he displayed most aptitude, it seems unlikely that any local committees will actively campaign to have a monument erected in his honour, especially as the most appropriate memorial would probably be a row of raven-haired scalps. Not that the population of the Golden State has much to be proud of when it comes to the wholesale slaughter of Native Americans during the nineteenth century.

Kirker was one of many Irishmen who made a career out of murdering Indians and, therefore, made a contribution to the attempted genocide of the indigenous American races. He was a ruthless, efficient and avaricious killer, but he was also a product of his time and his geographical location and must be seen in that context.

Johnny Healy: whiskey peddler

John Jerome Healy was named after two hallowed saints but never aspired to canonisation himself. In fact, in some inverted universe he might well have been a candidate for demonisation. He was born in the parish of Donoughmore in County Cork in 1840 and, like hundreds of thousands of Irish people of his generation, he was forced into exile with his family in 1853 by the continuing effects of the Great Famine. In common with many other Irish families who landed at Ellis Island, they didn't stray far. They settled in Brooklyn. Five years later Healy was on the move. In a country beset by fears of being overrun by immigrants, and where 'No Irish Need Apply' signs proliferated, the US Army tended not to discriminate, at least in its 'other' ranks. Healy, now eighteen years old, joined up. He was quickly despatched westwards to join in a campaign against the troublesome Mormons in Utah, who were deemed to be defying the constitution by practising polygamy and rejecting the authority of the federal government.

During the early part of his sojourn in the West, Healy became yet another Irishman to come in contact with the monumental Jim Bridger. His unit was stationed at Camp Scott near Fort Bridger and the veteran trapper and guide was a frequent visitor to the military camp. By the time Healy was discharged in 1860 he had, courtesy of his army training, developed many of the skills of the men in Bridger's profession and he decided to remain on the frontier. With an Irish friend, John Kennedy, smitten by the prospect of making his fortune as a gold miner, he headed to the wild and unpredictable American Northwest. His new life eventually brought him to Fort Benton in Montana. It was an unprepossessing boom town, relying on mining and the fur trade for its existence, but it became the focus of much of Healy's activities from 1862.

Prior to settling permanently in the West, he returned to New York with the modest proceeds of his prospecting and managed to persuade his brother Thomas, an uncle and two nephews to return to Montana with him. He also cajoled an Irishwoman, Mary Frances Wilson, into marrying him and going west. The Civil War was raging at the time, but Healy, a good Irish Democrat, had done his stint in the army and was clearly not sufficiently persuaded of the righteousness of the northern cause to risk his neck again.

In 1864 Healy became an employee of the Indian agent Gad E. Upson on the Blackfoot reservation at Sun River in Montana Territory. His terms of employment allowed him to carry on trading. Like most Indian reservations, Sun River left everything to be desired. Although the Blackfeet were expected to learn to grow crops, the area was subject to flash flooding that routinely washed away their produce before it could be got out of the ground.

By 1869 Healy had graduated to trading with the Blackfoot, Crow and Gros Ventre tribes on foot of a permit issued by his fellow countryman, Acting Governor Thomas Francis Meagher. One of his jobs was to oversee the safety of a herd of government-owned horses on the reservation. He also ran a well-protected store in Sun River. The security arrangements at his home/place of business would have been impressive at a military fort, but then, military forts were not as close to the 'front line' as Healy and his family were.

'Fortress Healy' proved its defensive capabilities in 1871 when a raiding party of Flatheads tried to 'liberate' the herd of federal horses. Among Healy's lodgers at the time were his brother Tom and his Irish friend John Kennedy. When Healy tried to prevent the Flatheads taking the horses, the attempted theft turned into a pitched battle. Healy and his allies barely made the safety of the fortified house. Fortunately a nearby camp of friendly Canadian Blood Indians joined in on the Irish side and the Flatheads fled. After the skirmish Healy came across a dying Blood Indian who extracted a promise from him to look after his motherless child. The young Blood boy was later christened Joseph Healy.

In the early 1870s Healy reverted to what he did best. In the 1920s it became known as bootlegging. In the latter part of the nineteenth century it was whiskey peddling. Enterprising Montanans had always made money selling illicit liquor on Indian reservations. By the 1860s it was almost considered to be their birthright. But in the decade that followed, the federal government began to flex its muscles and rein in some of that old frontier spirit. The army, which had often incurred the wrath of the Territory's traders, miners and ranchers by its apparent unwillingness to protect settlers from Indian attack, proved to be much more competent in its interdiction of supplies of whiskey to the Native American tribes of Montana.

At around that time the Hudson's Bay Company retrenched, pulled out of the Canadian prairie states and handed over a million square miles of land to the government. Healy saw an opportunity immediately. With the HBC gone there was no one left to police an extensive area of Canadian territory. A resourceful 'trader' was no longer going to get roughed up by the agents of the HBC and the Canadian federal government was in no position to monitor this vast region efficiently. So it was open season. Healy could switch his attention to a new market, the Native Americans of the Canadian prairie. All he had to do was get supplies of liquor across the border into Canada under the noses of American military overseers who knew exactly what he had in mind. His plan was simple. He obtained a licence to trade 'six wagons loaded with supplies, provided there is no spirituous liquors in the wagons except a small quantity which may be taken safely for medicinal purposes'.[6] The party of men Healy brought with him must have been distinctly unhealthy specimens, as the cargo contained few solids.

Healy reached Canada by means of two cunning ruses. He stashed his wagons close to his Sun River store and headed for Fort Benton. From there he telegraphed his partner A.B. Hamilton and instructed him to meet him east of the town. As he had been instructed to do by the US Army, the telegraph clerk alerted the troops at Fort Shaw, fifty miles southwest of Benton, about Healy's intentions. Of course there was to be no rendezvous with Hamilton. Instead Healy recovered his liquid cache and headed for Canada by an alternative route. In case the army realised it had been duped, he added a further refinement. All of his wagons were equipped with long poles that trailed behind the wheels, giving the impression to a tracker of an Indian village on the move. To the delight of many anarchic Montanans, Healy made it across the border with his whiskey, established a trading post in Alberta called Fort Hamilton (nicknamed Fort Whoop-Up) and made a profit of $50,000. Within months his escapade was being flattered by the imitation of a horde of other would-be bootleggers.

Before we get too carried away at the success of this anti-establishment Irishman, it would be wise to recall the effect the role this illicit trade played in the degradation of the Native American. Healy's profits came at great cost to the Indians. Much-sought-after trade goods (buffalo robes, blankets, horses, etc.) were handed over in exchange for whiskey. The value of these was then realised by Healy and Hamilton elsewhere. The net gain for them was considerable. But it was a minus sum game for the Indians. They gave up their valuable possessions in return for a few hours or days of oblivion and a lifelong addiction to alcohol. In modern terms Healy, and those like him, were the moral equivalent of twenty-first-century drug pushers.

According to his biographer, William R. Hunt:

> if Healy ever suffered any attacks of conscience for his long-term contribution to the degradation of the Indians he never admitted it. You had to be tough and indifferent to suffering to stay in the whiskey trade when you saw its effects. It helped too if you believed that the destruction of the Indians was inevitable, necessary to the advance of white civilisation.[7]

Indians, traditionally, had a low alcohol tolerance and would fight among themselves, and with white traders, when they became intoxicated. For example, during one winter, seventy members of the Blood tribe, which had come to Healy's aid on the Sun River reservation, died in drunken brawls. Healy must have been aware of the effect his biggest sales line was having on the Indians, but he was able to distance himself from it because Fort Whoop-Up functioned as a primitive off-licence. Customers were discouraged from drinking on or around the premises.

Healy acquired a reputation as a tough and resourceful opponent. He outwitted the US Army and, periodically, faced down challenges to his position from Indian and white alike. His 'enterprise' finally came to an end, due, indirectly, to a notorious massacre committed by a group of Montanans ill disposed towards him.

One of the less well-regarded professions on the northwestern frontier was that of 'wolfer'. These were men who acquired and sold wolf pelts. The acquisition of their stock involved killing a buffalo and poisoning his flesh with strychnine. The result would be the deaths of any scavenging wolves that tried to eat the dead beast. It was not an exact science and was an activity despised by Indians, who lost hundreds of their dogs to its indiscriminate nature. As a consequence the border tribes were on a permanent war footing with wolfers. Healy was hostile towards them as well. As a supplier of goods and services to Canadian Indians, he saw the wolfers as being bad for business. Furthermore, they took a dim view of another of the Irishman's sidelines, supplying the Indians with sophisticated firearms.

In 1873 a group of Fort Benton-based wolfers had their horses stolen by Indians. Unable to secure military assistance in recovering them, they took the law into their own hands. There are conflicting versions of what followed but, in what became known as the Cypress Hills Massacre, the wolfers crossed the international border into Canada and became embroiled in a skirmish with Indians. After forcing the withdrawal of the Indian warriors from their camp, the wolfers, according to witnesses, descended on the camp, murdered the children, raped the women and then murdered them too. Canadian estimates put the death count at more than forty; American sources insisted the toll was not much more than a dozen.

The wolfers' action went down well in Montana but was condemned by Canadians as a ruthless and provocative American incursion, tantamount to an act of war. Canadian press denunciations conveniently ignored the fact that some of the wolfers were from north of the international border.

Attempts were made by the Canadian government to extradite the wolfers. This was vigorously resisted in Montana. Tension along the Montana–Alberta border was exacerbated by the presence in the region of Irish-born lawyer John J. Donnelly, who had already attempted two Fenian invasions of Canada. He, and other Irish inhabitants of Fort Benton, stoked up hostility by turning the incident into an anti-British crusade. It was not a difficult thing to do in a state where the British-owned Hudson's Bay Company was not held in high esteem thanks to its history of exploiting the often fuzzy boundary between the USA and its northern neighbour. In the end, no one was extradited and a subsequent trial of three of the alleged murderers in Alberta was aborted for lack of prosecution witnesses.

However, the massacre itself, the apparent ease with which Americans could cross the border for illegal purposes and the lingering fear of Fenian invasion led to the establishment of the North West Mounted Police. Healy's fellow countrymen in the Fenian Brotherhood and the renegade wolfers had, between them, scuppered his highly profitable enterprise. With the elegantly scarlet-clad Mounties roaming the border on the lookout for Irish republicans and homicidal Americans, Fort Whoop-Up would not be able to continue its lucrative trade.

There was one brief moment of farce before reality dawned for Healy. The first force of Mounties sent west to close him down managed to get itself completely lost and was obliged to send scouts across the border to Fort Benton in order to find out how to get to Fort Hamilton. But they made it there eventually and 'got their man'. Healy was due for a mid-life career change.

Unable to continue his liquor trading with the Canadian Indians, he was left in an even worse position when demand for the buffalo robes he had taken in payment suddenly collapsed. He lost more than $12,000. He was reduced, in 1877, to returning to Fort Benton and touting for the local newspaper, the Fort Benton *Record*. His job was to collect money due and try to increase circulation. But, more importantly to the historian at least, he wrote a series of memoirs for the paper. In the main they were the sort of self-congratulatory pieces you might expect from a spiritual brother of Jim Bridger. But there was also a more subtle intent at work. Healy, despite having profited from Native Americans, conveys a sense of extreme distrust of them in his writing. Contradicting the current received wisdom, derived mainly from migrants' letters and diaries, Healy maintains that Indians had been responsible for a great number of deaths of westward migrants. In florid and emotive language he claims that 'hundreds upon hundreds of families, of whom nothing is known but that they died miserably upon the plains, have been found and buried or left to molder and mingle with the dust'.[8]

He also used his new platform to become a champion of the Fenians and took a few swipes at his old nemesis, the North West Mounted Police.

But it was the threat of Indian uprising that preoccupied most Montanans in the mid-1870s. Healy, in 1876, offered to emulate James Kirker in New Mexico by raising a civilian force not dissimilar to one assembled by Acting Governor Thomas Francis Meagher ten years earlier. The humiliation of the 7th Cavalry by Crazy Horse, Sitting Bull and Gall and their non-reservation force of Sioux and Cheyenne at the 'Greasy Grass' battle (Little Bighorn) caused further consternation among the already nervous inhabitants of Montana. The following year Chief Joseph and his Nez Perce conducted some of their epic and ultimately unsuccessful flight to Canada through the Territory of Montana. Joseph, with a constantly dwindling band of warriors, women and children, was trying to escape the confines of the tribe's Idaho reservation. The Nez Perce were eventually stopped a few agonising miles from sanctuary in Canada by a force led by Colonel

Nelson A. Miles, the man who had harassed the Sioux and Cheyenne war party into insignificance in the year after the Little Bighorn battle.

Healy was working as an army scout as the Nez Perce moved across Montana. He was present when Miles cornered Joseph and his band of 100 warriors and 200 women and children near the Bear Paw Mountains in October 1877.

Exhausted after a journey of 1,800 miles over hostile terrain and debilitated by hunger and the extreme cold of a fast-approaching Montana winter, the ragged group was forced to surrender. The Irishman had one of the great journalistic 'scoops' of the American West. Unusually for him he was prepared to acknowledge the nobility of the Indians after they reluctantly capitulated to Miles's force. He wrote:

> The Nez Perce, of course, deserve little sympathy; but they fought as bravely as any men could have fought, and conducted their warfare more like civilised people than savage Indians. During the siege they never harmed a wounded soldier, and on no occasion have they been known to take a scalp or otherwise mutilate a victim.[9]

That is about as charitable as Healy ever becomes with a race he himself had exploited shamelessly.

His next encounter with the Native American would be with the great Sitting Bull himself. The Lakota religious leader had been forced into Canada after the American military reaction to the Little Bighorn humiliation. The Canadian administration refused the US Army permission to pursue Sitting Bull and his Lakota band across the international frontier. However, given the record of this particular Sioux band, the government was reluctant to entertain it in Canada for long. A conference was organised involving, among others, General Alfred Terry and the Canadian Mounted Police Inspector J.M. Walsh. Terry was an amiable, gangling (six foot, six inches tall) bearded officer who had commanded one of the columns involved in the ill-fated 1876 punitive campaign against the Sioux and Cheyenne. Walsh, not one of Healy's favourite people, was a dedicated policeman of Irish descent, though his heritage looks to have had an interesting mix. Photographs of him reveal a man with very Latinised colouring and bone structure. He also sported a prominent moustache, a leafy forest on his upper lip.

The talks, which included Sitting Bull, were designed to persuade the Lakota chief to return to the USA with his warriors. The meeting took place at Fort Walsh in Canada and was conducted in a tense atmosphere amplified by the presence of twenty-five red-coated Mounties, three companies of the US 2nd Cavalry (which Terry had been allowed to bring for protection) and Sitting Bull's warriors. Also present were three reporters, one of whom was Johnny Healy.

Proceedings began with Terry requesting Sitting Bull to return to the USA and promising that no punitive action would be taken against him or any of his warriors. The atmosphere went sour very quickly when the Sioux chieftain made it abundantly clear that he had no intention of leaving Canada. Walsh tried to mediate, attempting privately to persuade Sitting Bull that a return to the Sioux reservation was his best long-term option.

At about this time the ever-belligerent Healy appears to have made a bizarre proposal to General Terry. He offered to kill Sitting Bull. Terry declined, pointing out that Healy would be charged with murder by the Mounted Police if he chose to go ahead with his threat. It remained hanging in the air only to evaporate when Healy was presented with an even more inviting challenge. He became involved in an argument with one of the other reporters. Healy insisted that he could ride the 340 miles to the nearest telegraph station, in Helena, Montana, within forty-eight hours and have the story of Sitting Bull's defiance in the New York *Daily Herald* within three days of the inconclusive ending of the negotiations. Terry, no doubt anxious for Healy to be elsewhere, dismissed the boast and Healy rose to the challenge.

Forty-three hours and five horses later Healy rode into Helena, hungry, exhausted and almost asleep in the saddle, and the *Daily Herald* had its unexpected scoop. At a rather more leisurely pace, Healy then wrote up his account of the negotiations for the Fort Benton *Record*. In it his dislike of Indians other than quiescent whiskey drinkers comes across in his descriptions of Sitting Bull. Like all white Montanans, Healy had been traumatised by Little Bighorn and his writing is informed by a sense of vulnerability and insecurity. Sitting Bull is disparaged. 'His fame is not all deserved. The report that he is a fine, intelligent half-breed, classically educated, is of course false. He is a full blooded Sioux and not a very remarkable one at that.'[10] Healy also takes the opportunity of sniping at Walsh, blaming him for encouraging the Lakota shaman in his defiance. In this he gives full vent to his antipathy towards the Mounties and expression to his Fenian anti-Britishness. Healy's contempt for an Irish Canadian in the service of the British Crown would have been almost as lip curling as his aversion towards Sitting Bull, which was ironic because Healy was about to become established in the same line of business.

The instances of lawbreaker turning law enforcer in the history of the American West are far too numerous to provoke much surprise. Poachers turned gamekeeper with regularity and, in most cases, came down hard on other poachers with the zeal of the convert. Who better than a former criminal to understand the criminal mentality? Furthermore, on the frontier, notions of legality were flexible, to say the least. Crimes such as whiskey peddling may have contravened federal laws, but the federal government had to make those laws stick in a society that only tolerated its irksome presence because of the military protection it afforded in a precarious environment.

As far as the people and, more importantly, the political élite of Choteau County were concerned, John Healy had two things going for him. He was tough – ruthless if required – and he was a Democrat. His exploits had turned him into something of a local hero and it was better to have him inside the kitchen spitting outwards than vice versa. He was first appointed to the job of sheriff in 1877, when the incumbent resigned over the escape of a prisoner. Healy got the prisoner back. He ran for the office in his own right in 1878 and was re-elected in 1880. During his term of office his stock in trade was to go about his business unarmed. He reasoned that 'no man who is sober will shoot down an unarmed man'.[11] It was a philosophy that reposed a lot of faith in his fellow man, but it seems to have worked for him. He generally managed to defuse situations. He had two things going for him: the first was his reputation for toughness, the second he never had to reveal. It was the fact that he always carried a small Derringer secreted about his person, just in case he was proved wrong.

For a man who had, very profitably, defied federal excise laws, he conducted his own tax-collecting activities with particular efficiency and gusto. This taxation was purely local. The Choteau County revenue stream had begun to dry up shortly into Healy's second full term as sheriff. Healy, who risked not being paid, heard of a group of Canadian buffalo hunters operating near Fort Benton. He decided that, as they were using roads built by Choteau County (as a matter of fact there were none), they were liable for tax. He marched straight into their camp and managed to separate them from more than $6,000 worth of their buffalo robes. When the exchequer was running down again after the proceeds of the first exercise had been distributed amongst county officials (fellow Democrats to a man), he tried it again. His second foray was not as successful. At first the new group of hunters, informed of their liability, reluctantly agreed to pay up to a well-armed posse. However, as soon as they were reinforced they demanded the return of their robes and Healy's tax gatherers barely managed to escape with their lives. The Irishman informed Choteau County officials that another revenue stream had just dried up and that they needed to consider alternatives. Healy's activities had also come to the attention of the federal authorities in Montana and, had he not lost office shortly afterwards, his unorthodox approach to tax collecting might have got him into difficulty with higher authority.

None of which is to suggest that Healy was not a good sheriff. He shared the ambiguous relationship of the average Montanan with the federal administration, but when it came to the maintenance of local law and order and the continued transition of Fort Benton from the wildness of his own early years there to something more resembling civilisation and gentility, he played his part. He was not re-elected in 1882 for a number of reasons. He was deemed by some to be spending too much county money enforcing the law. In one instance he was criticised by the local press for having gone to the expense of pursuing a prisoner into another county.

But the main reason for the loss of his position (he wasn't even nominated by the Democrats to run again) was his relationship with Montana stockmen. The theft of cattle and horses, mainly by Indians, from cattle ranches was rife. To the voters of Fort Benton, Healy was a little too enthusiastic in his efforts to restore stolen livestock to the big cattlemen. And of course not all of the rustling was down to the Native Americans tribes. His own constituents would have been responsible for a portion of it.

After his failure to be re-elected sheriff, Healy tried to establish an auctioneering business in the town, but if there was much to be auctioned the sellers obviously went elsewhere because Healy closed it down after a brief time in business. Shortly thereafter Healy decided that Montana had nothing left to offer him. He gradually sold out whatever interests he had left in the state and, when his wife died in 1883, Alaska beckoned. Some of his friends had already moved to the new boom territory of the Yukon. Healy decided to follow. His subsequent career in the frozen but potentially lucrative northernmost Territory of the Union was not without interest but falls outside the ambit of this work.

It seems that nothing became his time in Montana like the leaving of it. The Choteau *Calumet* paid him the kind of tribute, on the occasion of his final visit to Fort Benton, normally reserved for a remarkable corpse. An editorial sang his praises, recognising him as 'the originator and promoter of many successful enterprises for advancing the welfare of the communities in which he has resided'.[12] One can't help but suspect that the leader writer had his tongue sliding around his cheek in his reference to 'successful enterprises', given that Healy's most profitable venture had been the sale of illicit whiskey in an illegal market.

The *Calumet* praise was double edged, however. When the editorial said that he was 'one of the most prominent and heroic characters of our early civilisation', it was perhaps suggesting that the Irishman was a relic of a bygone and less respectable era, that he was a quasi-legal pioneer out of place in a more 'civilised' society. After his Alaskan adventure, Johnny Healy died in San Francisco in September 1908 at the age of sixty-eight. He is one of the most interesting and well-documented Irishmen to have made an impact on the frontier, and like many of the others, he is a highly ambivalent figure to twenty-first-century observers.

Like many Irishmen at home and abroad, circumstances had taught him to have little respect for civil authority. He came from a society that was not even allowed to legislate for itself and where the privileged few were identified with the colonial lawmakers. It was easy for someone like Healy to equate the US federal government, which exercised a control in the new territories disproportionate to that in the established states, with British governance of Ireland, all the more so when this irredentist Fenian lived in a state that bordered another British colony and did much of his illicit business there. That he then became an enthusiastic lawman is hardly surprising either. Just as there was a long tradition of Irishmen defying British authority in Ireland and elsewhere (Australia, South Africa and Canada, for example), there was an equally long tradition of Irishmen serving that very same authority in policing or the military.

What might be more dismaying for a twenty-first-century readership is Healy's treatment of and attitude towards the Native American.

The Indian constituted an American underclass, a conquered race, therefore the assumption is that an Irishman would have had an empathy or at the very least more sympathy with the members of that underclass. In practice it rarely worked out that way. As we have come to realise after some years of prosperity at home, there is nothing inherently empathetic in the Irish character. In a sense, the Irish experience in the West can be seen as a laboratory experiment or an examination of Irish tolerance of other cultures when directly confronted with diversity. In most instances the candidates can be said to have failed the exam.

Healy had opportunities to write sympathetically about two very real icons of Native American culture and history in Sitting Bull and Chief Joseph and chose not to do so. He saw the Native Americans less as a persecuted people than as a dangerous enemy, a competing underclass. To Healy his own people, i.e. white westerners, were the oppressed. Caught between a federal administration that was learning how to govern in a very interventionist, 'hands on' manner and hostile Indians who wanted to take back everything the white man had gained, Healy would have seen himself and his peers as victims. Given the tragic history of the Native American, it is not a sentiment that would be shared by many today.

However, it is generally a mistake to try and second-guess the past. Johnny Healy was a rogue who delighted in tweaking the noses of the federal authorities (it is an attitude of mind that exists in the West to this day). He was no lover of the Native American and may even have rationalised that he was best serving his own community by condemning Indian communities to an undignified life of alcoholism and thus pulling the teeth from any threat they posed. He was capable of operating on either side of the law and did so, over the years, with considerable success. But his triumphs were ephemeral and unlike someone of the calibre of Thomas Fitzpatrick, when he died he left behind little other than the memory of a 'colourful' character, one of many who populated the American West.

Paul Kane: painter of the mythic

Ireland has never been particularly noted for its visual artists, so it might come as a surprise that the man often entitled 'The Father of

Canadian Art' was born in Mallow, in County Cork, on 3 September 1810. Paul Kane's family moved to Canada when he was nine years old, but the young Kane later returned to Europe to study painting. Whether or not he fathered Canadian art is debatable, but three years of his life are of considerable interest to students of the American and Canadian West. They were years in which he emulated much of the work of American artists such as George Catlin and Europeans such as Karl Bodmer. He captured on canvas and in drawings a west that was already passing and he was, like Catlin, especially fascinated by the Native American. His paintings of Indians, though often highly romanticised, and his account of his three years in the West in his book *Wanderings of an Artist among the Indian Tribes of North America* are valuable, if flawed, anthropological documents.

Kane's family name had originally been Keane and his father had come to Ireland with the Royal Horse Artillery in 1798. The family migrated and settled in Toronto (then called York). Paul Kane, whose artistic tendencies were encouraged during his education, left school in 1826 and spent the next four years working in a furniture factory as a decorative painter. He spent at least four years working in the southern USA and exhibited in Toronto in 1834. At this point in his career he was a glorified copyist, his work consisting of imitations of European works. In the preface to his *Wanderings* Kane explains why he made the extraordinary journey that he did. During his schooling he spent much time with Mississauga Indians and noted that he had, in his youth, seen many Indians in or near Toronto. Now, however (he was writing in 1859):

> the face of the red man is no longer seen. All traces of his footsteps are fast being obliterated from his once favorite haunts, and those who would see the aboriginals of this country in their original state, or seek to study their native manners and customs must travel far through the pathless forest to find them.[13]

We can also assume that he saw his future reputation as an artist being established in this virgin territory.

Towards the end of the 1830s Kane left for Europe to study painting abroad. He travelled to France first. He then followed that up with a trip through Italy, during which he sketched copies of some of the most famous paintings of the Renaissance. He spent some time in London and it was there that he appears to have met George Catlin in 1842.

Catlin, the artist with whom Kane is most often compared, had spent some time in the 1830s travelling in the West, befriending trappers and Indians and sketching the western landscape and way of life. Now, as a gimmick to help sell his paintings and increase interest in Native Americans, he was travelling Europe with a troupe of Indian dancers.

In 1844 Kane returned to Canada with the intention of doing for Canadian Indians what Catlin had done for the American. As he later wrote, 'The principal object in my undertaking is to sketch pictures of the principal chiefs, and their original costumes, to illustrate their manners and customs, and to represent the scenery of an almost unknown country.'[14] His first trip was to the Great Lakes area in 1845, where he lived among the Ojibway, but if he thought he was going to meet the Noble Savage there he was quickly disillusioned. He found the Indians in that relatively accessible region to have been 'corrupted by whites'. He did, however, stage an exhibition of the work he completed on this expedition.

He decided to go further into the interior, which meant territory under the control of the Hudson's Bay Company. Here, as art historian Brian Lynch puts it, 'is the conjunction of art production with commerce'.[15] Kane needed the approval and co-operation of the company if he was to fulfil his ambitions. He was helped by the recommendation of a HBC agent to the Hudson Bay governor, Sir George Simpson, that he 'was prepared for the hardships of travel in the west'. In 1846 he met Simpson in the town of Lachine and showed him sketches he had already done. Simpson was impressed and commissioned a dozen paintings. Simpson provided Kane with a letter of introduction that meant he could use HBC transport to get him to wherever he wanted to go.

He visited the major HBC forts (Garry, Francis, Victoria and Vancouver) and near Fort Garry sketched scenes from what was, in effect, one of the last of the great traditional buffalo hunts on the North American continent. Kane himself took part and claimed to have killed two of the 500 or so buffalo slaughtered.

As he indicated in his preface to *Wanderings*, portraiture was his particular interest. His approach to his subjects was direct – he simply walked up to whomever he wanted to sketch and began. If there was any objection he would invoke the name of the Great White Mother (Queen Victoria) and claim to be on a mission from Her Majesty herself.

At that time Oregon was disputed territory, so Kane actually spent a considerable time in what is now Washington state in the USA. He visited the religious settlement of the remarkable and ill-fated couple Marcus and Narcissa Whitman. The Whitmans were on a mission from God. In the 1830s the Indian tribes in the Oregon Territory were deemed, by various religious groups, to be ripe for conversion. A society of Congregationalists and Presbyterians raised the money to establish their own mission in the far West and chose an eager young New York doctor, Marcus Whitman, as its first minister. Given previous experience of unmarried missionaries succumbing to the charms of native women, the society insisted Whitman could not remain single. A young woman, Narcissa Prentiss, was in a similar predicament, so the two agreed to get married. In 1836 they accompanied two other newly wed missionaries, Henry and Eliza Spalding, on the overland trail to Oregon.

Unfortunately the couples did not see eye to eye and when they arrived in the disputed territory began to behave in a most unchristian fashion and established missions as far away from each other as possible. The Whitmans settled in Waiilatpu, near modern day Walla Walla in Washington state. Equally unfortunately, the Whitmans didn't seem to get on much better with the poor souls, the Cayuse, among whom they had been sent to work. Over the next decade they converted a total of twenty Indians. The Whitmans saw the Cayuse as 'insolent, proud, domineering, arrogant, and ferocious' while the Cayuse thought the Whitmans were 'very severe and hard'.[16]

Like most unsuccessful missionaries before them, the Whitmans turned their attention to the spiritual needs of the growing white population in Oregon. Marcus Whitman even went east to promote Oregon as a settlement destination. However, the settlers he managed to attract to the West in 1847 brought smallpox with them and the disease decimated the Cayuse. The Indians, who blamed Whitman for their troubles, attacked his settlement and killed the reverend doctor, his wife and ten others. On his visit to the Waiilatpu settlement, Kane not only sketched the Whitmans (the only known life sketches) but, in a macabre twist, also sketched the two Cayuse men who, a few months later, would be hanged for killing the missionaries.

In the course of his three years in the Canadian and American West, Kane did in excess of 500 sketches, more than enough material to keep him painting for the rest of his life. Altogether, he produced Simpson's paintings, another dozen or so on commission from the Canadian government and more than 100 canvases that he sold to a wealthy Toronto resident, George W. Allan. Later, his paintings were sent by the Canadian government to the Paris World's Fair in 1853 and he became the most celebrated Canadian painter of his day. His account of his journey was published in 1859, though some have alleged that a careful reading of his contemporaneous journals suggests that *Wanderings of an Artist* may have been ghost written. It was a best seller in Canada and a French edition was published in 1861.

If the seed of Kane's career had been sown in the Northwest, so had the blight that would end it. He suffered snow blindness during his time spent in the Rockies and it curtailed his career as a painter. With his eyesight failing he was forced to give up painting in the 1860s. He began to drink heavily,[17] possibly because of his inability to paint. He died of liver failure in February 1871.

Kane was one of the first artists to portray the Northwest and, as the period of his travels there (1845–8) was pre-photographic, we are over-reliant on him for an accurate portrayal of Indian and trapper lifestyles at that time. So do we get any great measure of accuracy? Not really. Kane made hundreds of drawings during those three years, but he was an artist. He was not necessarily depicting reality. What he represented on canvas was reality seen through his own romantic prism, informed by his own agenda and his own sensibilities. As Kane once said himself, 'I turned my sketches into the kind of paintings people wanted to see' – his field sketches are often radically different from his studio work, which depicted, in the words of one critic, 'Victorian parlour Indians'.[18] When you compare a Kane sketch with the resulting oil-on-canvas work (which it is possible to do in the Royal Ontario Museum in Toronto), the warts have been removed. Portraits of individual Indians make them appear far more charismatic than the corresponding sketches.

In only one significant instance does Kane demonise as opposed to romanticise a subject. With the two Cayuse men responsible for the murders of the Whitmans, the touches Kane adds to the originals turn two neutral sketches into finished portraits from a chamber of horrors. The two are given, *ex post facto*, the clichéd baleful stare, simian features and threatening mien of the stereotypical killer.

Kane's romanticising of most of his subjects may have been for the sake of romanticism itself or it may have been a simple commercial calculation that the kind of people who would buy paintings or portraits of Native Americans were disposed to view them as 'noble savages'. Accordingly Kane may have felt compelled to introduce nobility where it does not appear in the sketches. In this he may have been doing, for largely mercenary reasons, what Catlin was doing out of greater conviction.

Kane's writing often suggests someone with an, at best, ambiguous attitude towards his subjects. His art seems to embrace the Native American while his words often express revulsion at their lives and rituals. There are many references to violence or the threat of violence. He describes a 'scalp dance' of the Chualpay tribe, after one of their hunting parties gives the scalp of a dead Blackfoot to a woman whose husband was himself killed by members of that tribe some years before. The scalp was

> stretched upon a small hoop ... and thus carried by the afflicted woman to a place where a large fire was kindled: here she commenced singing and dancing, swaying the scalp violently about and kicking it, whilst eight women, hideously painted, chanted and danced round her and the fire.

He adds, somewhat sarcastically:

> Having witnessed the performance for about four or five hours, seeing no variation in it, nor any likelihood of its termination, I returned, deeply impressed with the sincerity of a grief which could endure such violent monotony for so long a period.[19]

He reserves much of his bile for the Chinooks, highlighting their practice of binding the heads of infants to give them a distinctive angled forehead, enslaving members of their own and other tribes and certain 'filthy' habits – 'their persons abounding with vermin and one of the chief amusements consists in picking these disgusting insects from each other's heads and eating them'.[20] There is no suggestion of this disapproval or distaste in his portraits.

Kane was also a champion of the Hudson's Bay Company. At a time in the mid-nineteenth century when the British government was reassessing the HBC monopoly of the Canadian fur trade, Kane's *Wanderings* provided ready-made propaganda for the company. Kane held it up as an example of good governance, particularly when it came to its dealings with Indians. However, Kane could hardly be accepted as a neutral witness. He would never have been able to carry out his work without HBC help and he had received a hefty commission from its governor, Sir George Simpson (who, incidentally, was not above asking Kane to modify some of his paintings). It has even been suggested that the hand of Simpson can be traced between the lines of *Wanderings*.

Whatever his relations with the company and whatever his real motives were in heading west (his professed reason coming, after all, more than ten years after his journey), there is no doubt that he made a significant contribution to the recording of images from the American and Canadian Northwest that would not have survived without him.

Michael Meagher: gunfighter and lawman

Before beginning an account of the career of one of the few *bona fide* Irish-born gunmen in the American West (there were many more second-generation Irish who qualified for the description), it is worth clearing up a few misconceptions about the nature of one-on-one combat in the Wild West foisted upon us by Hollywood.

In the first place, the classic Colt .45 'fast draw' shootout of the western movie, which takes place between a square-jawed, white-hatted lawman and a surly, snarling, malevolent, mean-spirited bandit in the dusty main street of a wild cattle town, is a complete invention. Towns such as Abilene, Tombstone and Dodge City could be dangerous places, but it was rare for arguments to be settled in such a dramatic fashion. Gunfighters tended to use rifles or shotguns as their weapon of choice, avoided set-piece shoot-outs and eschewed the theatrics of the fast draw in favour of accuracy. Nineteenth-century weaponry and a distinct lack of skilled marksmanship meant that merely hitting your opponent was something of a bonus – blinding speed was superfluous.

Gunfighters were rarely involved in the 'profession' on a full-time basis. In general, they worked in areas that required them to carry a gun. Many were law officers, more were cowboys, some were criminals. Sometimes it was difficult to tell which was which and some gunfighters would regularly cross the line of legality, dividing their time between flouting and serving the law. There were probably no more than about 250 men who would, by any stretch of the imagination, qualify for the description of 'gunfighter'.[21] Statistics show that it was a dangerous calling, with almost two-thirds of those so-described dying violent deaths, mostly in firefights (about 5 per cent were executed). Less than a quarter died of natural causes. One of those who died by the gun was Irishman Michael Meagher.

Meagher was born in Cavan in 1843 or 1844, emigrated to the USA with his father and his younger brother John and settled in Illinois. The Meagher brothers fought on the Union side in the Civil War and in the aftermath of that conflict moved west to become stage drivers in Kansas.[22]

With the building of the transcontinental railroads, Kansas railhead settlements such as Wichita became vitally important cattle towns. They were at the end of the great cattle trails along which thousands of steers would be driven from states such as Texas, where they could only be sold at uneconomically low prices. From the cow-town railheads they would be shipped east, where prices were higher. The railroads utterly transformed the fortunes of towns that often had not even featured on maps before the arrival of the Iron Horse. The downside of this new prosperity was the influx of hundreds of cowboys. At the end of a dangerous, dusty drive they were unleashed, with money in their pockets, from the fatigue and perils of the trail and were frequently responsible for mayhem and crime. Officers of the law in cattle towns were busy men.

In 1871 Michael Meagher was appointed marshal of Wichita, Kansas. His brother John became his deputy. Even though the town was built on the Chisholm Trail, nearby Abilene benefited more from the cattle trade. But Wichita was still a town inured to violence. Meagher was the third town marshal within a nine-month period. His predecessor had lasted all of three days.

At least the city fathers seemed to take law enforcement more seriously once Meagher became marshal. A local ordinance was passed banning the 'carrying of deadly weapons concealed or otherwise'[23] within the city boundary and money was allocated for the building of a jail. On the orders of the city council, on 28 June 1871 Meagher demonstrated that Wichita meant business when it came to keeping guns out of the town. The Irishman erected pine boards outside the city limits that read, 'All persons are hereby forbidden the carrying of firearms or other dangerous weapons within the city limits of Wichita under penalty of fine and imprisonment. M. Meagher, City Marshal.'[24] Charlton Heston and the National Rifle Association would not have approved, but now Meagher had to make the ordinance stick.

That he did so through the summer of 1871 probably had more to do with the fact that the cattle trade still bypassed the town for Abilene. Things began to change when the town was connected to the Santa Fe line in 1872 and more and more cowboys started to frequent the town's saloons. They were the kind of people who, like Mr Heston, were loath to be parted from their firearms. Meagher, however, earned a reputation for defusing potentially dangerous situations without the use of violence and without resorting to his own gun. (He and his ten-strong police force were the only men allowed to carry weapons in Wichita.)

In 1874 Meagher abandoned law enforcement and the town of Wichita in favour of a move to Indian territory, where he drove a freight wagon. His departure may not have been entirely voluntary. Despite a good record as city marshal, he was passed over for reappointment by the new mayor, elected in April 1874. One of his policemen, William Smith, was appointed over his head and Meagher seems to have decided not to acquiesce in his demotion. That his interest in the job remained intact is borne out by the fact that in 1875, when the position of marshal was, once again, an elective office, he decided to stand against Smith and another former policeman, Dan Parks. He was duly elected by 340 votes to 311 for Smith and 65 for Parks.[25] Among the policemen appointed by the city council to assist him was a twenty-seven-year-old who hailed originally from Illinois, a certain Wyatt Berry Stapp Earp, who would have his own date with destiny at the OK Corral in Tombstone, Arizona on 26 October 1881.

Completely ignorant of the fact that he was now the boss of one of the great legends of the Wild West, Meagher went about the task of policing Wichita as efficiently as he had done in his first term. He also found time to get married, in August 1875, to a twenty-four-year-old Ohio lady named Jenny. Twelve months after his election Meagher stood against Smith once again. His cause was not helped by Earp, who got into a fight with the rival candidate, punched Smith and, in consequence, damaged the Irishman's prospects. Despite this, Meagher won comfortably by 477 votes to 249. It was an electoral victory that would lead to his first killing.

On New Year's Day 1877, a Wichita stage driver named Sylvester Powell went on a bender with a friend. The binge ended in an assault that got him arrested by Meagher. After being bailed by his boss, Powell swore vengeance on the marshal. Later that evening he, quite literally, caught the Irishman with his pants down, in the WC outside a Wichita saloon. He opened fire, hitting the marshal in the leg. A second bullet sailed harmlessly through his coat. Despite the bullet in his leg, Meagher instantly launched himself at Powell and the two men began to grapple for the stage-driver's gun. A third shot grazed the marshal's hand before Powell fled into an alleyway. Now Meagher reached for his own handgun and fired after the retreating Powell. He missed and limped off in pursuit of his assailant who, bizarrely, dawdled in front of a drug store and allowed Meagher to surprise him. The marshal, spotting Powell in the street, didn't wait to be fired on again and, abandoning his standard operating procedure when faced with danger, took aim and shot Powell dead with a bullet through the heart.

As the local newspaper, the Wichita *Eagle*, noted on 4 January 1877, Meagher had 'always succeeded by his imperturbable coolness to not only come off without a scratch, but to hold and confine his assailants without resort to deadly means ... we know he regrets as much as anyone, the sad issue'.[26]

Whether it was this salutary experience or, more likely, the beginning of a 'bust' cycle in the economy of Wichita as cattle numbers declined, Meagher moved to the growing town of Caldwell, Kansas in the late 1870s. He was elected mayor of the town in 1880 – the same year his former employee, Wyatt Earp, became deputy sheriff of Tombstone, Arizona. The dizzy heights of this public office did not prevent Meagher from falling foul of the law. In August 1880 he was fined for running an illegal gambling operation. Despite this he was, briefly, appointed city marshal in late July 1881. He served only five days and was, ultimately, replaced by John Wilson. It was while assisting Wilson in an arrest that Meagher was killed on 17 December.

A Texan cowboy named Jim Talbot, who lived locally with his wife and children, had been on a month-long bender during the course of which he would periodically become violent, issue threats and intimidate Caldwell citizens. In one reported instance he attended a local play in a drunken state, took exception to what he saw on stage and threatened to kill the author.

Marshal Wilson made numerous attempts to arrest Talbot and his equally raucous drinking partners. In one of these he was assisted by Meagher, who had been threatened by Talbot. As the marshal and his Irish predecessor chased Talbot through the streets of Caldwell, the Texan turned and fired at Meagher with his Winchester rifle. The shot slammed into the fleshy part of the Irishman's right arm and continued into his lungs. Contemporary accounts, which tend towards the dramatic, suggest that Meagher dropped the rifle and handgun he was carrying and groaned out a cry for help. His last recorded words were to one of Wilson's deputies. 'Tell my wife I have got it at last,' he muttered as he slumped to the ground. He was helped to a nearby barber's shop, the local barber often being the closest thing to a town surgeon, but within less than half an hour he was dead.

One member of Talbot's gang was shot before he managed to escape town and the rest were pursued into Indian territory by the county sheriff. They escaped the posse but many, including Talbot, were subsequently arrested and charged with various crimes associated with the death of Meagher. Talbot himself did not face trial until 1895; by that time all sorts of rumours had grown up around him, one of which held that he had been a member of Billy the Kid's gang. Talbot was tried under his real name of James D. Sherman and was ultimately acquitted after the jury in his first trial failed to reach a verdict. But he didn't last much longer anyway. Within the year he had returned to California. There he himself was gunned down in the town of Ukiah, apparently by his wife's lover.

Meagher's body was returned to Wichita for burial on 20 December 1881. Two days later his obituary positively leaped from the pages of the *Eagle*, which commented:

> With nothing of the dare-devil or reckless bravado in his composition, nevertheless Mike Meagher did not know the meaning of personal fear ... Many a time and oft has he faced death upon these streets with a bravery, fortitude and composure beyond the power of words to describe.

Thomas Francis Meagher: drunken politician or murdered reformer?

Why is one of the counties of the state of Montana named after the Irish revolutionary Thomas Francis Meagher? Because, for a brief and turbulent period in the mid-1860s, he was governor of the state.

Meagher is, of course, a hugely significant figure in Irish and in Irish American history but his fleeting role in the history of the American West offers an interesting and ultimately fatal cameo. Born in Waterford in 1823, he had been sentenced to death for his activities in the Young Ireland rebellion in 1848 but was transported to Tasmania instead. He escaped from there, made his way to the USA in 1852 and during the Civil War led the Irish Brigade in the Union Army. At the conclusion of the war, in 1865, he was appointed Military Secretary to the Montana Territory. His arrival in the territory gave the incumbent Governor Edgerton his excuse to depart (by the same stagecoach on which the Irishman arrived) and Meagher, almost immediately, became acting governor of Montana.

In the aftermath of the Civil War Meagher had sought some form of political reward for services rendered during the conflict. Attendance at a lecture by frontiersman James Fiske had stoked his enthusiasm for the far West. He may well have had a Messianic notion of populating the vast open spaces of Idaho or Montana with Irish settlers, much as the Mormons had done in Utah.

Meagher was not to know it when he took on the job of military secretary, but in travelling to Montana he was entering a political snake-pit. He would have problems with 'renegade' Indians, but these paled into insignificance in comparison with the hostility he would face from vigilantes and Republicans. In addition he had to confront an animosity towards government-appointed territorial administrators that was typical of the West. The term 'carpetbagger' was coined in the Reconstruction South to describe Yankees exploiting the economic and political weakness of the southern states. Western territorial governors were often portrayed in similar terms. There was much resentment among eastern migrants that, albeit through their own free choice, they now lived in a mere territory rather than a fully fledged state. Making matters worse, as Patricia Limerick has noted, 'the imposed governments of Southern Reconstruction did resemble the territorial system, and that resemblance could make it look as if the West was receiving gratuitously what the South earned as punishment'.[27]

The Territory of Montana was a Republican Party fiefdom in the aftermath of the Civil War, though large numbers of Union and some Confederate Democrats had begun to settle there. Before the departure of Edgerton, the incumbent governor, many of the Republican judicial and executive stakeholders had voted themselves large salaries from territorial funds. The official Republican administration was shadowed by a powerful but illegal vigilance committee that, in effect, took care of law and order in Montana. But it did so according to criteria laid down by the powerful and privileged. Soon after his arrival, Meagher received self-serving judicial advice that he did not have the power to summon the territorial legislature and deal with such abuses of power. Initially, as he felt his way into the job, he went along with this advice. Soon, however, he realised that, as he put it to a crowd in the town of Helena, he had 'fallen into the hands of a bad adviser'.[28]

In order to break the power of the Republican élite and the secretive vigilance committee, Meagher wrote to the president informing him that he had decided to summon the legislature at the earliest opportunity in 1866 (i.e. when the bitter Montana winter was over) and that he was also calling a convention that would (and did) formulate an application for statehood. To an influential and powerful constituency in Montana, Meagher's decision to assert his independent authority was tantamount to a declaration of war.

The first accusation against Meagher was one of gross egotism. He was accused of hankering after the first Senate seat that would accrue to Montana in the event of statehood. In fact, as he became more enamoured of the state, he probably did cherish such ambitions. Another charge commonly levelled against him was that of drunkenness. Meagher was, undoubtedly, fond of his liquor and had been known in the past to go on almighty benders. But his fondness for the bottle was greatly exaggerated by his political enemies during his twenty months in Montana. Such was the persuasive influence of the vigilante supporters that Meagher is dismissed in many quarters in Montana to this day as a mindless, self-aggrandising drunk.

Just as his nationality assisted in the creation of the image of the stereotypical Irish drunk, so was it used by his enemies to suggest that he was a proponent of the Fenian notion of an invasion of Canada. He denied this charge in personal letters to President Johnson and Secretary of State Seward. In this climate of mutual animosity, matters between Meagher and his Republican opponents were brought to a head by the so-called Daniels affair.

James Daniels was, depending on your point of view, a double murderer who had knifed an honest Montana citizen or an unfortunate victim of vigilante violence. In the winter of 1865–6 he killed one Andrew Gaitley in a knife fight in Helena. He had also been responsible for the death of a man in California. In the trial that followed the Montana killing, Daniels was sentenced to three years in jail for manslaughter. Following representations from Daniels's friends and business associates, Meagher reviewed the case and pardoned the prisoner. The petitioners persuaded the acting governor to exercise clemency on the grounds that 'the circumstances under which the aforesaid offence was committed were most provoking on the part of the deceased'.[29] Daniels's advocates were mostly well-known opponents of vigilance-committee rule. The response of the vigilantes was to lynch the unfortunate Daniels on his release from custody. A note was pinned to his body reading 'The governor is next'. The note did not refer to Governor Edgerton.

While all this was going on, the 'Indian problem' intensified. The leaders of the Blackfoot tribe had been intimidated into the signing of a typically disadvantageous treaty. This ceded thousands of square miles of traditional land north and east of Virginia City and Helena. But many groups of recalcitrant warriors refused to accept the terms of the agreement and began to attack and kill individual settlers and miners. Meagher sought army help from General William Tecumseh Sherman, commander of the Department of the Missouri. Sherman was impressed neither by the request nor by the source from which it emanated. 'I fear civilians in the style of T. Francis Meagher may involve the frontier in needless war,' he wrote to a friend in 1866.[30] The application for a force of 850 soldiers was turned down.

In his dealings with Native Americans, Meagher did not exhibit any of the supposed Irish empathy with the underdog. Of the young and angry Blackfoot tribesmen, he said:

> The rascalities in crimes, robberies and murders, with which the liberality of the United States was repaid, might well be cited with condemnation of the costly and wasteful policy with which it was believed in Washington the Indians could be tamed and subsidised.[31]

The so-called 'liberality' of which he wrote was the usual re-grant of a small portion of their traditional land to the Blackfoot in the form of the Fort Peck reservation.

In a series of pseudonymous writings as 'Colonel O'Keefe', Meagher refers to a visit to a Jesuit-run Flathead tribe reservation at St Ignatius in Idaho. His lack of sympathy for Native Americans comes across clearly when he describes this relatively well-run reservation as 'an extravagant franchise', some of whose land should be made available to white settlers because the Flathead people 'virtually do not hold, and most certainly do not turn to advantage, one sixteenth of it'.[32] His sympathy for the dispossessed does not appear to have extended far beyond a fellow feeling with the landless in his own native country.

Amidst rumours in the winter of 1866–7 that Red Cloud and his potent force of Sioux warriors was about to go to war, there was even greater nervousness among Montanans. Meagher decided to change tack and called for the raising and arming of a militia. He wrote to the new president, Ulysses S. Grant:

> The most populous and prosperous portion of our territory ... is threatened by the Sioux. The greatest alarm reasonably prevails ... danger is imminent ... we earnestly entreat permission from the War Department to raise a force of one thousand volunteers for menaced quarters to be paid by General Government.[33]

The rumours proved to be well founded and after the February 1867 Fetterman Massacre of three officers and ninety men from Fort Phil Kearny in Dakota Territory (later part of Wyoming), the nervousness was ratcheted up to near hysteria. Meagher called for 600 militia volunteers to offer three months' service. Some of Meagher's political enemies took the opportunity to accuse him of grandstanding. This view was shared by Sherman. However, the military commander did promise a consignment of more than 2,000 rifles to the newly created force.

The claims of Meagher's detractors, that he was hyping up the threat so that he could emerge as Defender of Montana, might have had some validity because his force did not manage to come in contact with any hostile Indians. Gradually, as the snows of winter melted away, so did the militia. Many would later return to the areas they had been patrolling to pan for gold in sites they had identified during their militia stint.

In June 1867, still concerned at the Sioux threat and aware of the positive impact on morale of a consignment of arms, Meagher went looking for the guns promised by Sherman. He set out from Virginia City to make the 200-mile journey to Fort Benton on the Missouri River. By the time he arrived in the riverside town, the acting governor was in bad health. His detractors claimed that he was, by now, permanently drunk, but it is far more likely that he was suffering from a severe stomach and bowel complaint brought on from drinking fouled water along the hot, arid route to Benton.

He arrived in the town on 1 July and went straight to the three steamers tied up in the river. To his disappointment and chagrin there were no federal guns on any of them. While riding through the streets of the town he seems to have interpreted a relatively innocent remark shouted out to him ('There he goes') as some form of death threat. The vigilante version of Montana history claims that it was a bad case of the DT's that brought out this latent paranoia. An equally likely explanation is that it was the distraction of severe stomach cramps.

The master of one of the three steamboats, the *G.A. Thompson*, John Doran, was Irish and familiar with Meagher by reputation. He invited the general on board the boat and when the latter claimed in agitation, 'Johnny, they threatened my life in that town,' Doran invited Meagher to sleep in one of the rooms on board.

Doran much later (1913) wrote an account of the acting governor's last day. He insists that, despite many offers of hospitality from Fort Bentonites, Meagher was sober when he arrived and drank nothing stronger than tea. After a light meal Meagher was led to a stateroom that locked from the inside and the two Irishmen said goodnight. It was the last time anyone admits to seeing Meagher alive. His death remains a much-debated mystery to this day.

That night Doran, walking the lower deck, heard an unmistakeable splash and knew that someone was overboard. A search of the water began but no one, alive or dead, was found. The waters of the Missouri were still very full and choppy at that time of year and only a very good and extremely fortunate swimmer would have survived for long. Meagher's stateroom was empty and there was no sign of him on board so it was assumed that it was he who had gone over the side. No body was ever found.

Since his disappearance there has been endless speculation as to the cause of his death. Was he drunk and did he stagger along the upper deck only to fall into the water? This was certainly a theory canvassed by vigilante elements in the state. Did his illness cause him to fall overboard? There were reports, not confirmed by Doran and others in Benton, of a coil of rope temporarily substituting for a broken rail on the upper deck that might have led to a tragic accident. Another contemporary theory was that Meagher had been summoned back to Washington in disgrace and had chosen to commit suicide instead. However, no such summons had been issued.

Then there are the inevitable conspiracy theories. The most compelling one, proposed by Democratic Party supporters of Meagher's policies (and sustained to this day by others), was that he had been murdered by assassins sent by the vigilance committee. One variant of this theory has the Irish general being killed by a coalition of vigilantes, Freemasons and a member of the Pinkertons.[34] Many contemporary Irish Americans not resident in Montana clung to the belief that he had been assassinated by agents of the British government. A much more fanciful hypothesis sees Meagher as a victim of the Fenian Brotherhood because of his influential opposition to an invasion of Canada. But while Meagher may have fallen out with the notion of using the territory of the USA to launch an invasion of a British colony, he was not at odds with the leadership of the Fenian movement in America.

In a gruesome postscript to the acting governor's death, a petrified body was found downriver from Fort Benton in 1899. It had a neat bullet wound in the middle of the skull. The body was purchased from the finder and exhibited in shows and fairs around the country as that of General Meagher. In an ironic twist, the body was brought to Australia, scene of Meagher's incarceration, and shown there as well. If it did nothing else, it reopened the debate on the enigma of his death.

Meagher died young and he died mysteriously but, ironically, he is probably better known today (outside of his native Waterford) in Montana than he is in Ireland. Whether or not they actually killed him, he had his final revenge on the vigilantes when his statue was erected in front of the Montana State Legislature in Helena in 1905. It had to be thoroughly cleaned recently but it is still there.

James Harvey Strobridge: railroad builder[35]

The influence of the Irish in the American West is often understated except in one important area: the building of the transcontinental railroad. Here it is frequently exaggerated. The received wisdom is that it was Chinese labour that built the Central Pacific railroad from California to Utah and Irish labour that built the Union Pacific in the opposite direction. The latter would not have been built but for its huge corps of Irish navvies, but there were other nationalities involved in the epic UP enterprise. Having said that, we will now, largely, ignore them.

The building of the railroad, long a dream of a rail lawyer and aspiring Illinois politician named Abraham Lincoln, created a truly 'United' States of America. Prior to its construction, you got to the West by wagon train, hand-cart or by ship (via Cape Horn if you were a good sailor or Panama if you felt immune to malaria or other tropical diseases). The Central Pacific–Union Pacific line preceded most urban settlement (other than its termini in Omaha and Sacramento, Salt Lake City was the only sizeable urban area on or near its route), created towns along its track, made millions of dollars for a small number of entrepreneurs, employed thousands of demobilised Civil War veterans who might otherwise have become a focus of social discontent and finally brought about the division of the continental USA into organised time zones.

Work commenced while that other small matter, secession, was being dealt with in the Civil War. The outset of that conflict had finally determined the route that would be followed. In the late 1850s the then Secretary of War, Jefferson Davis, had advocated a southern route from New Orleans to Los Angeles. It would, he claimed, be more viable from an engineering standpoint and a lot cheaper to construct. Left unsaid was that it would also increase the economic and political power of the southern slave states. But in the 1860s, when Congress was taking important votes that would make the transcontinental railroad a reality, there were no southern legislators left in Washington to oppose the choice of a northern route. Jefferson Davis was otherwise occupied in his new but short-lived position as president of the Confederate States of America. The chosen route went from eastern Nebraska, through Wyoming, Utah and Nevada to Sacramento.

Everyone was agreed upon one thing: if a transcontinental railroad was going to be built, there was only one man who could do it – Uncle Sam. The federal government owned the land over which track would be laid and had pockets deep enough to see the project through. In the end the feat was accomplished by means of what, today, would probably be called a Public Private Partnership. The logistics of surveying, planning and construction were left to the two companies that would, ultimately, run the railroad line, the Central Pacific and the Union Pacific. As an incentive, each was given huge tracts of federal land on either side of the tracks being built: 6,400 acres for every completed mile. The principal investors in the enterprise might just as well have been led by the hand to a new Comstock lode or granted permission to print their own currency. In Illinois in 1852, land had been worth about $1.25 an acre. In 1853, when construction began on the Illinois Central Railroad, land adjacent to the track route had shot up to $6 an acre. By 1856 it was fetching $25 an acre.

In addition to the land, soft federal loans were advanced for every mile of track laid, anything from $16,000 to $48,000, depending on the gradient. The Central Pacific, with the connivance of an acquiescent geologist, Josiah Whitney, managed to persuade the government that the Sierra Nevada began somewhere in the Sacramento valley and so earned $48,000 in loans for virtually every mile of track it laid until it reached Nevada.[36] It was for rendering this invaluable service that Mr Whitney had the highest mountain in the continental USA named after him.

The Union Pacific Railroad was established in 1862. One of its earliest investors was the Mormon leader Brigham Young, who took five of the first fifty shares issued. It may have augured well that another twenty shares were purchased by a man called Train. Its financial structures and the way its founders and principal backers made money (including George Francis Train) became a controversial and indeed scandalous subject in nineteenth-century America. But from the point of view of this narrative, the importance of the Union Pacific lies in the numbers of Irish labourers it employed. Most of their names are recorded, but the overwhelming majority are still anonymous repositories of the muscle and brawn that the capitalists at the helm of the Union Pacific required to realise their financial ambitions. Few, if any, of these Irish 'navvies' wrote any letters, memoirs or journals that have survived. Many were probably illiterate anyway, even if they had had the time and the luxury to commit their thoughts to paper. Had they done so, they would probably have written about very hard times indeed, of backbreaking labour, physical peril from machinery, explosives, Indian attack, blistering heat, searing cold and disease, the infrequency of contact with women other than the hundreds of prostitutes who followed the track-laying teams, drunkenness, loneliness, venereal disease, lack of privacy or intimacy and the constant demands of foremen and engineers for ever speedier progress.

The Central Pacific was controlled by a group that became known as the Big Four: they were four California-based businessmen who would use their wealth to bribe, corrupt and exert political power in their attempts to add greatly to that wealth. Chief among them were Leland Stanford, who became governor of California, and Charles Crocker, one of the real driving forces behind the whole enterprise. Work on the Central Pacific began in 1863, while war was raging in the East and South, and utilised the services of hundreds of Irish immigrants. They were signed up by Crocker on the east coast before they could be cajoled into enlisting in the Union Army or disappear into the Irish ghettoes of New York, Boston and Philadelphia. Once engaged, they were then shipped west at considerable cost. It was not a very successful operation, the Irishmen proving recalcitrant and intemperate. They drank too much, went on strike too easily and many of them simply deserted the railroad construction sites for the California and Nevada gold mines shortly after they arrived.

However, one man who served the Central Pacific loyally was the engineer James Harvey Strobridge. According to historian Stephen Ambrose, in 1862 'he was thirty seven years old, out of Ireland [other sources cite Vermont as his place of birth], over six feet in height, agile, energetic'. Strobridge was a commanding presence who mercilessly drove the men under his charge. He could always point to himself as someone who had made huge sacrifices for the company – he had lost an eye in an explosion early in the track-laying process. So bad tempered and profane was he in his dealings with his labourers that Crocker frequently upbraided him for the way he treated them.

Strobridge once responded, 'You cannot talk to them as though you were talking to gentlemen, because they are not gentlemen. They are about as near brutes as you can get.'[37]

Brutish they may have been, but Strobridge couldn't get enough of them. In January 1865, two years after construction had begun and with the Central Pacific about to begin the painstaking construction of track through the forbidding Sierra Nevada, he advertised for '5000 laborers for constant and permanent work'. He got about 2,000, most of whom were out-of-work miners who needed a few weeks' work to raise the money to get them from California to Nevada where a new gold rush had begun. Within weeks Strobridge had lost all but 100 of his 2,000 new recruits.

Crocker tentatively suggested an alternative: Chinese. There were about 60,000 of them in California by 1865, mostly men. Many were involved in mining but such was the level of discrimination against them there (they were subject to all sorts of levies and taxes from which white miners were exempt and were banned from working mother-lodes) that they would probably be willing to adapt to railroad construction. But Strobridge was unwilling to adapt to the Chinese. He argued, not unreasonably, that they had no experience of railroad construction and that with an average weight of less than nine stone each they were not, physically, up to the strength-sapping labour. 'I will not boss Chinese,' was his final word on the matter. Crocker pointed out that 'They built the Great Wall of China, didn't they?' Whether or not it was the Great Wall argument that swung it or whether Crocker simply pulled rank, Strobridge agreed to take on fifty Chinese 'coolies' (the term had actually come, via the British, from India).

The experiment, despite Strobridge's misgivings, was a spectacular success. The Chinese, mostly speaking only very basic English, organ-ised themselves into gangs or teams. They worked continuously and quickly became expert in the use of explosives, a prerequisite for success in the Sierra Nevada with the Central Pacific blasting and gouging its way through solid granite tunnels on a daily basis. Strobridge, in spite of himself, was impressed with the work-rate of his new Chinese employees. They were content to earn about a dollar a day (the Central Pacific had been forced to pay some white labourers up to $3 a day), never seemed to get sick (although they died in acci-dents in their hundreds), never went on strike and never complained.

By the end of 1865 the Chinese complement in the Central Pacific workforce had risen from fifty to 7,000 as against 2,000 whites. Many of those were Irish-born bosses of Chinese work gangs.

One of the most difficult sections of the railroad in the high Sierras was a stretch known as Cape Horn. Here, instead of boring a tunnel through the mountains, the Central Pacific was forced to carve out room for its tracks along the side of a precipitous slope that formed part of a gorge along the American River. The river surged through a narrow valley 2,000 feet below. Labourers had to be lowered from the tops of the mountains, drill holes for the black powder explosive, set light to it and holler so that they could be rapidly hoisted out of danger. It was highly dangerous work: many Central Pacific engineers thought the task of building this three-mile stretch would be beyond them. Then the Chinese approached Strobridge and volunteered to do the job. They asked only that reeds be sent from San Francisco for the weaving of traditional baskets that would be used to lower them into the danger zone.

A mutual respect quickly grew up between Strobridge and his Chinese workers. They gave him the nickname 'One Eyed Bossy Man' and, on the rare occasions when trouble emerged from their ranks, he would sort it out with a pickaxe handle. After only a few months working with them, Strobridge was able to say of the men whose capabilities he had doubted, 'They learn quickly, do not fight, have no strikes that amount to anything, and are very cleanly in their habits. They will gamble and do quarrel among themselves – but harmlessly.'[38]

Strobridge's own countrymen on the Union Pacific were no less efficient in their own way than the Chinese on the Central Pacific. Their jobs were quite different. The Central Pacific was laying tracks along difficult, some said impossible, terrain. Progress, measured in terms of miles of track laid, was tortuously slow, often only inches per day. For the employees of the Union Pacific, often laying tracks across open prairie or along river valleys, it was measured in miles per day. These men were paid an average of about $3 a day (good wages at the time) but could earn up to $4 depending on their trade. Of that they were charged $5 a month for food and board in the rail cars that accompanied the track-laying gangs. They worked almost from dawn until noon, were given a one-hour break to eat and then worked on for another five to six hours. The work was truly gruelling and photographs of the men who worked for the Union Pacific depict sinewy, fleshless types with broad shoulders, narrow waists and muscular arms and legs. These men were the inspiration for songs such as 'Paddy Works on the Railroad' and provided virtually the only mechanical power available to complete one of the most astonishing engineering feats of the nineteenth century.

Eventually, fifteen tunnels later, in September 1868, the Central Pacific left the high Sierras behind and started to sprint across the arid desert state of Nevada. Here it faced a whole new set of problems, but progress could once again be measured in miles per day. As the rival companies reached Utah the surveyors and graders (the men who built up or cut out the route along which tracks were laid) passed each other and continued their work. Here the Union Pacific's Irishmen and the Central Pacific's Chinese met for the first time and it was not love at first sight. The Irish were quickly rattled by the speed and energy with which the Chinese graders cleared or prepared the way for the track-layers who followed. They resorted to jeering their rivals and throwing clods of earth at them. When this had no effect they tried all out attack. To their consternation the Chinese had the effrontery to defend themselves. The tension was ratcheted up still further when the Irish grading crews started to set off explosives too close to the Chinese for comfort. Despite complaints from the Central Pacific and orders to the Irish from their own superintendents, the practice continued until the Chinese responded in kind, setting off one explosion that buried a number of Irish alive. That brought a rapid end to hostilities.

Eventually Congress stepped in and ended the waste of time and resources involved in the parallel grading by both companies. They were told to direct their lines towards Promontory Summit in Utah. This brought the race between the competing companies to fever pitch. With less than 100 miles left, the faster of the two sets of track-layers would garner more land and loan revenue for its employers. The superintendents and foremen on both sides began to call for super-human efforts.

The Union Pacific held the record for miles of track laid in a single day, at four and a half miles. As the end of construction approached, that bar was raised on a number of occasions. The Central Pacific managed six miles in one day. Then the Union Pacific, by dint of starting work by lantern light at 3.00 a.m and continuing until midnight, managed eight. Strobridge and Crocker were convinced they could lay ten miles. They left it until a few weeks before the two lines met at Promontory Point. The bulk of the work was done by 3,000 Chinese. They laid down wooden sleepers and hammered spikes but a crucial role was played by a gang of Irish track-layers who hauled the 560-pound rails and put them into place. Thomas Daley, George Elliott, Michael Kennedy, Edward Killeen, Patrick Joyce, Fred McNamara, Michael Shay and Michael Sullivan spent the day picking up thirty-foot rails with their tongs, running to get them into place, lowering them when they heard the instruction 'down' and then repeating the process. That day the Central Pacific laid ten miles and fifty-six feet of track.

According to Stephen Ambrose:

> Each man among the Irish track layers had lifted 125 tons of iron, plus the weight of the tongs. That was 11.2 short tons per man per hour. Each had covered ten miles forward and the Lord only knows how much running back for the next rail. They moved the track at a rate of almost a mile an hour. They laid at a rate of approximately 240 feet every seventy five seconds.[39]

And even though they were Irish, they weren't working for the Union Pacific.

When the tracks were joined on 10 May 1869, at a ceremony at Promontory Point in Utah, James Strobridge was given the honour of driving in one of the last spikes. The final Golden Spike was left for Leland Stanford of the Central Pacific, who swung and missed. Between them the two companies had built 1,775 miles of railway line. Both the Irish and the Chinese continued to work on railroad construction, with the more malleable Orientals being favoured over the Irish, even by the successors of the Union Pacific. One of the founders of the Union Pacific observed that 'Irish labor, with its strikes, its dead fall whiskey shops and reckless disregard of all our interests, must be gotten out of the way'.[40] Many unemployed Irish construction workers turned to mining instead. It has been suggested that the building of the transcontinental railroad, 'the grandest enterprise under God', turned many thousands of Irish labourers into Americans. In truth the Irish who built the Union Pacific had far less of a stake in its completion than the men who drove them to complete it.

But for the USA, so recently divided North and South, the building of the transcontinental railroad had united it East and West.

REEL EIGHT

THE LINCOLN COUNTY WAR:
MURPHY, DOLAN, RILEY, BRADY AND BILLY THE KID

I t has become one of the most famous lines in a Hollywood western – proof, if any were required, that the American film industry knew exactly what it was doing and where it was going with the genre. In *The Man Who Shot Liberty Valance*, a newspaper editor refuses to print James Stewart's 'confession' that it was not he who disposed of the outlaw Liberty Valance, on the basis that the lie has already gained currency and acceptance. 'When the legend becomes fact,' he observes, 'print the legend.' If this axiom could be applied to the repeated recounting of any western story, then it has to be to the events of the so-called Lincoln County War.

As a 'war' it would hardly rate a mention. It was really three over-lapping feuds, fought out in an unwieldy and remote county in a wild and isolated US territory by uncompromising and vicious protagonists. Casualties were heavy, but only relative to the sparse population of southern New Mexico and were far lighter than for the parallel Mescalero Apache Indian uprising of 1879–80.

As a war it was a hit-and-miss affair that produced no heroes and a surfeit of villains. It has led to a raft of films that romanticise and misrepresent its course, as well as a plethora of books that teem with subjectivity and inaccuracy.

Why so much interest? Because it produced Billy the Kid.

That fact alone has guaranteed that in the 120 years since it petered out it has not been forgotten. It may well be enough to maintain sustained interest through the twenty-first century.

Ironically, the Kid (aka William Bonney, aka Henry McCarty or McCarthy) was, at best, a supporting player who has been erroneously credited with heroics and a homicide rate far in excess of what can be established beyond reasonable doubt. But if any legend has become fact, it is the legend of Billy the Kid, the wronged and misunderstood delinquent saved by a righteous and protective Englishman, lost again after his patron's treacherous murder and finally drifting into vicious psychopathy and self-destruction. It is a legend that has launched a thousand metaphors. But it is just that, a legend.

The Lincoln County War is as much about the rekindling in New Mexico of antagonisms accruing from centuries of Anglo-Irish conflict as it is a story of the end of lawlessness in the Old West or the betrayal of the small rancher by powerful moneyed interests. It is a multicul-tural and multinational story, combining many of the ethnic elements that enriched the history of the West. It includes Irish, English, Canadians, Germans, Mexicans, Apaches, Navajos and even a few Americans. Democrats take on Republicans; Protestants confront Catholics. To reduce it to the story of one young gunman, however romantic a figure he might have been, is to do it a grave disservice. But it keeps coming back to Billy the Kid.

Lincoln County is in southern New Mexico. In the 1870s it almost *was* southern New Mexico. In area it was upwards of 25,000 square miles and made up a quarter of the landmass of the vast territory. It was both wilderness and garden, with high country to the west, well-drained pasture to the east (through which flowed rivers like the Pecos, the Ruidoso, the Bonito and the Hondo), as well as patches of arid desert, including the White Sands region, many years later to witness the birth of the Atomic Age. What it had in land it lacked in population. During the period of this narrative, the population hovered around 3,000 – with around 600 living in or near La Placita (later renamed Lincoln). Other centres of population included Roswell, San Patricio (established by Irish-born ex-servicemen mustered out of the Union Army in 1866) and White Oaks. However, they didn't boast populations of more than a few hundred. It was bilingual, with Spanish the native tongue of a huge percentage of the small population. The western part of the county was where much of the Mexican settlement had taken place; it was also the location of the Mescalero Apache reservation.

Its remoteness and the sparseness of its population, however, were not a protection against violence. With the end of the Civil War, the rule of law was slowly being re-established in the more settled parts of the American Southwest. Lincoln County's vastness and inaccessibility acted as a magnet for outlaws who were falling on harder times in Arizona and Texas.

The eastern part of the county had seen an influx of Texan cattlemen in the post-Civil War period. The most prominent of these was John Chisum. In 1970 a form of immortality would be conferred upon him when he was portrayed in the film *Chisum* by the great John Wayne himself. But he was unconscious of that future honour when he and his brothers, Pitzer and James, drove their huge herd of more than 50,000 cattle from Texas into New Mexico in 1867. They began to graze them along the Pecos River, a stretch of over 100 miles. Chisum based his claim to graze this land on what he called 'right of discovery'.[1] In effect, he was a squatter on a gargantuan scale, occupying land that had not yet been opened up by the federal government to settlers. Chisum was an effective and unscrupulous operator. He often boasted that he never carried a gun. This was probably because he didn't need to. He employed more than enough cowboys who, if required, would pull a trigger on his behalf. In 1877 he is alleged to have ordered his men to launch a murderous punitive raid on the Mescalero Apache reservation in retaliation for that tribe's suspected involvement in the theft of his cattle.[2]

At the time this narrative begins, Chisum was in his early fifties (he died at the age of sixty) and unlike John Wayne, who always seemed to have the dimensions of a medium-sized mountain range, was small in stature. He was also balding, sported a characteristic moustache of the period and his most notable physical attribute was his ears, prominent and presumably kept close to the ground at all times.

If Chisum was the dominant figure in the eastern part of the county, he was matched in power and influence to the west by Lawrence Gustave Murphy, based in the town of Lincoln and boasting a far more modest ranch of his own nearer to White Oaks. Born in County Wexford in 1831, Murphy is quite a study. He was like an east-coast Irish political 'Boss' transported to the sagebrush and tumble-weed of New Mexico. One unsubstantiated rumour has him attending the Seminary at Maynooth College in his youth in Ireland. If it is true, then he had shaken off most of his godliness by the time he reached Lincoln County. Sometime between the ages of seventeen and twenty he emigrated to the USA and discovered, like many an Irishman before and since, that the steadiest employment was to be found in the army. His second five-year stint in the pay of the federal government had just ended when the Confederates fired on Fort Sumter and the Civil War began. Having made his way to Santa Fe, Murphy accepted a commission as a lieutenant in the New Mexico Volunteers being organised by the famous army scout Lt Col. Christopher 'Kit' Carson.

During the War between the States (as the Confederates characterised it) he saw plenty of action, mostly, however, against Apache and Navajo warriors. He seems to have spent much of his time on logistics and thus acquired some of the skills in feeding and clothing army units and reservation Indians that would serve him well after demobilisation.

After the war he went into partnership with a German fellow soldier named Emil Fritz and they established a trading post/store at Fort Stanton. At that time the fort was the key to whatever economic prosperity was enjoyed by Lincoln County. Only the federal government had the funds to make anyone in Lincoln rich. The army controlled the fort, and the Bureau of Indian Affairs, with the assistance of the army, ran the Indian reservation system. Supplying both with beef and grain was crucial to anyone who wanted to operate much above subsistence level. Murphy had that ambition and much more besides, as well as the will and the capability to achieve it.

By 1868, largely based on their own army records and their admirable contacts, the enterprise of Fritz and Murphy (the latter by now a dapper, prosperous-looking man of high forehead and bushy moustache) was thriving. In a pattern that was to be repeated later, when the enterprise moved to the town of Lincoln, the firm sold high and bought low. As an effective monopoly it could dictate whatever prices it wished. Local farmers had few realistic competing options. The store offered credit where cash flow was a problem – in return, farmers would repay in cash or kind at high rates of interest. They would also buy goods at purchase prices set by the Murphy–Fritz store. If you were Murphy, it was a virtuous and profitable circular arrangement; if you were an impecunious customer, it was simply a vicious circle.

A young Irishwoman, Amelia Bolton Church, daughter of the quartermaster's clerk at Fort Stanton, summed up the relative poverty of even the minority 'Anglo' community in the area of Fort Stanton–Lincoln in the early 1870s. She wrote:

> everything not raised locally was very expensive … men worked for $1 a day and women for 50 cents. However, few people could afford paid help. Everyone kept one or more milk cows, some hens, pigs, a few sheep, and raised their own beef when possible.[3]

By that period Murphy was running a store, a brewery, a saloon and a hotel (of sorts) as well as trading with the Mescalero. He was becoming an economic and a political power in the community. In 1868 Congress had allocated $2 million to be thrown at the 'Indian problem' and Murphy decided he wanted a share. The reservation system was in its infancy, but already treaties had been drawn up that obliged the federal government to allocate money to some Indian tribes. An Indian agent was appointed, based in Fort Stanton. Murphy was aware that this functionary would have to be kept onside. One of the first agents, despite bearing the feisty name of Andrew Jackson Curtis, proved eminently biddable. Murphy became supplier to the Mescalero. Coincidentally, a bill to the federal government for the furnishing of goods to 325 Mescalero Apaches in 1871 become a bill for the supply of 2,679 members of that clearly fertile nation the following year. 'A rapidity of increase which leaves rabbits, rats and mice in the shade,' as one later, less pliable agent observed.[4]

In 1869, as he bamboozled his way to relative wealth and power, Murphy had taken on an employee who would change his circumstances. James Joseph Dolan was a fellow Irishman. Born in Loughrea in County Galway in 1848 – at around the time Murphy left Ireland – Dolan's family may have emigrated before he was ten years old. He too joined the army and was mustered out in 1869 at Fort Stanton. He applied for a job with L.G. Murphy & Co. and was appointed clerk.

At the time Dolan was an energetic and clearly ambitious young man. Small in stature, he possessed a full head of wavy dark hair, was clean-shaven and blue eyed. As time would prove, his undoubted energy could rapidly switch to intense aggression. Thanks in no small part to the diligent nourishment of an impressive drinking habit (a characteristic he shared with his patron, L.G. Murphy), the longer he spent on the frontier, the nastier he seemed to become. But at the start of his employment with L.G. Murphy & Co. he was more promising material. Murphy appears to have been very taken with his new clerk – so much so that subsequent commentators have suggested that their relationship might have been homosexual. This allegation is based on the fact that Murphy remained unmarried until his death (Dolan married twice). However, though Murphy never went through a marriage ceremony, he did have a permanent female partner. It is far more likely that Murphy's loyalty to Dolan was based on the latter's Irishness and, more particularly, his resourcefulness, even though that nous came in tandem with an often ugly and troublesome nature.

Sometime in 1873, an ailing Fritz returned to his native Germany to die and Murphy (owing to some injudicious belligerence from Dolan) found it politic to relocate the retail element of his business to the county town, Lincoln, a short distance from Fort Stanton. What he built there was a credit to an impoverished Irish immigrant. The Murphy store stood at the western end of the small town and was by far the largest building for miles around. It was a two-storey structure with more than 5,000 square feet of floor space – the rooms had eleven-foot ceilings. It was a spacious edifice in a county and a state that valued space but was not accustomed to buildings of such impressive internal dimensions. It had no equal in Lincoln and was only surpassed by a few structures in Santa Fe. The tall and dapper, shrewd and ruthless boy from County Wexford had come a long way.

The pattern of violence in Lincoln County that would persist through most of the 1870s began in March 1873 with what had many of the hallmarks of a race war. It involved a clannish Texan family known as the Harrells (or Horrells or Harrolds – clearly no one ever nailed down the spelling) who fled the law in the Lone Star state and moved west into New Mexico. They had killed five lawmen in a shootout in the town of Lampasas, so their future in Texas did not look auspicious.

They purchased land in the Ruidoso Valley and it wasn't long before they began to make enemies of the Hispanic population in Lincoln County. Texans were not popular among native-born Mexicans. They had treated the Hispanic population of New Mexico badly during the Civil War and memories of their arrogant and homicidal behaviour still rankled. Before the arrival of the Harrell family, inter-racial tensions had already been rising. Two young Hispanics had been killed and one of those responsible, Irish-born John H. Riley (a twenty-three-year-old native of Valentia Island in County Kerry, of whom much more anon), had only escaped death at the hands of an Hispanic posse led by Lincoln County Probate Clerk Juan Patron when (just like in the movies) the army arrived in the nick of time and probably prevented his summary 'execution'.

In such an atmosphere, the introduction of a family such as the Harrells was tantamount to tossing dry wood on a smouldering fire. There had already been some nasty incidents when, in December 1873, one of the Harrell clan and some associates, during a bout of drinking, began to shoot up the town of Lincoln. Among the citizens disturbed by the gang was Irishman John Bolton, who managed to placate them and send them on their way. The fact that he was white probably ensured his survival. Lincoln Constable Juan Martin was not so fortunate. He set out to arrest members of the drunken group and the result was four deaths, including his own and that of Ben Harrell.

Two days later, two Hispanics were randomly killed on their ranch. The Harrells denied any involvement but the gloves were off. Feelings were running high and members of the Hispanic community even contemplated attempting to rid Lincoln County of its entire Anglo population. The Harrells would have been happy for the Mexicans to start with L.G. Murphy, whose various business enterprises had attracted their antipathy. This was as a consequence of one of the few worthwhile alliances they had managed to forge.

The Harrells had another Lincoln County Irishman in their camp. Rancher Robert Casey, who was born in Ireland in 1828,[5] was a neighbour of the Harrells and wielded considerable influence over them. Casey too had come from Texas some years before the Harrells and may have been egging them on in their animosity towards Murphy. He had no time for the monopolistic business practices of his fellow countryman and was one of Murphy's principal antagonists in the political and economic affairs of Lincoln County.

The next link in the cycle of killings was the most horrifying. On 20 December 1873 the Harrells rode into Lincoln and found a Mexican wedding party in progress. They opened fire on the revellers indiscriminately and killed four men, including the father of Juan Patron. This flagrant atrocity drew a response from the governor of New Mexico, who put a price on the heads of each of the Harrell family and their known associates. The Texan clan decided that the time had come to leave the state. They sold up their stock as quickly as they could and moved from their Ruidoso spread to the Casey ranch for some protection.

On 25 January 1874 a posse led by Jimmy Dolan sacked the Harrell ranch, tearing down each of the buildings and burning all the crops. On hearing of this the Harrells decided on one final act of revenge before their departure from Lincoln County. This involved the killing of a number of people, including Murphy, Dolan and Patron. Before they could reach Lincoln, however, Robert Casey managed to persuade them that such a course of action would be unwise and that they would be best advised to return to Texas. Instead of punitive action against the town of Lincoln, the Harrells, on their journey back to the state where they had recently slaughtered five law officers, intercepted a party of Hispanics transporting grain to the Chisum ranch and murdered five of them.

They then decamped for Texas and were not heard of in New Mexico again.

The so-called Harrell War was unconnected with much of the more-celebrated violence that followed some years later, but it had left sixteen people dead within a very short period, had destabilised an already volatile section and led to the beginning of alliances that would continue the sort of mindless, endless blood feud that results in victory for neither side and ruination for all involved.

Its conclusion also coincided with the death in Stuttgart in Germany of Emil Fritz and the beginning of the partnership that would prosecute the most lethal phase of the Lincoln County War, that of Lawrence Gustave Murphy and James Joseph Dolan.

Lincoln County in the 1870s and 1880s was a largely unregulated society stalked by violence and where killing was tolerated to an extent that would not have been acceptable in most other states, even in the Wild West. It was governed by the same laws as the other states and territories of the Union, had a similar legal infrastructure and employed the same officials to ensure that those laws were carried out, but therein lay the problem. Enforcement of the law in such a vast territory with insufficient taxation resources was inadequate. In many cases it barely existed above the level of the vigilante, relying as it often did on volunteer posses to pursue wrongdoers. The administration of the law could also be highly partial. Many law-enforcement positions were elective and those elections could produce highly partisan winners. Disputes over jurisdiction added further confusion where the boundaries between federal, state and local authority were not clearly defined. In the Lincoln County War it was not unusual for someone who was being pursued by one posse to become a member of another posse raised by a rival legal official.

But the problem with lawlessness in Lincoln County was not entirely a function of undefined legal boundaries or inadequate enforcement. If there had been no crime, there would have been no law to enforce in the first place. But there was crime in abundance. Lincoln County citizens displayed a unique talent for transgression. It was to violent crime what California was to earthquakes. There were two principal reasons for this: alcohol and guns.

New Mexico may have been inaccessible to the law and to many routine goods and services, but there was no shortage of liquor. The consumption of ninety-proof whiskey products such as Double

Anchor and Pike's Magnolia was one of the few recreations available to both the hard-working and the felonious citizens of the county. It was available wholesale at $2.50 a gallon, though it was sold over the counter at a multiple of that figure (at least $20 a gallon).[6]

The omnipresence of the gun in US society and the American obsession with gun ownership and gun control have their roots not simply in the inclusion by the founding fathers in the constitution of the right to bear arms, but of the unprecedented access to modern weapons in the wake of the Civil War. Millions of American men learned to use weapons in that war and many took weapons home with them when they were demobilised. The war itself had sparked an upsurge in weapons research and development and the emergence of more efficient handguns, rifles and shotguns. Guns were produced that were more capable of hitting a target, even if the shooters themselves were lacking in expertise.

In a frontier society such as that of New Mexico, there were many compelling reasons for carrying a gun and few encouragements to leave one's weapon at home. The regular excursions of Apache and Navajo raiders from their reservations resulted in far fewer fatalities than is the common perception. However, their frequency introduced a fear factor into the logistical equation. Perception was all, and if a man felt that he was going to have to protect his stock or his family against Indian depredations, then he would hold and probably carry a gun. The same was true for the activities of rustlers.

Much of the animosity that led to gunfights was fuelled by alcohol consumption. With their faculties dimmed by Pike's Magnolia, few would-be gunfighters could achieve sufficient accuracy to fell a stationary elephant, let alone another human being. As will be apparent from many of the murders that took place during the Lincoln County War, most killings were either of unarmed opponents, from well-protected positions or with the advantage of the element of surprise.

However, even though guns and booze tended to cancel each other out when it came to incendiary situations, insults traded or challenges issued while under the influence could be carried as long-standing grudges or become the basis for vendettas and blood feuds. It was the lawless atmosphere that pervaded Lincoln County that prompted the second and least sanguinary eruption of violence, the so-called

'Chisum War' or 'The War on the Pecos'. Like so many other major and minor conflicts in the American West, this pitted the mega-rancher against the smallholder.

In 1875 John Chisum sold his vast herd to a St Louis-based cattle brokerage firm, Hunter and Evans. He'd been caught short when a Mescalero Apache raid robbed him of all his horses and deprived his hundred or so cowboys of the means to round up beef on the hoof and supply it to the army at Fort Stanton. As a result he only managed to bring in one-third of the cattle for which he had contracted and found himself with severe cash-flow problems. His decision to sell to Hunter and Evans for a price of around $300,000 sparked a series of demands for the settling of long-standing but disputed debts from his days in Texas. Many of the demands came through a Santa Fe legal firm owned by one of the rising political powers in the state of New Mexico, Thomas B. Catron.

The sale of the herd was like a Rustlers' Charter. Those who had spent the years since his arrival picking off Chisum's cattle assumed, now that the beef was no longer his, that he would be less than vigi-lant when it came to the protection of the scattered herd. In doing so they totally misread the man with whom they were dealing. Chisum had taken a relatively relaxed attitude to the annual loss of a propor-tion of his herd, just as a storeowner budgets for inevitable losses to shoplifters. But having sold the herd and incurred an obligation to deliver 30,000-odd head of cattle to Hunter and Evans ranches over a period of time, Chisum became altogether more aggressive in his efforts to stem his losses.

He was losing his stock to a variety of felons. Professional rustlers would always find a ready market for stolen beef. Some even stole to order. There has been much speculation over the years about the source of the beef supplied to the army and the Mescalero reservation by Lawrence G. Murphy. He was not well known for the vastness of his herd. There is little doubt but that Murphy, from time to time, called on the services of a gang of rustlers known collectively as 'The Boys'. This gang, led by Jesse Evans, Frank Baker and Tom Hill, would steal cattle from Chisum. They were then sold on by Murphy to the army. Evans, in his mid-twenties and with multiple bullet scars testifying to a lengthy career in the business of rustling, was the acknowledged leader of the group.[7]

Towards the southern extremity of Chisum's vast grazing area along the Pecos was a region known as Seven Rivers. This area was populated by smaller ranchers who would, from time to time, augment their own herds by engaging in some amateur rustling. These included men such as Robert Beckwith and Dick Smith. By 1877 Chisum was on a war footing with many of the Seven Rivers ranchers, as more and more of his cattle were being run off and sold in Texas. His hundred-strong workforce had, in effect, become a private army. It was operating in a section where the forces of the law were woefully inadequate to cope with rustling and where Chisum's colossal herd was seen as fair game for the 'small man'.

To combat rebranding (the system by which, for example, the RC brand of Robert Casey would be turned into a spurious 'BO' by over-writing the original brand) Chisum had developed the 'jinglebob' earmark as a means of identifying his cattle. This involved a slit along the edge of the ear that left part of it dangling. As there was nothing to over-burn, it meant that the only means of disguising Chisum's ownership of an animal was to cut its ear off. This in itself was tanta-mount to an admission of theft.

The War on the Pecos began with the murder of one of Chisum's foremen in October 1876, continued with the killing of Dick Smith by one of Chisum's men and culminated in a siege of Robert Beckwith's Seven Rivers ranch house. The latter event resulted in an inconclusive stand-off. The War on the Pecos petered out. But it would be refought in a different context. A foundation for many of the personal, political and economic antagonisms that fuelled the later Dolan–Tunstall conflict were laid down in the skirmishes of the War on the Pecos.

While Chisum attempted to sort out his difficulties with the Seven Rivers ranchers aggressively, Lawrence Murphy and his mercurial new business partner, Jimmy Dolan, were solidifying their hold on the economy and the politics of Lincoln County. Though Murphy is often depicted as the 'boss' of the enterprise, by the time of the War on the Pecos he was beginning to fade into the background, allowing Dolan to assert himself. Murphy's health was beginning to fail by the late 1870s and he was starting to pass less time overseeing the retail busi-ness that had become known locally simply as the House and spend more time on his ranch. Dolan was more than ready to take up the slack. He had graduated from lowly clerk to partner with startling rapidity.

The Galway-born Dolan was a bantam cock of a man. Despite his small stature and the fact that he looked almost absurdly young (he was in fact thirty years of age in 1878), he was sufficiently able, confident and assertive to command the respect of his allies and the fear of his enemies. He had a capacity for intrigue that probably exceeded even that of his older mentor. If confronted he would never back down from a situation of physical danger. In that regard, he was probably too hot-tempered and apt to make enemies unnecessarily. By 1877 he already had one killing to his 'credit' – that of a Mexican man, Hiraldo Jaramillo. He insisted that he had killed the man in self-defence and escaped any legal sanction, but his assertion was widely disbelieved.

In addition to the economic hegemony of the House, there was the issue of the pervasive political influence of Murphy and Dolan. Both were Democrats and their highly efficient partisanship ensured that the public administration of Lincoln County was largely peopled by fellow partisans. Ironically, their power in southern New Mexico derived from their association with a shadowy Masonic group of politicians and businessmen known as the Santa Fe Ring. Despite his Catholicism, Murphy was believed to be a member of the Masonic Order. His membership was likely to have been one of convenience. But the real irony lay in the politics of this covert political cabal. It was overwhelmingly Republican. However, in the face of opposition in Lincoln County from powerful individuals such as John Chisum, the Santa Fe Ring was content to back the local Democratic 'machine' (for want of a better word – Lawrence Murphy was no 'Boss' Murphy of Tammany fame). The man who was their principal ally in Santa Fe and who occupied the influential position of US District Attorney was Thomas B. Catron, a rich and powerful business figure who dominated New Mexican politics for the best part of two decades.

When it came to the preservation of their political and economic stranglehold on the county, Murphy and Dolan could be utterly ruthless. The Irish-born Texan rancher Robert Casey, who had been an associate of the Harrells, was a vocal opponent of their dominance. In August 1875, after making a virulently anti-Murphy speech at a political nominating convention, Casey was ambushed from behind an adobe wall (a killing technique favoured by New Mexican gunmen over the face-to-face duel) by a former employee of his, William Wilson. Wilson's story was that Casey owed him $8 and that the dispute over this sum had escalated. No one believed him. It was widely assumed that he had been paid by Murphy to nip in the bud Casey's leadership of political opposition to the House in the most permanent manner possible.

The execution of Wilson bears out this suspicion. Strenuous efforts were made to have his death sentence commuted. In the end he was hanged anyway – had the sentence not been carried out he most likely would have been lynched. His execution, however, turned into a ghoulish affair. It was a very public hanging. Casey family rumour has it that on the scaffold Wilson turned to Murphy and whispered bitterly, 'Major [Murphy's brevet rank from the Civil War], you know you are the cause of this. You promised to save me but …'.[8] Unfortunately he never got to finish the sentence, as Murphy is then said to have kicked the lever that sprang the trapdoor and gravity did the rest. It may be a fanciful story, but it does have a ring of moral if not factual truth about it.

What is not disputed is what happened next. After about ten minutes, ample time in which to die, Wilson was cut down and placed in a coffin. It was then discovered that either gravity or the hangman had failed in their duty. Wilson was still alive. At this point Murphy, who was a duly elected judge, insisted that Wilson, having already been legally hanged, could not be hanged again. This was stretching the notion of double jeopardy too far and Murphy was overruled by the citizenry. Second time around, Wilson was left suspended from the rope for a good twenty minutes. This time there was no doubt about his morbidity when he was cut down.

Sometime in the late 1870s Murphy and Dolan acquired another important employee/ally, John H. Riley. Riley and Dolan could have been hewn from the same block of wood. Riley, a Kerry man two years younger than Dolan, was hard-nosed and belligerent, though he appeared to lack much of the latter's raw physical courage. His family had emigrated to the USA when he was twelve years old and settled in Baltimore. As a teenager he had been a railway construction worker in Colorado. He became a partner in the firm of L.G. Murphy in 1876. Riley had proffered his credentials in September 1876 by shooting another outspoken political opponent of Murphy's, Juan Patron. Patron had made common cause with Robert Casey and others before he was shot and almost killed by Riley. The Irishman pleaded self-defence and was not charged with any crime. This is all the more astonishing in that Patron had been shot in the back.

One of the questions that has dogged scholars and researchers into the Lincoln County War is the question of whether this unsavoury Irish 'triangle' was in fact a quadrilateral. A fourth Irishman features prominently in the history of the conflict. He was perhaps the most famous victim of Billy the Kid, the two-term Lincoln County sheriff William Brady. Most commentators have no doubt about Brady's complicity with his fellow Irishmen. One of the most credible, Maurice Fulton, is unambiguous. He observes that 'it was commonly recognised that Brady was a Murphy henchman and took his orders from the man who had been responsible for placing him in office'.[9] However, one of Brady's successors, Pat Garrett, says in his ghost written *The Authentic Life of Billy the Kid* (actually penned by local journalist and writer 'Ash' Upson) that he 'was an excellent citizen and a brave and honest man. He was a good officer and endeavoured to do his duty with impartiality.'[10] Garrett, famously, became the man who killed the man who killed Brady when he hunted down and shot Billy the Kid in 1881.

Brady's Irishness and his support for the Democratic Party has ensured that he has been painted with the same brush with which most chroniclers have, deservedly, tarred his three compatriots. But, according to his defenders, at all times Brady was a decent, independent, impartial lawman who found himself mediating between two devious, brutal and uncompromising factions. He was doing a difficult job because economic circumstances meant he could not hope to make a living from ranching. The defence of Brady is always passionate, but the arguments advanced in his favour are often less than compelling.

Brady was born on 16 August 1829 in Cavan town. The eldest of eight children, he emigrated to America when he was twenty-two years old. His history is similar to that of Murphy. He joined the army straight away and served for ten years, becoming a sergeant. During the Civil War he served with the Second New Mexico Volunteer Infantry as a first lieutenant. In 1862 he married a local New Mexican woman (a widow), Maria Bonifacio Chaves Montoya. After the war, he began ranching in Lincoln County on a spread of about 1,000 acres, four miles east of Lincoln, named Walnut Grove. Continuing in the post-war militia, he was promoted to major in 1865 and cited for bravery in the campaign against the Navajos. He was first elected sheriff in 1869 when Lincoln County was created and, after being succeeded by others, was re-elected in 1875. He also became the first elected representative from Lincoln to serve in the state legislature.

The most bloody and most notorious period of violence in southern New Mexico (the phase always recognised and described as the Lincoln County War) began with the arrival of two influential newcomers in Lincoln, John Henry Tunstall and Alexander McSween.

The first to show up in the county was McSween. Not a lot is known about many periods of his life. It is thought that he was Scots-Canadian Presbyterian, born on Prince Edward Island in 1843, though he may actually have been born in Scotland. He often referred to himself as Scottish, though this is a well-known trait of North Americans up to (and beyond) three generations removed from their European origins. A faded photograph of him shows a man with a high forehead, close-set eyes and a large, flamboyant, semi-circular moustache that, according to some accounts, had been shaved off before his arrival in New Mexico. McSween had married in 1873 and his wife Susan (two years his junior) was to have a powerful influence on the course of the Lincoln County War. She was a forceful and often vindictive woman who had a huge impact on the subsequent historical record because she survived well into the twentieth century and influenced the first disinterested chroniclers of the war.

In 1875 the McSweens were based in Eureka, Kansas, where Alexander had a law practice. Given the controversy that was to engulf McSween by the end of the decade, it is worth noting that he appears to have left the town under a cloud and in a hurry. He had been given money to invest on behalf of a client, a sum of about $750 – only $100 of which ever found its way back to the client. In his haste to leave Eureka, McSween left behind three unsold properties and a sizeable sum in unpaid taxes. The properties were later disposed of by the local sheriff and the proceeds put towards the tax bill.

The McSweens decamped for New Mexico, where they had the good fortune to impress a local congressman, Miguel Otero, who directed them to Lincoln and gave them a letter of introduction to Lawrence Murphy. The McSweens decided to try their luck, for a while at least, in New Mexico and thus began the chain of events that would lead to tragedy, bankruptcy, murder, mayhem and myth.

McSween could not have established a legal practice in a less competitive environment. There was no attorney for more than a hundred miles in any direction and there was, from McSween's point of view, a cornucopia of lawlessness. However, McSween first aligned himself with the most significant power in the land when he presented his letter of introduction and began working for the House. In effect he became Murphy's debt collector, ironically pursuing for payment many of those he would later seek out as allies when he fell out with the House. He retained 10 per cent of whatever he collected. It was convenient for McSween but it was not a marriage made in heaven. McSween's employers were rough and ready, hard-drinking Catholic Irish Democrats. He was a somewhat precious, abstemious Presbyterian Republican. It was a professional relationship that was not destined to last for long.

As McSween became more established and as his abilities as a defence counsel became known throughout the county (he specialised in acquittals arising from legal technicalities), his dependence on the patronage of Murphy and Dolan was reduced. He began to bridle at their political and economic dominance of the county in which he hoped to make his home. In an example of the sort of hubris that often characterised his WASPish underestimation of the political capabilities of Irish immigrants, he began to devise a plan by which he could supplant them. But for his strategy to succeed, he would require powerful allies and an abundance of cash.

His first step was to befriend the most powerful antagonist of the Murphy–Dolan faction in the county, John Chisum. The two men became occasional guests in each other's houses. On one visit to McSween's house in Lincoln, two local outlaws who nurtured a grievance against Chisum, Frank Freeman and Charlie Bowdre, broke into the house, shot up an innocent sewing machine and threatened the cattleman. When a Mexican servant wounded Freeman with a shotgun, they fled and were later arrested by Sheriff Brady.

Throughout the period that followed there was no doubt which side Chisum favoured. But at all times he was only a shadowy figure who made infrequent entrances into the action. He might have wished to become more involved in the struggle for dominance of the county, but his own financial difficulties and legal action by his would-be creditors ensured that he spent much of that time in custody.

John Henry Tunstall offered more direct and active support for the designs of Alexander McSween.

Tunstall was a young Englishman (born in 1853) from a well-to-do middle-class London family. The business interests of his father (also John) were lucrative enough to ensure that his son was able to undertake a grand tour of Europe in 1869. John Henry Tunstall was the only male in a family of five children. He was tall, slim, lightly bearded and had a somewhat aristocratic demeanour. At the age of nineteen he had left England to work for the family business in Canada. Tiring of this, he abandoned Canada for the USA, first arriving in California before acting on advice and heading for New Mexico to set up as a rancher. He was clearly doted on by his family and his father was prepared to offer financial support for almost any money-making scheme devised by Tunstall.

He arrived in Santa Fe in August 1876 and two chance encounters there sealed his immediate future and his ultimate fate. The first of these was with a well-educated but down-at-heel German, Robert Widenmann, who seems, from references made by Tunstall in his letters home, to have impressed the Englishman. When his luck ran out in Santa Fe, Widenmann would follow Tunstall down to Lincoln County and play a significant part in the hostilities that followed the Englishman's arrival.

The second encounter was with Alexander McSween. Tunstall wrote to his father in October 1876:

> I may start upon a trip down into Lincoln County the day after tomorrow ... There is a very nice young fellow here from Lincoln County just now, a lawyer by profession, who has the outward appearance of an honest man.[11]

McSween had clearly dangled some tempting bait before the Englishman. He saw in Tunstall a potential partner in his long-term business strategy. Tunstall's money would bankroll a campaign that would see the Murphy–Dolan enterprise totter. McSween knew how close it already was to the precipice. He had seen the books and had been employed to shore up the enterprise by collecting debts from farmers and small ranchers with no hope of paying. With a final push from a competitor financed by English money, the House of Murphy would topple. Long live the House of McSween!

The attorney was in Santa Fe on his way to New York. He had been employed by the estate of Emil Fritz to seek payment on an insurance policy amounting to $10,000. In his handling of the commission, McSween had already begun to thwart his former employers. Because the financial situation of the House was precarious, Murphy and Dolan had lodged claims against the Fritz estate for money they claimed the deceased German had owed the partnership. McSween considered this claim to be the spurious concoction of a cash-starved enterprise. If he had his way, the House would not see a cent of the Fritz estate. He had other plans for the money. The bulk would go to the deceased's sister, Emilie Fritz Scholand, and his brother Carl, minus a considerable fee for his own trouble.

McSween first crossed the House on an issue concerning his newly acquired friend, John Tunstall. Dolan had offered him $5,000 if he managed to persuade the Englishman to buy a ranch 'owned' by the House. Instead McSween warned Tunstall off. Murphy and Dolan had a habit of selling parcels of land of dubious title and there were good grounds for believing that they were attempting to repeat that process when it came to this transaction. Instead Tunstall purchased 4,000 acres in the valley of the Feliz River, eighty miles southeast of Lincoln. The first pawn had been captured in McSween's game of chess. Tunstall was ensconced. His ranch (complete with proper title) was well-watered grassland in a region where the man who controlled water controlled livelihoods.

The Tunstall–McSween strategy evolved quickly and was comprehensive in its intent. The object was, quite simply, to supplant the House and to concentrate the assets of Lincoln County in the hands of the two usurpers. Tunstall intended to finance the establishment of a retail outlet in the town of Lincoln that would undercut Murphy's store. He also proposed to compete with the House for the army and reservation beef trade. To apply the *coup de grâce* he intended to combat the stranglehold Murphy and Dolan had over so many heavily mortgaged properties in the county by setting up a rival bank that would further threaten the economic hegemony of the House. It was a sweeping and breathtaking plan that would be fuelled by Tunstall's money and which depended on the rapid bankrupting and disintegration of all the Murphy–Dolan enterprises.

Tunstall explained it to his family in the following terms:

> Everything in New Mexico that *pays* at all is worked by a '*ring*' ... to do any good, it is necessary to either get into a ring, or make one for yourself ... My ring is forming itself as fast and faster than I had ever hoped ... I propose to confine my operations to Lincoln County, but I intend to handle it in such a way, as to get the half of every dollar that is made in the county by *anyone*.[12]

The final assertion is revealing. Taken in conjunction with other hints and comments in his correspondence, it suggests that Tunstall and McSween would have been hardly less avaricious had their plan succeeded than the rapacious House that they intended to replace.

At the outset Tunstall's store offered lower prices for retail goods and higher rates for goods purchased than did the House. Tunstall was welcomed as an honest and fair trader, a desirable alternative to the grasping Dolan and Riley. This initial approach has created an assumption that the Englishman intended to continue as he had begun. It is supposed that he and McSween were, in some way, more ethical in their approach to business than the Irishmen. At least one exchange, in May 1877, between Tunstall Senior and Junior suggests otherwise. In one letter the father advised caution when it came to lending money to impoverished Hispanics. Tunstall Junior replied that Mexicans were 'as improvident as butterflies' and that the only trick he needed to know in his dealings with them was how much they were able to pay.[13] Tunstall was no Good Samaritan. Both he and McSween were undoubtedly prepared to sustain losses in the initial period of business in order to retain an appearance of generosity. But once the House had been routed it seems likely that they would simply have become the House by another name.

There were no saints on either side in the Lincoln County War. Murphy, Dolan and Riley are merely the more obviously villainous. Frederick Nolan, whose monumental *The Lincoln County War: A*

Documentary History is the best and most comprehensive survey of the conflict, is in no doubt that Tunstall and McSween were almost equally unscrupulous:

> Tunstall was clever, ambitious, and rich. Taking every leaf he turned out of the House's book, he intended to be as much the boss of Lincoln County as Murphy once had been, but hid that intention behind a façade of English dissimulation. McSween, his none-too-honest lawyer and partner, was equally ambitious for position and money, and not too particular about how he got either.[14]

Had the Tunstall–McSween strategy succeeded, it would probably have been a case of 'meet the new boss, same as the old boss'. But the strategy did not succeed.

Where it fell down was in the expectation that the Irishmen would simply step aside and bow to the inevitable mercantile rout. Susan McSween may have been more astute in her evaluation of the situation than her overly optimistic husband. She later claimed in an interview, 'I told Tunstall and Mr. McSwain [her pronunciation of the family name] they would be murdered if they went into the store business.'[15] If this is not simply self-aggrandising hindsight (which can never be ruled out in her case), then she was more prescient than the new business partners.

Their tactics also failed on the level of astuteness. Tunstall and McSween assumed that the *coup* would come as a surprise to the House, which would be unable to respond to the commercial pressure. However, ironically, it was Tunstall's penchant for regular and indiscreet correspondence with England that proved to be his undoing. That correspondence has been a treasure trove for historians but, given that the Lincoln County Post Office was located in the Murphy–Dolan building, the first people to read Tunstall's letters to his father outlining his increasingly ambitious plans were Jimmy Dolan and John Riley.

In March 1877 there was a slight realignment of the forces that would contest the war. Lawrence G. Murphy bowed out before a shot was fired. On 14 March he formally withdrew from the partnership of

Murphy and Dolan; his health had been failing and, in fact, he would only live for another eighteen months. The name of the business was changed to J.J. Dolan & Co., with Dolan and Riley as partners. For the Tunstall faction, the line-up of principals was completed with the arrival from Santa Fe of the shady Robert Widenmann in early 1877 and the inclusion in their ranks of one of the few unambiguously decent figures in the conflict, Dick Brewer.

Widenmann had clearly made an impression on Tunstall in Santa Fe and he continued to ingratiate himself in Lincoln. The Englishman wrote of the German in far more fulsome terms than he ever did of McSween, his actual business partner. McSween was a nakedly ambitious, dourly Presbyterian entrepreneur intent on advancing the interests of Alexander McSween and with more than a whiff of the ideologue about him. In addition to his plans for securing economic supremacy in Lincoln County, the Scots-Canadian was also determined to build a Presbyterian church and school in a county that was not exactly teeming with non-Catholics. By the time he had concluded his grand plan, Lincoln County would be Republican, Anglo and Protestant. There are clear hints in Tunstall's letters that, while happy to be McSween's business partner, he wanted to keep him at arm's length.

Widenmann was more of a chameleon. He clearly saw Tunstall as a meal ticket but offered in return the displays of loyalty of which the self-important and self-serving McSween would have been incapable.

Dick Brewer was to prove every bit as loyal as Widenmann. Loyalty was only one of his admirable qualities. A simple man and something of a 'gentle giant', Brewer, originally from Wisconsin (in New Mexico, everyone who was not Indian or Hispanic was from somewhere else), was one of many small ranchers who had been shamelessly exploited by the House. He ranched on the Ruidoso River where the Harrell clan had settled briefly before taking their homicidal tendencies back to Texas. He had been sold the land by the House and was in hock to them despite the fact that, unbeknownst to Brewer, Murphy and Dolan had no title to the land that they had sold him. The prices they paid him for his grain ensured that he would never clear himself of the 'debt' he owed them.

McSween gave Brewer an opportunity to exit the vicious circle. He pointed out the House's dubious title and he suggested that the farmer would get a better price for his produce from Tunstall's store than from Dolan's. Brewer's default in his repayments and his defection to the Tunstall store did not go unnoticed. Dolan, along with two of his associates, Billy Matthews and William Morton, rode over to the Ruidoso ranch and threatened Brewer. The big Wisconsin farmer faced them down, telling them that he would make no more repayments to them for land they did not own and that he would sell his produce where he could get the best price. In doing so he added himself to a growing Dolan 'blacklist', atop which stood the names of McSween and Tunstall. Brewer soon began to work for Tunstall, becoming, in effect, his foreman.

Of course there is still one missing piece of the jigsaw, the most colourful one if not necessarily the most consequential. No one knows exactly when Henry McCarty, aka Henry Antrim, aka William Bonney, aka Billy the Kid, arrived in Lincoln County or in what circumstances. There are suggestions that he rode with the Boys and was close to Jesse Evans, who introduced him to the county. If he did, then his subsequent history would make such an association, however brief, richly ironic.

What we do know about the Kid is that he was born in New York City in 1859, probably on 20 November, to Catherine McCarty (or McCarthy). No father's name is listed on his birth certificate. He was brought up in the lower east side of the city in an area recently made famous in the Martin Scorsese movie *Gangs of New York*, the notorious Five Points. By 1864 Catherine McCarty was living in Indiana, where she met and moved in with a William Antrim. By 1873 they were in New Mexico, where they got married before settling down in Silver City. At that stage, according to Silver City sources, young Henry was a sociable child of small to average height with blue eyes, fair hair and prominent teeth, who was ambidextrous (hence the later 'left handed gun' mythology) and liked to sing and dance.

In 1874 Catherine Antrim died. Whether this event helped turn Henry into the disturbed and violent personality of the late 1870s is down to conjecture. Certainly his stepfather claimed to have had great difficulty in controlling the boy after his mother's death, as his entire character seemed to change. Various myths surround the reason for the Kid's departure from Silver City, the most widely believed being that, at the age of twelve, he stabbed to death a man who had insulted his mother and was forced to go on the run. However, at the time (1871) the family had not even settled in Silver City. The truth is more mundane. He appears to have become involved in petty crime, been arrested and escaped, and subsequently left town to avoid his stepfather's wrath.

The most celebrated and persistent myth about the Kid is that he killed a man for every year of his short life (he was dead by the age of twenty-one). This tall tale may have been propagated by the Kid himself to belie his callow appearance and enhance his aura of invincibility, but it is well wide of the mark. He is known to have been personally responsible for the deaths of four men and was complicit in the killing of four more.

His first victim was a thirty-two-year-old Irishman, Frank Cahill, a native of Galway. After leaving Silver City, the Kid deserted New Mexico entirely and headed for Arizona. There he worked as a teamster in Graham County. In August 1877 he became involved in an argument with Cahill, a blacksmith and former soldier. Cahill had a reputation for needling the Kid and probably pushed him too far. By the dead man's own account (published as 'the deceased's last words' in the Arizona *Weekly Star*), Cahill called the Kid a 'pimp' and 'Antrem' [*sic*] responded by calling him a 'son of a bitch'. The Kid went for his gun and Cahill tried to get hold of it; in the fracas that followed the gun went off, mortally wounding the Irishman. The Kid was immediately arrested but, once again, displayed his knack for escaping custody. Facing a murder charge in Arizona, he returned to New Mexico. He stayed at various ranches along the Pecos and Ruidoso rivers in the autumn of 1877 (including that of John Chisum). He may have worked for Chisum for a while, he may even have worked for William Brady, but Lincoln County cowboys insisted that his only involvement with cattle was when he stole them. He may, or may not, have participated in the activities of Jesse Evans and the Boys, but eventually he ended up in the employment of John Henry Tunstall and the rest is legend.

Tunstall, at the time of the Kid's arrival, was suffering from the depredations of the Evans gang and other rustlers. Tunstall was convinced, like Chisum before him, that the Boys were stealing cattle to order and that the proceeds of their raids were supplementing the Murphy 'Miracle Herd', an assortment of cattle of dubious provenance used to supply the army and the Mescalero. Murphy, though retired from the store, still continued his ranching activities. A myth has grown up (encouraged by Hollywood) of an avuncular Tunstall taking a liking to the young Billy and acting *in loco parentis* towards him. An alternative and much more beguiling theory is that Tunstall took the Kid for a barely reformed rustler and hoped, by dint of good treatment and decent wages, that he would be able to persuade the Kid to blow the whistle on the 'Miracle Herd' and testify against Murphy.

Jimmy Dolan knew what John Henry Tunstall was planning almost as soon as Tunstall did himself. An energetic and unscrupulous post-master could acquaint himself with the private business of just about any literate person in the county. Tunstall might have been preparing the ground for his *coup*, but Dolan was in the game already with his counter-*coup*. And he didn't even have to wait for Tunstall and McSween to move first. In fact, his strike had to be pre-emptive.

As counsel for the Fritz estate, McSween, in August 1877, had successfully negotiated the payment of most of the $10,000 New York insurance policy on the German merchant's life. The proceeds were resting (temporarily, he insisted) in an account in his name in a St Louis bank. McSween was adamant that the money would remain there until all possible beneficiaries of Fritz's estate had been located. He suspected that, in addition to the two siblings resident in the USA, there might be more heirs in Germany. Perhaps McSween was being scrupulous to a fault, but there are two alternative possibilities. By retaining the money he might have been guarding against its appro-priation by Dolan, who could probably rely on the Lincoln County courts to get access to it. Or he may well have been guilty of the charge of which he would later stand accused, namely that he intended to leave the jurisdiction and appropriate the money for his own use. The fact of the money being lodged out of state would tend to support either contention.

As soon as McSween had secured the insurance money, Dolan entered a claim for the entire amount, based on Fritz's mysterious indebtedness to the House. McSween rejected this as spurious and entered a counter claim against the House on behalf of Fritz's heirs for more than $20,000. This represented his assessment of the German's equity in the firm of L.G. Murphy & Co. If McSween could make his counter-claim stick, the days of House domination of the mercantile affairs of Lincoln County would be at an end.

But Dolan wasn't about to give up that easily. He exploited the impatience of Emilie Fritz Scholand to get her hands on her inheritance. Both she and her brother had been pressing McSween to release the funds, but he had demurred. In December 1877 he announced plans to vacation in St Louis with his wife. He made no secret of his travel arrangements and Dolan managed to persuade Emilie Scholand, now prepared to think the worst of McSween, that the lawyer was leaving the jurisdiction to make off with the Fritz insurance funds and would not return to Lincoln County. Scholand signed an affidavit alleging that McSween intended to embezzle the inheritance and that he should be prevented from leaving the territory.

Dolan now called on the services of some prominent members of the Santa Fe Ring. He took the Scholand affidavit straight to District Attorney William Rynerson, a prominent ally of T.B. Catron and a friend of the Murphy faction. The result was highly satisfactory for the Ring because McSween was travelling with another of its principal adversaries, John Chisum. Both men were violently intercepted near Las Vegas (New Mexico). McSween was arrested on foot of Scholand's injunction. Chisum was taken as well to prevent him leaving the jurisdiction when proceedings were pending against him over a number of old cattle deals. The Murphy–Dolan faction and the Santa Fe Ring had two of their most prominent and resourceful enemies exactly where they wanted them.

McSween sent his wife on to St Louis and insisted on returning to Lincoln and facing any charges that might be brought forward. Chisum, obstinate and intractable, chose to spend eight weeks in the Las Vegas jailhouse rather than comply with a court order to list his assets. McSween was fortunate in that he was placed in the custody of a well-meaning deputy sheriff, A.P. Barrier. When he was returned to Lincoln, McSween should have been handed over to Sheriff William Brady until a punitive $8,000 bond was paid, but he managed to convince Barrier that his life was in danger if he spent any time in the Lincoln jailhouse. Barrier agreed to allow him to remain at large, in his custody, and effectively became McSween's bodyguard for upwards of three months.

His decision may have been influenced by threats issued by Dolan to McSween and Tunstall on the road between Las Vegas and Lincoln.

Dolan, accompanied by Jesse Evans, stalked his enemies before bursting into their camp and threatening Tunstall (who had travelled to Las Vegas to escort McSween home). Barrier intervened to prevent violence but Dolan's verbal parting shot to the Englishman was an ominous 'I'll get you soon.' He was to be as good as his word.

Over the next few days the animosity between the two factions went beyond words and threats and escalated to a state of all-out war. When McSween got back to Lincoln on Sunday, 10 February 1878, it was to find that Sheriff Brady was already busying himself assembling the collateral for the $8,000 bond. This had been imposed by Judge Bristol, a supporter of the House, in his court in the town of Mesilla. A tally was being made of the lawyer's assets. It began with his house and furnishings and was about to encompass the Tunstall store when Robert Widenmann, left in charge in the Englishman's absence, protested that the store had nothing to do with McSween. Brady, however, insisted that it was well known that McSween was a partner in the enterprise so the assessment should continue.

By Wednesday, 13 February the action had shifted to the Tunstall ranch on the Rio Feliz. At this point Tunstall was beginning to issue threats against anyone who would attempt to appropriate any of his property 'for a debt of McSween's'.[16] The Englishman claimed that the ranch was entirely his own and that McSween had no financial interest in the spread. Tunstall saw Brady's activities as an act of harassment, an attempt to persuade him that his future prosperity lay elsewhere than Lincoln County.

Brady himself did not venture out to the Rio Feliz; instead he deputised a number of Lincoln citizens and sent them out to seize Tunstall's cattle on the dubious basis that McSween had a pecuniary interest in the herd. Leading the posse was Billy Matthews, an ally of Dolan's and a silent partner in J.J. Dolan & Co. Included in its ranks were George Hindman, one of Brady's deputies, William Morton, an employee of Dolan's, and Andrew 'Buckshot' Roberts. The posse also included, incredibly, Jesse Evans, Frank Baker and another of the Boys, Tom Hill. Brady later claimed that he had been unaware that fugitives from justice had been used to augment a sheriff's posse.

Waiting for them on the Rio Feliz ranch was a group of Tunstall employees that included Dick Brewer, Robert Widenmann and William Bonney – the name by which Henry McCarty now went. Tensions were sufficiently high and there was enough hardware in evidence for the war to have begun then and there. It was Dick Brewer who managed to broker an arrangement that averted a confrontation. He refused to allow any cattle to be taken but agreed that Matthews could place a deputy on the ranch to ensure that the herd was not disposed of before the entire matter was settled. Matthews and his posse left and returned to Lincoln.

When Tunstall was informed by Widenmann of what had happened, he moved to enlist the aid of John Chisum. He rode to the Pecos ranch but Chisum was still in jail in Las Vegas and his brothers were not co-operative. Tunstall rode for his own ranch, reaching it late on the night of 17 February. He decided to abide by the agreement reached between Brewer and Matthews but realised that no deal had been made regarding his small herd of horses. These he decided to remove from the ranch. At 8.30 a.m. on Monday, 18 February, Tunstall, along with Brewer and Widenmann, headed for Lincoln with the horses; about 500 yards behind them were Bonney and another employee, John Middleton.

After almost nine hours of riding they had failed to make much progress with the herd. Sometime after five in the afternoon Brewer and Widenmann chased after a flock of wild turkeys in the undergrowth. This left Tunstall on his own with the herd. At that precise moment, when he was at his most vulnerable, a group of riders came over a nearby hill and made straight for Tunstall. It was part of a second posse that had been despatched by Brady. It was led by William Morton, included Jesse Evans and numbered up to twenty men. The rest of the posse, led by Matthews and Jimmy Dolan, was already at Tunstall's ranch. What followed has been the subject of much dispute, debate and controversy ever since.

All that is known for certain is that when the posse approached, Brewer and Widenmann sought the sanctuary of some nearby rocks. Bonney and Middleton, bringing up the rear, didn't make it to Tunstall in time. None of them saw exactly what happened. The Englishman was approached by an element of the posse, two or three shots were fired at him and he was killed instantly. His associates fled, unwilling to take on the superior numbers in the posse. The story Morton told Matthews and which found its way into Brady's report (once again, the sheriff had not accompanied the posse) was that a detachment from the larger group had been fired on by Tunstall. Fire had been returned and Tunstall had been killed. The three men who had separated from the posse and approached Tunstall were Morton himself, Jesse Evans and Tom Hill, another of the Boys. They were the only three men who witnessed what had happened. Given that two of them were wanted criminals with a history of animosity towards Tunstall, their claim to have been shot at first was widely disbelieved.

The body of Tunstall lay where he died in the canyon for some hours before it was recovered and brought to McSween's house. There a preliminary post-mortem was performed by Rev. Taylor Ealy, a Presbyterian missionary minister, doctor and close personal friend of McSween's. His examination and subsequent report gave birth to two myths about the killing. These were that Tunstall had been 'finished off' at close range and that his body, specifically his head, had been brutalised after his death. A more objective autopsy was performed by the assistant surgeon of Fort Stanton, Dr Daniel Appel. It revealed no scorch marks in the vicinity of either of the two bullet wounds on Tunstall's body, indicating that the shots had been fired, probably from a rifle, at long range. The victim's head had not been mutilated and, Appel added for good measure, there was 'evidence' of venereal disease'.[17]

John Henry Tunstall, who had come to New Mexico full of high hopes and intent on making his fortune, had died three weeks shy of his twenty-fifth birthday. He was buried a short distance from the store that was to have been the cornerstone of his prosperity.

Recriminations and preparations for war began immediately.

As Tunstall's coffin was lowered into the ground on Friday, 22 February, the normally mild-mannered Dick Brewer made a public vow that 'every one of the men who had had a hand in Tunstall's death would pay for it with his life'.[18] McSween, who had been finding himself on the wrong side of the law for too long now, put his knowledge of that law to good use. Concluding that it would be futile to approach Sheriff Brady or Judge Bristol for justice, McSween took an alternative route. Dick Brewer and Billy the Kid were brought before a local Lincoln justice of the peace, J.B. Wilson, and swore affidavits identifying the members of the posse that had slain Tunstall. Warrants were then issued by Wilson, who placed these in the hands, not of the sheriff, but of the town constable.

McSween's tactics were simple but highly creative. Given, as he saw it, his lack of access to a just and fair system of law enforcement, he was going to create his own. Wilson was prevailed upon, in his capacity as justice of the peace, to appoint Brewer as a town constable. Brewer duly deputised a number of McSween supporters. It was the birth of the group known to western history as 'the Regulators'. Lincoln County now had, in effect, two alternative and competing law forces, one with the authority of the county and the other, notionally at least, based in the town of Lincoln. Whatever about the alignment of Brady and his deputies, no claims of impartiality can be made for the Regulators. They were a pro-McSween militia dedicated to the capture and killing of the men they saw as being responsible for the murder of John Tunstall. They included men who were angry at the death of Tunstall and guilty at their own inability to protect him. The names of the members of the Regulators (there were ten to fifteen of them at different times) have been immortalised in dime novels and Hollywood movies. Led by an angry and implacable Brewer, the most celebrated Regulator was Billy the Kid, but this quasi-legal group also included another Tunstall loyalist, John Middleton, as well as men such as Josiah 'Doc' Scurlock and Charlie Bowdre, who were motivated by antipathy towards Dolan and Riley.

While all this was going on, Dolan had travelled to the neighbouring Dona Ana County with a double mission. He was going to attempt to have McSween rearrested on the embezzlement charges and handed over to Brady. McSween was still, officially, in the custody of the highly protective and aptly named Barrier. But Dolan also had a more sinister purpose. It had been clear to him from popular reaction to the murder of Tunstall that the worm was turning. Dozens of men had pledged their support to McSween if a shooting war broke out. These were people who were tired of the oppressive tactics of the House. Dolan realised that, despite the support of the Evans gang, he was short of manpower if a full-scale war broke out. He could not depend entirely on the good offices of Brady. His journey to Dona Ana

County was dictated by his need to engage the services of an 'enforcer' of his own, one John Kinney, 'a brutal and reckless ruffian who usually had at his beck and call a band of fellows as desperate as himself'.[19] Dolan now had the hardware for an extended war. What he lacked was the finance to sustain it.

As originally conceived, the Regulators were closer to a vigilante group than a lynch mob. Later they would go down the latter route but, as envisaged by Brewer, they were simply doing a job that county officials didn't seem prepared to do – namely, to deliver the alleged killers of John Tunstall for a session of the county court due in April. That resolve was quickly put to the test when news reached the Regulators that members of the Matthews posse were encamped on the Pecos River at a cattle station owned by Jimmy Dolan. A forced ride to the Pecos and an extended chase netted William 'Buck' Morton and Frank Baker, the former directly and the other more peripherally involved in the death of their mentor.

The prisoners were first taken to the Chisum ranch, where Morton took the opportunity to write a letter to a cousin in Virginia. It was tantamount to a deathbed *apologia*, as it is clear from the tone of the letter that Morton did not think he would live for much longer. The letter, which was later posted in Roswell in the post office run by the writer Ash Upson, offered Morton's account of the killing of Tunstall (which was that the Englishman had fired first) and named the members of the Regulators posse that now held him and Baker. The final line of the penultimate paragraph is significant: 'If I am taken safely to Lincoln, I will have no trouble.'[20] It was a big 'if', but Morton seems to have been certain that he would not remain in Brady's custody for long were the Regulator posse to actually bring him back to Lincoln.

His problem was that the same notion had occurred to some of the members of the posse. Brewer was committed to the maintenance of some semblance of law and order and assumed that Brady would hold on to Regulator prisoners once the job of apprehending them had been done for him. Others, like the Kid, thought Brewer was being naïve and advocated taking the law into their own hands and disposing of Morton and Baker themselves. Also, a rumour had reached the Chisum ranch that Dolan and Riley were assembling a troupe of their own gunmen to ensure that the Regulators didn't get to Lincoln with their charges. Brewer, however, won the argument. On 9 March 1878 the posse set out from the Chisum ranch for Lincoln with Morton and Baker in tow. Tagging along was a former Tunstall employee of dubious loyalty, William McCloskey.

Once again, no one knows exactly what happened next – there are many stories and many theories. The facts of the case are simply outlined. The posse never made it to Lincoln and Morton, Baker and McCloskey were killed en route. The McSween faction's story was that Morton had managed to snatch McCloskey's pistol as they rode side by side, had killed McCloskey and, along with Baker, had tried to escape. Some of the Regulators had given chase and managed to shoot them down.

It is as plausible a story as Morton's version of the Tunstall killing. Morton's body contained nine bullet holes. All were in his back. It suggests that he might have been shot while trying to escape, but it would have required standards of marksmanship that, despite Hollywood suggestions to the contrary, would have been out of the ordinary in the West. Dolan and Riley's lurid version of events (not that there were any of their acolytes present) was that Morton and Baker had been shot in cold blood, on their knees, begging for their lives. McCloskey had been despatched because he had tried to protect them. The truth is probably somewhere in between. In most film versions of the event, the fatal shots are fired by the Kid (there is no evidence to this effect) while McCloskey is killed because he is suspected of being a 'fifth columnist'. It is significant that Dick Brewer was riding in the rear of the group when the killings took place and was not a witness to what went on. It suggests that the vengeful element within the Regulators took the opportunity of exacting their own penalty while Brewer's attention was elsewhere.

Suddenly the war had escalated. But the Regulators' bloodlust had not yet been sated.

Dolan had been caught off guard by McSween's legal manoeuvre that gave the lawyer his own quasi-legal force. He moved quickly to restore the status quo. In doing so, he wielded all the political influence at the disposal of the House and went all the way to the top.

On the same day that Morton, Baker and McCloskey were meeting their maker, Governor Samuel B. Axtell was paying a visit to Lincoln to see for himself what was happening in this remote part of the territory over which he held executive power. His visit was imperious in nature and short in duration. His notion of local consultation didn't go beyond a three-hour chat with Lawrence G. Murphy. As a result of that conversation, before he left Lincoln County he issued a number of proclamations, the most important of which revoked the appointment of J.B. Wilson as justice of the peace and nullified all actions taken by him. This included the deputising of Brewer.

The proclamation went on to threaten the introduction of troops to restore order (House order was the clear implication) and decreed that Judge Bristol was the only judicial force in the county and Brady and his deputies the only law-enforcement authorities. The fact that there were four other justices of the peace, in addition to Wilson, was conveniently overlooked by the governor. In taking action that was highhanded, possibly corrupt and definitely one-sided, Axtell left himself wide open to the humiliating fate that was to befall him. That came when outside, impartial observers began to officially investigate the causes of the unrest in a region that was still, in effect, a protectorate of the federal government. Axtell got what he deserved when he was later recalled and replaced.

The proclamation had the immediate effect of stripping the Regulators of any legal authority for their avowed intentions. Arguably it had also, retrospectively, criminalised their killing of Morton and Baker, assuming those deaths had not been extra-judicial in the first place. It also stripped McSween of his quasi-legal protectors (other than the doughty Barrier) and gave the initiative back to Dolan and Riley.

The killing of Morton, Baker and McCloskey and the implications of the governor's proclamation persuaded McSween that he would be wise to leave Lincoln. Taking Barrier, his faithful guard dog, with him, he sought refuge at the ranch house of John Chisum, who had just been released from jail in Las Vegas. Here McSween would be safe from Dolan's associates and mercenaries, protected not just by the Regulators, but also by Chisum's formidable force of cowboys. While he was there a bungled attempt at cattle rustling by Jesse Evans and Tom Hill cost Hill his life. Another of the alleged killers of John

Tunstall had been killed in his turn, this one without the assistance of the Regulators. But Tunstall's avengers, now stripped of any legal validation, had not yet finished upping the ante.

April Fool's Day 1878 was not a day for merriment in Lincoln County. It was one of bloodiest days in the gory history of the region. The roots of what happened that day may well stretch back to the house imprisonment or protective custody of Alexander McSween on John Chisum's ranch.

The lawyer knew that the April session of the Lincoln court would require his presence in the town for the embezzlement hearing. A misunderstanding resulted in the McSween faction being under the impression that the court would begin sitting on 1 April 1878. In fact the date had been changed to 8 April. However, ignorant of the change of date, McSween intended to be in Lincoln on the first day of the month and a number of Regulators planned to be there with him. Many of them arrived in the town on Sunday, 31 March and spent the night in the Tunstall store.

The following morning at about 9.00 a.m. Sheriff Brady, along with his deputies Billy Matthews, George Hindman, John Long and George Peppin, walked out of the Murphy–Dolan store on the western edge of the town, towards the building used as a temporary courthouse in the town's centre. They may have been distributing bills alerting the citizens to the change of court date or they may have been going to wait on the eastern edge of the town for the arrival of McSween from the direction of Roswell. In his pocket Brady carried a warrant for the arrest of the lawyer.

Their route took them past the Tunstall store. They walked, in an open, casual formation, past the corral at the rear of the store. It was on the northern side of the street. Without warning they were hit by a fusillade of rifle shots from behind an adobe wall. Sheltering there were Billy the Kid and a number of the more hot-headed Regulators, including John Middleton. The main target was clearly Brady because he fell instantly, hit in the head, back and left side. He died on the spot within seconds and was soon followed by Hindman, who was hit once and only survived long enough to cry out for water. Long was also wounded.

A question has been posed many times but never satisfactorily answered. Was the killing of Brady a calculated or purely opportunistic act? If it was premeditated, was it done on the initiative of the Regulators themselves or had the plan been conceived on John Chisum's ranch with the collusion of McSween and possibly Chisum himself?

There is credible evidence that the assassination of the sheriff was not simple opportunism. The absence of Dick Brewer may be significant. The acknowledged leader of the group and its main modifying influence had returned to his ranch rather than travel to Lincoln on that fateful All Fool's Day. Did his absence allow Billy the Kid or one of the other Regulators an opportunity to advocate this further escalation of a conflict that was already spiralling out of control? Or was there a more sinister reason for his non-appearance at what was assumed would be McSween's arrest? Was Brewer refusing to be party to an assassination that had been ordered and paid for by McSween?

By April 1878 the Regulators had been augmented by a number of Hispanics, notably Jose Chaves y Chaves and Francisco Trujillo. None were in Lincoln on 1 April – all had left the Chisum ranch and travelled to the town of Patricio. The suspicion is that they too did not have the stomach for the cold-blooded murder of a man who had a Mexican wife. Doc Scurlock was not in attendance either and he, like Brady, was married to an Hispanic woman. Almost sixty years after the events of that day, Francisco Trujillo, a man by then in his eighties, gave an interview in which he claimed that McSween had told the Regulators of his intention to return to Lincoln on 1 April and had added, 'As soon as I arrive, Brady is going to try and arrest me. You shouldn't let him get away with it. If I am arrested they'll lynch me, while if you kill Brady, you shall earn a reward.'[21]

It is impossible to know if Trujillo's allegation can be trusted. Either way, the absence of Brewer was probably crucial. It is highly unlikely that he would have sanctioned a killing that was only indirect vengeance for the murder of John Tunstall.

In killing Brady, did the Regulators rid Lincoln County of a well-placed Dolan stooge or of a decent lawman overwhelmed by forces that he could not hope to control? Certainly he had not unleashed those forces himself. Dolan and McSween bear most of the responsibility for that. But had he fanned the flames by his partiality towards one side over the other? In most historical works, fictional writing and cine-matic representations of the Lincoln County War, Brady is depicted as a creature of the House. In most accounts it is assumed that he remained loyal to his Irish ethnicity as well as benefiting financially from the hegemony of the House. It is also alleged that he turned a blind eye to the composition of the Matthews posse and thus effec-tively colluded in the murder of Tunstall.

The best that his critics have to say about him is that he showed weakness in the face of the power of the House and chose the line of least resistance – co-operation with the business interests of Murphy and Dolan. One New Mexican historian thinks otherwise. Donald R. Lavash has written a short biography of Brady, calling him the *Tragic Hero of the Lincoln County War* – it is a work that would be more convincing if it didn't gloss over certain events that do not depict Brady in an advantageous light. In his own wildly inaccurate *The Authentic Life of Billy the Kid*, Pat Garrett becomes an advocate for Brady. Garrett acknowledges accusations against Brady of partiality towards the Murphy–Dolan faction, but observes that 'the citizens of New Mexico will unite in rendering honor to the memory of an honest, conscien-tious, kind hearted gentleman'.[22] Not that Garrett can be seen as exactly impartial himself, given his relentless pursuit of the Regulators and later of Billy the Kid (with whom he had once been friendly) when he himself subsequently became sheriff of Lincoln County.

Perhaps the judgement of history has been harsh where William Brady is concerned. His military record and his conduct of the role of sheriff suggest that, whatever else his flaws may have been, he did not lack physical courage. However, he may have lacked the moral courage to resist his fellow countrymen, Murphy, Dolan and Riley. Neither would it have been in his interests to oppose them. Certainly any polit-ical ambitions he might have harboured (he had already served in the Territorial Legislature) would probably have been stillborn without their co-operation.

But as a man of some means who owned a fair-sized ranch, he would have been less financially dependent on the House than many of his neighbours. Perhaps his actions were symptomatic of personal prejudices that overlapped with the interests of the House. There is ample evidence that he had an intense dislike for both McSween and Tunstall. Could it have been that he allowed this animus to come between him and the impartial enactment of his duty? Brady was, after all, an Irish emigrant who had been (albeit indirectly) forced out of Ireland by the activities of acquisitive Englishmen like Tunstall. He would also have had a fervent dislike for the pious religiosity of the Presbyterian McSween. Brady may well have carried his duties too far where both were concerned out of a sense of personal animosity that happened to coincide with the interests of the House.

The next episode in the drama was enacted at an isolated hamlet called Blazer's Mill and must be counted as a setback for the Regulators. In attempting to 'arrest' Andrew 'Buckshot' Roberts (so-called because of the quantity of that particular kind of ammunition lodged in different parts of his body during an eventful life), Dick Brewer was killed and three others were wounded, including the Kid. Roberts had been a member of the Matthews posse and, given the fate of Morton and Baker, decided there was not much percentage in being taken alive. He wasn't. Although he managed to reach the relative safety of the mill owner's home, he died of his wounds after the Regulators withdrew.

Dick Brewer was described by a distraught Alexander McSween in the Cimarron *News and Press* as 'generous to a fault; a giant in friendship … kind, amiable and gentle in disposition … a man of kingly nature'.[23] No such panegyrics were penned for 'Buckshot' Roberts, who died without an epitaph. But then, the loss of Brewer to the McSween faction was of far more consequence than that of Roberts to the Dolan–Riley faction. Both men were buried at Blazer's Mill. They lie side by side to this day – however, no one knows which grave is which.

The convening of the Lincoln County grand jury (ironically under the guidance of Dr Joseph Blazer, owner of Blazer's Mill, as foreman) on 8 April was to prove to be the next major setback for the Dolan–Riley faction. Judge Bristol travelled to Lincoln County for the grand jury session but felt it politic to lodge in Fort Stanton each night and journey to Lincoln each day under armed military escort. The Regulators, although licking their wounds, were still at large and Bristol had already been accused of siding with the Dolan faction to such an extent that he might well have been a target for their wrath.

But nothing that Bristol had already done prepared the people of Lincoln for the partiality shown by him in his address to the grand jury. He asked its members to investigate a number of incidents, including the murders of Tunstall, Brady and Hindman. But this injunction to the jury was despatched rapidly (in about a minute) as Bristol wound himself up for a lengthy and undisguised attack on McSween (close to seven minutes) in his request to the grand jury of citizens of Lincoln County to examine whether or not McSween had embezzled money from the Fritz insurance claim. His address reads like the opening submission of a prosecuting attorney, as he practically instructed the grand jury to find that McSween should face criminal charges.

Furthermore, he went on, essentially, to order the grand jury to find McSween morally responsible for the violence in Lincoln County. As an afterthought, the allegations against Murphy and Dolan of receiving stolen cattle from Jesse Evans and his gang and of supplying these to fulfil government contracts were also to be investigated.

It was clear from its findings that the grand jury (which included Juan Patron) did not share the judge's prejudices. By 18 April it had completed its investigations and in its report it first attacked the governor for his proclamation of 9 March that effectively outlawed the Regulators; it then exonerated McSween completely from all charges of embezzlement; and it indicted Dolan and Riley on charges of knowingly receiving stolen cattle. In the case of the killing of Tunstall, indictments were brought against Evans and three others. Dolan and Billy Matthews were cited as accessories. The Kid and John Middleton were among those charged with the murder of Brady and Hindman. The Regulators were not to go unpunished for the killing of Andrew 'Buckshot' Roberts either. Charlie Bowdre and others (including the Kid and Middleton) were indicted for his murder.

The grand jury also highlighted the corrupt administration of the Mescalero Apache reservation – even though this, being a federal institution, fell outside of their jurisdiction – pointing to 'evidence that the Indians are systematically robbed by their agent of a large and varied assortment of supplies. We mention this here for the reason that it will explain why the Indians are migrating marauders and steal from and murder our citizens.'[24]

The Irish-owned House had made a substantial contribution to the systematic plundering of the entitlements of the Mescalero, but by the time the grand jury sent its report to Judge Bristol, Dolan and Riley were, temporarily at least, out of business. They were financially indebted to the real power broker in New Mexico, Thomas Catron, and he, fearing that they faced imminent bankruptcy, had taken control of their assets. Catron himself must have been concerned at the interest now being displayed by the federal government in the affairs of New Mexico and in the convulsions of Lincoln County. Sparked by British diplomatic concern over the death of Tunstall and by numerous appeals to the Department of the Interior and to President Rutherford Hayes himself, Washington had decided to find out exactly what was going on. The Department of Justice despatched a special investigator, thirty-three-year-old New York attorney Frank Warner Angel, to examine the condition of Lincoln County and report back. His impending arrival was making a lot of prominent people very nervous indeed. The momentum was starting to swing towards Alexander McSween.

A normally lawless society was now dogged by two blocs, both claiming to represent the forces of law and order. On the McSween side were the Regulators, while Dolan and Riley had the self-serving support of the Evans gang as well as that of the mercenary band led by John Kinney.

The two factions clashed, finally and conclusively, on 19 July 1878 in an encounter that became known as the 'Big Killing'.

It was a day of reckoning for both sides in the Lincoln County War and, as far as 'body count' was concerned, it was a clear victory for one side. It had been apparent for days that both parties were intent on bringing the hostilities to a final and bloody conclusion. The town of Lincoln was getting crowded. Armed men were arriving as if by some extra-sensory form of communication known only to those spoiling for a fight.

With George Peppin back in the saddle as the new sheriff, the legal campaign against McSween was renewed. Despite the grand jury's finding, the embezzlement charges were renewed. Warrants were also outstanding against many of the other members of the McSween faction for the deaths of Brady, Hindman and 'Buckshot' Roberts. McSween felt it necessary to leave Lincoln in early July for his own safety. He headed, once again, for the Chisum ranch. On 14 July he returned to Lincoln with a group of about forty supporters. His move took Peppin and Dolan's goon, John Kinney, by surprise. The McSween men were distributed about the town, with fourteen or so (including the Kid) joining McSween in fortifying his own house. Windows were barricaded with dismantled adobe bricks and portholes drilled through the walls. McSween was getting ready for a siege. Peppin (in reality, an agent of Dolan's) was happy to oblige once he got his forces together.

Within twenty-four hours of the return of McSween and his force, all but a handful of the forty or so families living in Lincoln had left the town to avoid the major gun battle they knew to be imminent. As 'civilians' left, new members of the Dolan faction arrived to reinforce Peppin's retinue. By 15 July the sides were numerically even and sporadic shooting had begun.

The loyalty or partiality of the officers at Fort Stanton had swung in both directions over the preceding months but now, under the command of a Colonel Dudley, it was swinging away from McSween. The lawyer blamed this on the intrigues of Dolan. This may well have been the case, but McSween had a peculiar gift for alienating influential figures that often rendered Jimmy Dolan's machinations unnecessary. Dudley, who had been praised for his neutrality when he took command of the fort, may have been genuinely irate at McSween's continued association with the likes of the Kid and the increasingly lawless and uncontrollable Regulators. Certainly Dudley, only newly arrived in the territory and determinedly neutral at the time of the grand jury report, was looking for a way of intervening on behalf of the newly appointed sheriff of Lincoln County, George Peppin.

He got the excuse he wanted when a member or members of the McSween faction, ill advisedly, took a pot shot at a serving soldier who happened to be in the tense and trigger-happy town of Lincoln. Dudley, who had refused all Peppin's calls for military assistance up to that point, now availed of the opportunity to send a detachment of troops to Lincoln to protect 'helpless women and children'.

All the pent-up tension of the five-day 'phoney war' was released on Friday, 19 July. Firing began at 7.00 a.m. With the army on the way, the Dolan faction was intent on bringing things to a head. Colonel Dudley had obtained a warrant for the arrest of McSween in connection with the shots fired at the soldier. He arrived in Lincoln at about 10.30 a.m. with a Gatling machine gun, 2,000 rounds of ammunition and a Howitzer artillery piece. Dolan hoped that the arrival of the military would affect the morale of some of McSween's men. He was optimistic that his adversary would be abandoned by the large number of Mexican supporters he had gathered. Dudley's troops marched past the McSween house and made camp at a point directly between McSween's three principal positions. By placing his troops in their line of fire, he was sending a clear signal that, while officially neutral, he was looking for the slightest excuse to engage McSween's men in defence of his own personnel.

The ploy had desirable consequences for Dolan. As he expected, most of McSween's Mexican supporters, overawed by the military presence, deserted his cause. More surprisingly perhaps, they were accompanied in their flight out of Lincoln by Charlie Bowdre, Doc Scurlock and John Middleton. The odds now favoured Dolan – only the men inside the McSween house and the nearby Tunstall warehouse remained to be dealt with. The decision was taken to set the lawyer's residence on fire and smoke him out along with his dozen or so remaining supporters.

At around midday, following one abortive attempt to fire the house, a Scottish-born member of the Dolan faction, Andrew Boyle (who had served ten years in the British Army in India), managed to get close enough to the west wing of the McSween building to start a fire. Attempts by those in the house to extinguish the flames were hampered by sustained firing from Peppin's men, who now surrounded the McSween house.

The fire took hold slowly, the prevailing wind retarding its progress. Nonetheless, it was clear to the defenders of the McSween household that their options were limited and lessening by the hour. It would not be dark until nearly nine o'clock and to emerge from the burning building in daylight would have been suicidal. Legend has it that at this point Billy the Kid took command of the situation and suggested that when darkness fell he and three others would take their chances with a dash for safety towards the Tunstall store to the east before cutting north and seeking the sanctuary of the Bonito River. This move would draw the fire of Peppin's deputies and the rest of the men, including McSween, might be able to make their escape.

As no one came up with a better idea, this became the default escape plan. It almost worked. The Kid, along with two or three others, raced from the burning building as twilight thickened into darkness. Only one man (Harvey Morris, a clerk in McSween's law practice) was killed as they crossed the yard toward the east gate and disappeared into the scrub along the riverbanks. But McSween and three others waited too long to make their move. The posse had ceased firing after Billy and the other decoy escapers by the time the lawyer bolted for safety. His group was spotted, fired on and forced to take cover. What happened after that is shrouded in mystery and controversy. But the balance of probability and the weight of the available evidence suggest that someone in the McSween group offered to surrender if one of Peppin's deputies would come forward and guarantee their safety. Robert Beckwith agreed to accept their surrender and stepped out from behind his own cover. He was killed almost immediately and this sparked off sustained firing that left McSween and his three companions dead.

The death of the lawyer led to an orgy of celebration on the part of the Dolan faction and the wholesale looting of the Tunstall store and bank. Susan McSween, who had been allowed to leave the burning house soon after it was fired, was now permitted to bury her husband. He was interred by her two black servants beside the grave of John Tunstall.

The Big Killing of 19 July (in addition to the deaths already mentioned, there may have been two more bodies in the embers of the McSween house) didn't end the Lincoln County War, but with the two principals on the Tunstall–McSween side removed from the picture, it now began to degenerate into disorganised lawlessness before fizzling out altogether. The removal of Governor Axtell from power and the appointment in his place, by the Hayes administration in Washington, of Lew Wallace, a much-decorated soldier and the author of *Ben Hur*, helped restore order. Washington stopped short of establishing martial law in the region but, in October 1879, threatened military intervention if hostilities did not cease. The action had the desired effect on most of the participants.

At the end of it all, no one had gained much from the war. Susan McSween profited in spite of it (Dick Brewer's parents gave her the deeds to his ranch – she went on to become one of the biggest cattle-women in the West). Jesse Evans returned to rustling and robbery, before ending up in Huntsville Prison in Texas after an encounter with the Texas Rangers. He escaped from prison and managed to fade into obscurity.

Billy the Kid never quite managed to achieve that sort of anonymity. His legend is largely built on his post-Lincoln County War history, as he descended into a pattern of violent criminal activities that included his later escape from custody in Lincoln when he murdered the two deputies guarding him, Bell and Ollinger. As is well known he, and many of the now thoroughly criminalised Regulators, was hunted down. The task was left to his famous nemesis, the former buffalo hunter Pat Garrett, elected sheriff of Lincoln County in 1880. The death of the Kid came as a great relief to John Chisum. The Kid had assumed that, after the death of McSween, Chisum would become the standard bearer of the McSween–Tunstall faction. But the wily Texan cattleman had more interest in peace than a renewal of war. The hostilities had forced him to move a large part of his herd back to Texas. When they were returned to New Mexico, Chisum was more concerned with keeping the likes of the Kid well away from his stock. The old alliances were no more. Chisum only lived for five years after the collapse of the faction that he had helped put together. He died of a cancerous tumour in 1884.

Jimmy Dolan and John Riley lost their heavily indebted store to their political ally and creditor, Thomas B. Catron. Dolan later went back into business in Lincoln County, ironically buying the Tunstall store and setting up another mercantile business. He also, heaping irony upon irony, bought Tunstall's ranch on the river Feliz. Clearly Dolan was an Irishman unaffected by ghosts. He served in various state political capacities and died in 1898. His friend and associate John Riley remained close to Catron but largely abandoned Lincoln County. He was elected Dona Ana County tax assessor in 1889. In the mid-1890s he moved to Colorado and died there in February 1916 at the age of sixty-five.

For Lawrence Gustave Murphy, there was no future of any description. He had left Lincoln County for Santa Fe before the Big Killing. He was already far gone at that stage, a broken alcoholic, finally unnerved by the carnage that he had caused. If the death of John Tunstall started the Lincoln County War, then it had come full circle by the time Murphy succumbed to the excesses of his alcoholic lifestyle in a Santa Fe hospital on 20 October 1879. He was a broken man by then, spiritually and financially.

A detailed examination of the complexities of the collective American psyche that elevates a thuggish killer of the likes of Henry McCarty, aka Antrim, aka William Bonney, aka Billy the Kid, to iconic status is, thankfully, well beyond the scope of this work. But the ubiquitous dime novelists of the day, as well as Pat Garrett's *The Authentic Life of Billy the Kid* (published in 1882), ensured his national celebrity. Garret was slower on the draw with his memoir than he had been on the night of 14 July 1881 when he shot the Kid dead in Fort Sumner. Eight novels were written between the time of the Kid's death and the publication of Garret and Upson's account of the young gunfighter's life.

So the Kid's reputation was well established before Hollywood got a lease on him in the twentieth century. There are conflicting figures for the number of movies featuring or concerning the Kid, but it is certainly more than fifty. Needless to say, there is a huge variation in degrees of historical accuracy.

In virtually all the films dealing with the Lincoln County War and Billy the Kid, the supporters of the House wear black hats and those of Tunstall and McSween wear white. Murphy and Dolan (or their renamed equivalents) are depicted as venal tyrants while Tunstall is portrayed as an idealistic and peaceable man with a paternal regard for the young cowboys (in particular the Kid) in his employ. In all representations of him, Tunstall is far too old – presumably on the basis that you can't be avuncular when you are in your mid-twenties and younger than many of your own cowboy employees. Most of the films ignore the ethnic origins of the protagonists, even where their actual names are used. There are few, if any, Irish or English accents and relatively few Mexicans.

Billy the Kid, made in 1941, features Robert Taylor in the lead role. It was one of *six* movies made that year about the Kid. Taylor is a singularly unconvincing nineteen-year-old. The angle taken by the film is that the Kid is a 'free spirit' who stays one step ahead of the authoritarian forces taming the Old West. The opening voiceover describes him as 'a young outlaw who lived his violent hour in defiance of an advancing civilization'. The Kid teeters on the edge of being an anti-hero but never quite falls into that particular chasm. He does a lot of killing but most of it is 'justified' in the context of the film and we never actually see the results of his violent acts. In the end he gets his just desserts, with the closing titles telling us that his fate was inevitable: 'Thus as the ways of the law came to the last frontier, the last of the men of violence found his peace.'

Arthur Penn's *Left Handed Gun*, filmed in black and white in 1957, is a much grittier and moodier piece. A young Paul Newman plays a Kid who is taken under the wing of a Scottish Tunstall (from Ayrshire), learns to read under his tutelage and goes completely off the rails when his mentor is murdered. Newman (and the script) manages to capture some of the irrationality and impulsiveness of the Kid and suggest that he is not entirely a victim of circumstance. For the record, Murphy becomes 'Martin' in this depiction of the war and if he was ever Irish he has lost all trace of his accent.

In Andrew McLaglen's *Chisum* from 1970, John Wayne plays the eponymous cattle baron and the Lincoln County War is seen from his perspective. Tunstall (played by Patric Knowles) is a pipe-smoking, neighbourly type who teaches Billy to read and the Kid and Pat Garrett vie for the attentions of Chisum's niece, Sally. Lawrence Gustave Murphy, played by Forrest Tucker, is as American as Joseph McCarthy and even less amiable. The local Indians have morphed into Comanches and Chisum himself becomes a Regulator when Judge Wilson deputises him to take a posse and pursue Morton and Baker after the killing of Tunstall. In the end Billy kills Jesse Evans, Chisum kills Murphy, Governor Wallace declares an amnesty and there it ends – long before the Kid goes to the bad. The best line in the film goes to western character actor Ben Johnson, a veteran of John Ford's 'stock company', who, as Chisum's crochety foreman, intones, 'There's no law west of Dodge and no God west of the Pecos' – which is supposed to justify all the extra-legal activity that takes place.

Sam Peckinpah's *Pat Garret and Billy the Kid* (1973) is, as are many of Peckinpah's movies, an exploration of the nature of violence and capitalism in American society. Kris Kristofferson is, like Robert Taylor in the 1941 film, a 'free spirit'. Had Billy lived in the decade in which the film was made he might have completely forsworn violence and become a harmless dropout. He has much of the idealism of the sixties (the 1960s, that is) and refuses to submit to the authority of his erstwhile friend Pat Garrett (played by James Coburn) and his rich, stock-owning employers led by John Chisum (lumped in, for convenience, with the Santa Fe Ring). Garret is represented as having sold out to the interests of capitalists. He informs one critic of his decision to accept the position of sheriff of Lincoln County that 'It's a job – there's an age in a man's life where you don't want to spend time figuring what comes next.'

Ironically, one of the most accurate representations of the struggle comes from a period when the western had long since passed its sell-by date. *Young Guns*, made in 1988, could just as easily have been called 'The Brat Pack Goes West', starring as it does Emilio Estevez as Billy, his brother Charlie Sheen as Dick Brewer and Kiefer Sutherland as 'Doc' Scurlock. In *Young Guns*, Murphy is played by Jack Palance with an Irish accent, Terence Stamp plays Tunstall as an aristocratic Englishman, 'Buckshot' Roberts kills Brewer, the Regulators are trapped in McSween's house with the army and John Kinney's mercenaries outside and many other things happen that are also historically accurate. In a salute to another era, Pat Garrett is played by Patrick Wayne (son of 'The Duke'). However, to give its audience the ending they desire, Murphy does not die in a Santa Fe hospital but is killed in the streets of Lincoln by a nicely manic Billy the Kid after the escape of the Regulators from the burning ruins of the McSween house (in broad daylight).

How serious a conflict was the Lincoln County War? All told there were sixty-three violent deaths between the time of the murder of Tunstall on 18 Feb 1878 and the killing of the Kid on 14 July 1881. Arguably the latter date falls well outside the bounds of the war. There were twenty-three violent deaths between 18 February and the Big Killing of 19 July 1878. This compares with over 100 killed in the US and Mexican cavalry war against the Mescalero Apache under the leadership of Victorio between September 1879 and October 1880, most of those deaths being among the Apache insurgents.

As we've seen, Hollywood has never come close to doing justice to the Lincoln County War. That is not entirely the fault of the American film industry. To begin with, part of its self-imposed brief has been to enhance the 'myth of the frontier', to create a mythology for a young country with no Arthurian, Roman or Viking past. That mission is often antithetical to historical reality. Furthermore, it would not be possible to encompass the complexity of the Lincoln conflict within the frame allowed by 120 minutes of screen time. Neither would any cinema-going audience be interested in a story in which there were no good guys, just bad guys and even worse guys, subtle gradations of felonious and homicidal culpability.

Regrettably, much of the writing about the war seems to fall into a similar trap. For a start, most of it focuses on the role of Billy the Kid in the conflict. This is understandable if you want to sell books but not if the object is a balanced account of a series of historical events. Many of the more wide-ranging accounts tend to view the conflict in terms of 'black and white', with most opting for the Murphy–Dolan faction as the exploitative tyrants and the Tunstall–McSween bloc as the oppressed underdogs. It is possible that any account of the Lincoln County War is doomed to failure. Just as it is difficult to find a jury to try a case that has received blanket media coverage, it may be impossible to bring the right perspective to a story already dominated by such an iconic figure as Billy the Kid. There were few neutrals in the war itself. There are few neutrals in the historical debate that followed.

The available documentary evidence suggests that both sides were equally unscrupulous but that Tunstall and McSween, as the newcomers with no obvious track record in venality, garnered a lot of support from hopeful inhabitants of Lincoln County and the benefit of doubt from later historians. Crucially, they also commanded a lot of support from the indigenous Mexican population of the county.

Equally, the Hollywood depiction of Billy as a misunderstood figure – a youthfully anti-authoritarian 'ordinary decent bandit' – requires that he be aligned with the 'good guys'. That particular thesis – that he was 'turned' into a psychopath by the killing of Tunstall and that his subsequent actions were simply revenge for the murder of his mentor – condemns the Murphy–Dolan faction and, more unjustly, Sheriff Brady without trial. It skews folk memory and, inevitably, leaks into the historical record as well. Not that Lawrence G. Murphy, James Dolan and John Riley aren't richly deserving of our opprobrium. The fact that they fled poverty and want in a small, politically oppressed country was no excuse for their calculated exploitation, oppression and avarice. But was it any more calculated than the subtle but equally ambitious manipulations of the tyro 'Boss' of Lincoln County, John Henry Tunstall, and his devious ward heeler, Alexander McSween? Under either dispensation the people of Lincoln County would still have owed their souls to the 'company store'. The only difference would have been the identity of the store owner.

When assessing the role of Tunstall and McSween in the conflict, one salient fact must be borne in mind. Susan McSween became a much-sought-after oral resource for chroniclers of the conflict in the early part of the twentieth century. She lived on until 1931, a period when movies were already being made about the war, and consistently 'set the record straight' when it came to the role of her husband and his English partner. What she was not able to do to Murphy, Dolan and others while they were alive, she was in a position to do to their memories after they died. She must have revelled in the fact that her longevity allowed her to pay her enemies back for the murder of her husband.

Frank Warner Angel, in his report to the Justice Department, reserved his most particular words of opprobrium for the Murphy–Dolan faction. But were Tunstall and McSween the plain dealers that Angel believed them to be? There is no doubt that Murphy, Dolan and Riley were unscrupulous and corrupt. They robbed from the federal government and extorted from the ordinary people of Lincoln County. They were determined to keep a closed shop, all the more so when the man trying to open up the market was an aristocratic Protestant Englishman, representing everything men of their ethnic backgrounds despised. But would their plausible, cultured opponent have proved any better in the long run? The last word on this subject should be left to the man who knows more than anyone about the Lincoln County War, himself an Englishman, Frederick Nolan.

In the valedictory chapter of his comprehensive *The Lincoln County War: A Documentary History*, he concludes:

> it is quite obvious that Tunstall and McSween were intent upon
> a domination of Lincoln County as complete as that of Murphy
> and Dolan. Perhaps, of the two, they might have been more
> benevolent ... but that is about all.[25]

In many ways the struggle for economic and political power in southern New Mexico that was at the heart of the Lincoln County

War was paradigmatic – a microcosm of the history of the West itself. It was brutish and violent, born out of a desire, on the one hand, to defend what had been won, or stolen, from others and, on the other, to tap into and exploit a promising opportunity. It also begot an overweening mythical figure. No western story would be complete without its icon – which is why we keep coming back to Billy the Kid. The Lincoln County War conferred immortality on this belligerent and enigmatic figure and he, in turn, has conferred immortality on the Lincoln County War.

REEL NINE

CAMEOS:
PIONEERS, PLUTOCRATS, POPINJAYS AND POPULISTS

At the end of a movie there are those of us who like to sit in our seats until the lights come up. This allows us to absorb what we've just seen, find out what that song was we really liked and enjoy the litany of amazing names people have dreamed up and bestowed on their unfortunate children. They scroll past our eyes from floor to ceiling, the stuntmen, electricians, wardrobe assistants – mere footnotes to us, but 'players' in their own movie.

So, for your consideration, here are a few final members of the supporting cast. Some are one-trick ponies, men and women who have earned a very post-modern fifteen minutes in the limelight. Others are shadowy extras who might be of greater interest if only we could find out more about them. All add something to the detail of our widescreen presentation.

Paul Boyton: floater

To begin with the more than faintly ridiculous, Boyton was born in Dublin in 1848 and emigrated to the USA before the Civil War, serving one year of the war in the Union navy. He had an adventurous life that included service in the Mexican revolution, prospecting for diamonds in South Africa and diving in the Caribbean. His connection with the West comes from his experimentation with a primitive form of rubber wet suit. To advertise himself and the suit, he undertook one of the most bizarre journeys of the nineteenth century. Starting in Glendive, Montana, he floated down the Yellowstone and Missouri rivers armed with a bugle and a knife. He took the precaution before setting off of identifying his own Boswell in the form of journalist James Creelman of the New York *Herald*, who turned him into a short-lived celebrity.

By his own account Boyton had a series of hazardous encounters with wildlife, Indians and rustlers as well as adverse weather conditions and perilous currents. But he survived all those vicissitudes to reach St Louis after sixty-four days in the water. Thanks to Creelman he was greeted by a huge crowd at his journey's end.

On the strength of his notoriety he opened a bar in New York and died there in 1924.[1]

Frank Butler: sharpshooter and husband

Butler's claim to fame is by association. He was the husband and manager of the great western sharpshooter Annie Oakley. Born in Ireland around 1840, he emigrated at the age of twenty-three, settling first in New York. There he took on a number of menial jobs that included working with horses – as in cleaning up after them. He then entered the entertainment business as a dog trainer and trick shooter. In 1876 he met the then sixteen-year-old Phoebe Annie Oakley Moses in a shooting contest. He was a professional marksman by then and toured the music halls and theatres of the West issuing challenges to local people from the stage. In Cincinatti, Ohio, Annie was persuaded to take up the gauntlet. She beat him, relieving him of $100 in the process, and either he wanted his money back or it was love at first sight. He married her on 22 June 1876 and became her manager and on-stage partner as half of 'Butler and Oakley'. His careful nurturing of her career contributed to her international fame, but it was her phenomenal eye that really made her famous. At first the pair worked with the Sells Brothers Circus, at which point Frank exited the act and Annie went solo. They then took the step that guaranteed Oakley immortality by throwing in their lot with one of the true creators of the Wild West, Buffalo Bill Cody, in 1885. 'Little Miss Sureshot' (she is supposed to have earned the name from Sitting Bull) and her Irish manager remained with Buffalo Bill for seventeen years. They toured the USA, Canada, England, France, Germany, Spain and Italy. In the course of her European tours she met Queen Victoria in 1887 and two years later shot a cigarette from between the lips of the then Crown Prince Wilhelm of Germany. Given his subsequent career, one wonders how European history would have changed if she had missed by about an inch.

The Butlers didn't finally retire from show business until 1922. They settled first in Leesburg in Florida but soon returned to Annie's home state of Ohio and settled in Dayton. Little Miss Sureshot died there in November 1926. Her beloved and disconsolate husband Frank, twenty years her senior, followed her three weeks later.[2]

Pat Coghlan: cattleman

Cork-born Coghlan was a post-Famine Irish economic refugee who reached the USA in 1848 at the age of twenty-six. Like a lot of his fellow Irishmen at the time, he joined the US Army. A large (six-foot plus) man with a powerful and athletic build who claimed never to have been beaten in a race, he served in its ranks until 1852 (although one report has him still in the army until 1872). Either way, he settled in Tularosa, New Mexico in 1874, buying a ranch there and raising cattle, some of which were actually his own. In this he anticipated the more organised activities of his fellow countryman Lawrence Gustave Murphy prior to the Lincoln County War. By 1878 he had acquired a sizeable herd (mostly from Texan rustlers) and attempted to cash in by driving the cattle to Fort Stanton. However, he was spectacularly hoist with his own petard when the herd was rustled from under his nose by a group led by one Jake Owens, who attempted to sell them to that other great New Mexican purchaser of beef, the Mescalero Apache reservation. Coghlan, cleverly realising that there was only one viable outlet for the herd other than Fort Stanton, secured the aid of the army and had Owens and his gang arrested.

The Cork man subsequently sold his Tularosa spread for a sum reported to be in the region of $200,000 and spent a long retirement in New Mexico. He didn't die until January 1911, aged sixty-three, and is buried in El Paso.[3]

The Connemaras: fishermen cut adrift

Some immigrants from Ireland bypassed New York, Boston and Philadelphia entirely and were resettled in places such as Minnesota (at the time a frontier state) by benefactors such as Archbishop John Ireland of Minneapolis–St Paul. The Kilkenny-born archbishop was highly successful in populating the often inhospitable prairie with pockets of Irish settlement. Many of them remain relatively intact to this day.

Through the 1870s, Ireland established ten rural villages and farming communities with names such as Clontarf, Avoca and Iona in five Minnesota counties under the aegis of his Catholic Colonization Bureau in St Paul. Ireland's right-hand man in this enterprise (which used railroad land) was Roscommon man Dillon O'Brien, born into the Catholic landholding class, who had been ruined by the Famine and forced to emigrate.

However, the redoubtable archbishop had an unhappy experience with one group of impoverished fisherman from the West of Ireland that he ill-advisedly attempted to turn into frontier farmers. The fate of the 'Connemaras' is part of the lore of the American Midwest.

Ireland had to have his arm twisted to accept the group in the first place. Against his better judgement, he allowed himself to be persuaded to settle them. But the wisdom of his initial reluctance was quickly borne out. Fifty families came from Ireland with their agricultural experience limited to garden farming. O'Brien met them off the boat in Boston in 1880 and was not impressed. His son described the group as 'not the competent, but the incompetent; not the industrious but the shiftless; a group composed of mendicants who knew nothing about farming'.[4] They were settled near the Graceville colony and the settlers already there were even less enamoured of the new arrivals than O'Brien had been in Boston. The first harsh winter they spent on the prairie saw them consume or sell the seed crops allocated to them and Ireland was forced to find employment for them, mainly as labourers and domestic servants, in Minneapolis and St Paul. Despite his best efforts on their behalf, many of the Connemaras were critical of Ireland and publicly accused him of neglect. The stress of the whole affair may have shortened O'Brien's life. He died suddenly in 1882.

John Wallace Crawford – Captain Jack: scout and poet

It would perhaps be too cruel to suggest that Jack Crawford was to American poetry what William McGonagall was to Scottish verse, but it would not be far from the truth. Nevertheless, the work of Captain Jack, though hardly accomplished, was highly popular and among the earliest examples of 'cowboy' poetry.

Crawford was born in Donegal in 1847 and came to America with his family in 1858. He enlisted in the 48th Pennsylvania in the Civil War and was wounded in action twice. After the war he headed west and was probably one of the stampeders who entered the Black Hills panning for gold in the aftermath of the Custer expedition there in 1874. Two years later he was serving as an army scout with General Crook in the Bighorn–Yellowstone campaign but managed to avoid the fate of many of his fellow countrymen at the catastrophic Battle of the Little Bighorn in June 1876.

His career as a scout prospered, especially in the wake of the decision of Buffalo Bill Cody to move east and begin on the path that would lead to the Wild West Show. To mark Bill's departure, Crawford, who thereafter assumed a Cody-like appearance, right down to the beard and long hair, made one of his first attempts at poetry – the first stanza of 'Farewell to our Chief' reads:

Farewell! The boys will miss you Bill;
In haste let me express
The deep regret we all must feel

Since you have left our mess
While down the Yellowstone you glide
Old Pard, you'll find it true,
That there are thousands in the field
Whose hearts beat warm for you.[5]

(Afficionados of the work of the peerless McGonagall will already have noted the marked similarities, possibly even an overt homage.)

Crawford's scouting activities took him to the Southwest at one point, where he was involved in the search for the Apache leader Victorio. He was good or fortunate enough to track the rebel leader to within a mile of his camp in Mexico. Planned negotiations were aborted, however, when his military companions opted for discretion and declined to enter the Apache camp with Captain Jack.

Eventually Crawford established a ranch on the Rio Grande in 1886 and gave full vent to his poetic powers. His first book, *The Poet Scout*, had already been published, but he also wrote three more books of poetry as well as three plays (in which he appeared) and more than 100 short stories. Most of his poetry is sentimental in nature, but he did occasionally use his verse to advance social causes and he did have a feel for the underdog, as exemplified in the last verse of a poem from his first collection, 'Only a Miner Killed':

Only a miner killed!
Bury him quick,
Just write his name on
A piece of stick,
No matter how humble
Or plain the grave,
Beyond all are equal –
The master and slave.[6]

Charles David Curtis: soldier and lawman

Curtis, born in 1839, was from Cloyne in County Cork and was one of the hundreds of thousands who fled Ireland in the immediate after-math of the Famine. He arrived in the USA with his family in 1850. An intelligent young man, he later graduated from university in St Louis. He claims to have been an army scout and Indian fighter in Utah before illness forced him, in 1860, to resign a second lieutenant's commission, though this cannot be confirmed. He studied medicine for a while before moving to Montana in 1864. He became the first city clerk of Virginia City before heading for Helena and starting a business. It was around this time that his path crossed that of Thomas Francis Meagher, acting governor of the Territory of Montana from 1865–7. He became a recruiting officer for the Montana Militia raised by Meagher to counter the threat from Red Cloud and his Sioux warriors. He first had a captain's commission in the force but was later promoted by Meagher to the rank he had held himself in the Civil War, brigadier general. This was in spite of the fact that his entire force numbered less than 500 – the equivalent of about half a Civil War battalion. He saw no action whatever and after Meagher's death the new governor busted him back to captain.

In 1877 he was called up again when the threat of Chief Joseph and the Nez Perce materialised but, once again, his fighting abilities were not required. In the 1890s he served as sheriff of Lewis and Clark County in Montana, lending a hand in the capture of the Charley Jones gang. Jones, a thirty-something Texan outlaw, whose real name was Camillo Hanks, had ridden with the Wild Bunch and was arrested in 1892 on suspicion of involvement in the robbery of a Northern Pacific train on the Yellowstone River. Thanks, in part, to Curtis, Jones did a ten-year stretch in Deer Lodge Penitentiary.

Curtis died in Helena in 1910.[7]

Marcus Daly: the copper king

Marcus Daly tried hard to be a Silver King but had to settle for making a huge fortune from copper instead. Born in County Cavan around 1841, he was the youngest of eleven children and arrived in New York at the age of fifteen. He was in much the same state as most of his emigrant compatriots – dirt poor, uneducated and with few, if any, marketable employment skills. For five years he did labouring jobs in New York until he made enough money to buy passage to San Francisco and move in with an older sister who lived in California.

He began work in the mining industry in California before moving to the Comstock lode in Nevada. By 1871 he was working as a foreman for the Walker Brothers (miners and bankers) in Salt Lake City. He was sent by the Walkers to Montana in 1876 to buy up claims and mines. In the case of one purchase, the Alice Mine, Daly retained a 20 per cent interest for himself. After five years he was able to sell his stake in the Alice Mine and purchase the claim that would make his fortune, the Anaconda. It was a silver mine, or at least it was until the miners hit a copper vein 300 feet deep and 100 feet wide.

At the time, copper was coming into its own: Edison had developed the electric light and demand for the metal was increasing. The return to copper-mine owners was relatively small, however, because the mined ore had to be shipped to Wales to be smelted. Daly, in order to realise more of the profits from the exploitation of the metal, got funding from his investors for a copper smelter. Not only did he build the installation itself, but he built the town of Anaconda to support it. By 1890 Montana mines, mostly in the very Irish town of Butte, were producing over $17 million worth of copper every year. Through his Anaconda mine and his smelter, Daly was taking a generous share of that sum.

The uneducated Irishman who had made a vast fortune 'the American way' enjoyed his riches. One of his main extravagances was the building of a summer mansion in the late 1880s. It was remodelled twice, but after the second makeover it reminded Daly of a church so he had it redesigned all over again. This part-time residence is preserved today. It has over 24,000 square feet of floor space and more than fifty rooms.

But the ownership of a huge, pretentious mansion did not mean that the bluff, bulky Cavan man had suddenly become genteel. Daly managed to retain his hard-nosed, tobacco-chewing demeanour even as millions of dollars were added to his bank account. He liked to drink with his miners, though his cultivation of good relations with his employees did not go as far as tolerance of trade-union activity. He also had a great love of horse racing. His political affiliations and his tendency to take questionable short cuts in business and in politics can be seen in the name of his favourite racehorse, Tammany. He raced in copper and green colours and after winning a match against a highly rated eastern horse, Daly built Tammany a castle.

Politics to Daly were a means to a business-related end. His great rival was his fellow Montana copper magnate William Clark, who cherished political ambitions of his own. Daly preferred to work in the background, Tammany style. Both Clark and Daly were Democrats but led their own feuding factions of the Montana Democratic Party. Daly consistently managed to frustrate Clark's attempts at election to the US Senate, frequently resorting to corruption and vote buying in order to do so.

Their classic political duel was the fight for the state capital of Montana. Naturally Daly wanted Anaconda to be named principal city, while Clark championed the cause of Helena (Butte was also a contender). Huge sums of money were thrown at the campaign. In pursuit of their aim, both men either bought or established newspapers as propaganda outlets. In the referendum that followed, Clark, or rather Helena, won out by 2,000 votes.

Daly was an intensely private man with no desire to leave much information about himself to posterity. After his death, his papers were burned, even letters between himself and his wife, Margaret. He died of a heart-related ailment in New York in 1900, not far from where he had first arrived in the USA as a penniless immigrant. He was just fifty-eight years old. A year after his death, William Clark was finally elected to the US Senate.[8]

James 'Paddy' Graydon: farmer, soldier and Indian killer

James Graydon's date of birth is unknown but he was probably born somewhere in Ireland in the late 1830s or early 1840s. He appears to have been a well-to-do farmer in Arizona with property valued at over $13,000. He also ran a hotel near Fort Buchanan, Arizona. But it is for his military activities that he became notorious. In 1861, during the US Army's war with Cochise and the Apache nation, he was instrumental in capturing alive three Apache warriors. They were held as hostages and hanged in dubious retaliation for a supposed Apache atrocity.

The following year, during the Civil War in New Mexico, a vicious but largely irrelevant campaign, Graydon, a Union combatant, came up with the not-very-bright idea at the Battle of Valverde of loading down two mules with high explosives and directing them towards the Confederate lines. Not unnaturally, the two highly intelligent animals refused to budge. This precipitated a necessarily rapid withdrawal by the Union forces from the vicinity of the obdurate animals.

Graydon died in October 1862 as a direct result of an underhand attack on a Mescalero Apache camp near Galinas Springs in New

Mexico. The Mescalero were in transit to Santa Fe, seeking negotiations with Kit Carson. Graydon, a captain with the improbably named Independent Spy Company, talked his way into the camp with some of his men and then began firing. A dozen Apache died in the fire-fight and up to twenty more were wounded. Graydon was accused of cold-blooded murder by a Kentucky-born physician resident in New Mexico, Dr John Marmaduke Whitlock, and challenged to a duel at Fort Stanton. In the gunfight that followed, Graydon was shot through the lungs and fatally wounded. He died four days later. In retaliation, the wounded Whitlock was brutally murdered by Graydon's men.[9]

Nicholas 'Old Man' Hughes: cattleman

Hughes was born sometime in the early 1840s, probably around 1843. He came to the USA in 1858 and lied about his age in order to get into the army. He was attached to the 5th Cavalry, re-enlisted after his first tour and fought in the Civil War, mostly in New Mexico. Despite seven years as a soldier he got no higher in rank than corporal. On being mustered out of the army, he decided to try his luck as a rancher. He alternated between Mexico and New Mexico before eventually settling in Arizona in 1878.

Hughes must have expected a lot of trouble when he built his ranch house. It was constructed like a fortress, with thick, impenetrable adobe walls. Given the kind of company he often kept, his penchant for tight security was probably wise. Although Hughes remained neutral in the 'war' that followed the Earp–Clanton gunfight in Tombstone, many members of the Clanton–McLaury gang frequented his ranch. The likes of Johnny Ringo or 'Curly' Bill Brocius were regular visitors. By 1883 Hughes had left Arizona and returned to New Mexico, where he owned a couple of ranches. He died in Los Angeles in 1920.[10]

Denis Kearney: politician and racist

Denis Kearney was an Irish immigrant, having arrived in the USA in 1868 at the age of twenty-one. But this fact did not stop Kearney from calling for the expulsion from the USA of another group of immigrants: the Chinese. In a brief political career Kearney preached a gospel of bigotry and intolerance that is, sadly, not untypical of Irish attitudes to the economic underclass (be it Native American, African American or Chinese American) in the West.

Kearney was a self-taught man who ran a carting business in San Francisco when he became involved with and eventually leader of the California Workingmen's Party. Following anti-Chinese riots in the city in 1877, Kearney at first joined with a local Vigilance group to prevent further violence. But he quickly changed sides and became a champion of the rights of the unemployed, who saw the Chinese as a direct threat to their jobs. Chinese labour was considerably cheaper than that of other (often Irish) working-class San Franciscans. Kearney's main political slogan was simple and unvarnished – 'The Chinese must go.'

The Workingmen's Party (composed mainly of Irish and German immigrants) had a brief period of success in the late 1870s. During this time Kearney was repeatedly arrested for incitement to violence and repeatedly acquitted of all charges. Kearney's campaign was populist and quasi-collectivist in nature, in that it also had in its sights San Francisco's capitalist class. Employers were accused, with some justification, of fostering 'the introduction among the people of an alien class to compete with the intelligent labour of the land, regardless of all principles of humanity, progress and civilisation'.[11] Stripped of the florid language, what the Workingmen's Party was alleging was that the employers were using cheap Chinese labour to force down wages. It was, and remains, a familiar capitalist tactic. Kearney's approach to the problem was, and remains, a familiar populist response.

The Workingmen's Party had its day in San Francisco politics and it was a very short day indeed. By 1878, despite having aided in the election of a mayor sympathetic to its views, the Workingmen's Party returned to the obscurity from which it came and the politically inclined Irish began to drift into the arms of Democratic Party-machine politics. Kearney died in 1907.

Dan Kelly: outlaw

Nicknamed Yorky, Kelly might more appropriately have been called Corky, as he left Cork in 1881 at the age of twenty-two. He didn't last long in the West, coming to grief at the end of a hangman's noose within three years of his arrival. In December 1883 he was living in Clifton, Arizona when he joined a gang of outlaws who raided the nearby town of Bisbee. The raid was a shambolic exercise and ended in the deaths of a number of innocent Bisbee citizens. Kelly was suspected, along with two other members of the gang, of holding up a store. He made his escape northwards and avoided capture by any chasing lawmen when a vicious snowstorm hit the area.

But he then made the mistake of boarding a train, posing as a travelling hobo. He was caught, identified and brought to Tombstone to face trial. He insisted that he was innocent of any crime but was convicted and sentenced to hang in March 1884. Contemporary reports suggest that he confronted his fate with a certain bravado. 'I will walk uprightly,' he told a reporter a few days before his execution. He was nonchalant enough (reportedly) on the day of his execution to tell the hangman, 'Let her loose.' The executioner did just that and the Corkman's short and unsuccessful career as an outlaw came to a summary end.[12]

James Lee: hostler, miner and Indian killer

Lee is another undistinguished Irish member of the civilian population who enthusiastically assisted in the slaughter of Native Americans in the Southwest. He was a worthy successor to his compatriot James Kirker, though not nearly as prominent in the practice of genocide as the Antrim man. Lee was born in Derry in 1833 and emigrated to the USA after his teens. His first job in his adopted home of Arizona was as a stagecoach hostler with the Overland Mail Company. When that closed down in 1861 he took to mining and later began to operate a flour mill in Tucson.

In April 1871 he was involved in one of the worst atrocities in the Southwest: the Camp Grant Massacre. This slaughter was similar to the infamous Sand Creek Massacre of 1864 in Colorado. Camp Grant was a desert outpost established as a feeding station for reservation Apaches who had submitted to military rule. However, the Apache people it fed also became convenient scapegoats for Arizonans intent on revenge for the killing of whites by renegade Apaches. A force of whites, Mexicans and Papago Indians (traditional rivals of the Apache) assaulted the camp on 30 April. Not only did they kill between eighty and 150 Apache people, they also mutilated their bodies and raped a number of female survivors. One account tells of a ten-month-old child being shot twice and having its leg cut off. Those merely wounded by gunshot were finished off by Papago arrows. One of the leaders of the massacre referred to the day's work as 'that memorable and glorious morning ... when swift punishment was dealt out to these red-handed butchers'.[13]

Such was the barbarity of the attack that President Grant was forced, mainly by eastern opinion, to investigate the atrocity. Lee was among those arrested and charged with murder as a result of the investigation. Along with all the other accused, he was acquitted of all charges by a Tucson jury in December 1871. Three years later he ran as an independent candidate for sheriff of Pima County, Arizona, but was defeated by a single vote. Lee died of pneumonia in 1884.[14]

Jim Levy: gunfighter

Although most western shootouts did not accord with the Hollywood model (a face-to-face duel in Main Street), one exception involved Dublin-born Jim Levy in 1877 in Cheyenne, Wyoming. Levy had a certain amount of 'previous' before he gunned down Charlie Harrison in the future state capital. He first came to public attention in the vicious mining town of Pioche, in Lincoln County, Nevada, in 1873. He got involved in a gunfight with another Irish American, David Neagle (born in Boston of Irish parents), who shot him in the jaw.[15] Neagle went on to become a deputy US marshal in Tombstone at the time of the Earp–Clanton rivalry. Levy's career went in a different direction. Before quitting Pioche he was responsible for the death of another Irish miner, Mike Casey (the town, like Bodie in California, was a violent mining town with Irish-born labourers forming the majority of the population).

By 1877 Levy was a fully fledged gunfighter and had fetched up in Cheyenne. He was drinking in Bowlby's Gambling Saloon in the town when he became involved in an argument with another gunman, Charlie Harrison. Both must have been off duty at the time as they were without their side-arms. The argument was fierce enough for both men to race off and gather up their weapons. While they were doing this the other denizens of the saloon opened a book on the outcome of the forthcoming duel. Because Levy was unknown, having only recently arrived from Deadwood, Harrison, in his absence, became the overwhelming favourite. So it was a good day for the bookies because in the gunfight that followed the return of the two men the Dubliner killed his opponent.[16]

The gun battle took place near Dyer House in Cheyenne and Harrison made the classic mistake of blazing away with his pistol at the earliest opportunity. While he emptied his barrel, Levy bided his time, aimed into the smoke screen caused by Harrison's fusillade and shot Harrison dead.

Levy, who was of Jewish extraction, met his end in Tucson when he got on the wrong side of a local gambler named John Murphy. Murphy challenged the Dubliner to a duel in Mexico but didn't wait for the face-off and killed Levy on 3 June 1882, with the help of two friends, while the Irishman was unarmed. All three of Levy's killers were arrested but escaped from jail and were never caught.

Jerry Lonergan: soldier and gunshot victim

Jerry Lonergan's sole claim to fame is because of the origin of the bullet that passed through his kneecap on 17 July 1870. Lonergan was a Cork man who was born in the early 1840s. In 1867 he enlisted in the 7th Cavalry, following the lead of hundreds of other Irishmen. He secured his status as a moderately interesting footnote in the history of the Irish in the American West in a saloon in Hays City, Kansas on the night in question. There he, very unwisely, got involved in a dispute with James Butler Hickok, known to all and sundry simply as 'Wild Bill'. Lonergan was lucky – he only sustained his knee wound; his partner in the fight, one John Kite, was fatally wounded.

Lonergan did not have long to enjoy the notoriety of being a living victim of Wild Bill: he was discharged from the army in 1871 and, according to one report, was killed in 1872 in Kansas by 'a man named Kelly belonging to an infantry regiment'.[17]

James McLoughlin: railroad worker and farmer

You will not find the name of James McLoughlin in any historical work. His life was not particularly colourful or eventful, but it was typical of many Irish in the American West and it has been recorded by his family. Consequently, it is of interest in that it represents the story of so many ordinary, unspectacular Irishmen who ventured west in search of wealth or of mere employment. He was born in 1846 in Moate in County Westmeath. He came to the USA in 1864 and worked his way to Omaha, Nebraska, where the Union Pacific was starting to build the new continental railroad to the West. As the railroad came through Nebraska, he met Sarah Daly and when the railroad got as far as Cheyenne, Wyoming in 1876, he decided to go back to Nebraska and marry her. Sarah was just sixteen years old. By the time the track had got as far as Granite Canyon, Wyoming in 1885, Sarah had four children. A local homesteader who was relinquishing his rights had a two-room house on his land so James bought the improvements and started homesteading in 1886. He added on to the house to accommodate his family and his last son, Maurice Frederick, was born in the log house in 1894.

While McLoughlin continued to work for the railroad, the family raised potatoes and milked cows. They took their milk, butter and cream to Granite, four miles by horse and wagon, to put it on the train for Cheyenne. They also sold hay that was cut from a large natural meadow. They cut ice on a lake near them and stored it in a cellar for the summer – it helped preserve their dairy products. After helping to build the Ames monument in 1882, James McLoughlin abandoned labouring and returned to his Twin Mountain ranch. He died in 1926 and his wife Sarah followed him in 1937. Their youngest son, Maurice, stayed on the ranch and died there in 1964. More than forty years later the ranch is still in the hands of a fourth generation of the McLoughlin family.[18]

Patrick McLoughlin and Peter O'Riley: the men who lost the Comstock lode

All miners and prospectors dream of the motherlode – the endless seam of silver or gold that will curtail their days of panhandling and digging and enable them to eat off silver plates for the rest of their lives. Two Irishmen, Patrick McLoughlin and Peter O'Riley, found the mother of all motherlodes but didn't realise what they'd got and sold it before they found out. Today the Comstock lode in Nevada doesn't even bear their names, but rather the name of the man who swindled them out of a fortune.

It was gold they were looking for. The precious metal had been discovered in Nevada two years after being found in profusion in Cailfornia. The early finds were located in the valley of the Carson River close to the Sierra Nevada by a group of migrating Mormons. By the mid-fifties a new settlement, Johntown, had been established and it was from this base that the two Irishmen scoured and worked the hills around the area for gold. In June 1859 they finally struck it rich in a region known as Six Mile Canyon. Had they discovered unadulterated gold or silver, the story might have been different, but what they came across instead was something they had not seen before and whose value they did not comprehend.

Digging down, they hit a layer of black sulphuret of silver – a decomposed ore of silver filled with spangles of gold. The two men were dubious about what they were digging out of the ground. They thought they might have struck a workable and opulent seam of gold but they feared that they might equally be mining some form of 'fool's gold'.[19]

Enter Henry Comstock, nicknamed 'Old Pancake' because he never managed to find the time to bake bread and used his supplies of flour to make pancakes.[20] Comstock spotted straight away what the two Irishmen had and immediately did what he did best. He began talking. He managed to convince the two Irishmen that he owned the land on which they were digging and the water that they were using to process their strange ore. Unsure both about what exactly they had and now about their right to exploit it, McLaughlin and O'Riley agreed to cut Comstock and his partner in on the profits from their claim. Their shareholding was ultimately reduced to one-sixth each in what was to become the lucrative Ophir mine.

Word of the discovery got out very quickly and other miners moved rapidly to stake claims close to the McLaughlin–O'Riley site. Because Comstock became the most familiar and celebrated member of the 'partnership', the vast seam came to be called after him rather than after the two men who had actually discovered it.

Deprived of their opportunity to go down in western history by a fast-talking con man, the two Irishmen also missed out on the possibility of untold wealth. In September 1859 Patrick McLaughlin sold his one-sixth interest in the Ophir mine for $3,500. O'Riley held on to his share far longer and eventually realised just under $50,000 for it, a huge amount of money in the 1860s but a tiny fraction of what was eventually earned from this colossal motherlode.

Eugene McNamara: mysterious priest

Could the Irish have saved California for Catholic Mexico? Was there a genuine attempt to 'plant' parts of the Golden State with Irish colonies in the mid-nineteenth century? Or was 'Father' Eugene McNamara a con man employed by property speculators to dupe Mexico into making sweeping land grants in advance of the annexation of the territory?

McNamara makes a brief and an enigmatic appearance in western history in 1846. He arrived in California onboard a British ship, *Juno*, to negotiate with the Mexican governor of California for tracts of land near San Francisco, Santa Barbara and Monterey for Irish colonies of 1,000 families. The inducement for the Mexican government was to have been 'to put an obstacle in the way of further usurpations on the part of an irreligious and anti-Catholic nation' and to halt the relentless advance of 'the Methodist wolves'. We can assume he was not referring to Canada.

The Mexican administration was sufficiently impressed with the proposal to grant the land but the creation of 'old Ireland over here' was put on hold almost immediately with the effective seizure of California by irregular American forces taking advantage of the Mexican–American War.

The status of this apparently legitimate attempt at an Irish plantation is still a mystery. McNamara disappeared, never to be heard of again, and the new administration was having nothing to do with land grants made by the Mexican government. There is speculation that the priest, or even the 'priest', had been put up to negotiating the deal by a London-based property syndicate who had foreseen the inevitable annexation of California by the USA and who sought to make a cheap pre-emptive land deal in the hope that their title would be recognised by the invaders.

The fact that the entire enterprise collapsed may well have resulted in the avoidance of a damaging Irish–American War for the future ownership of Silicon Valley.[21]

William Mulholland: engineer and water thief

If you are a fan of the Roman Polanski film *Chinatown*, then you will be interested in the career of the real Hollis Mulwray/Noah Cross – Irishman William Mulholland. Born in Belfast in 1855 and brought up in Dublin, he left home at the age of fifteen to become a sailor. He reached New York in the early 1870s and decided to try and earn a living in the USA instead of at sea. In 1877 he headed west, settling first in San Francisco before trying his hand at mining in Arizona. While there he was hired to fight the Apache.

By 1878 he had arrived in the city that was to be his home for most of the next sixty years: Los Angeles. At that time it was a small, inconsequential town, far adrift of San Francisco in terms of size, prestige and potential. Mulholland's first job was as a ditch cleaner for a private water company. He was ambitious, however, and had begun to educate himself. Eight years later he was an engineer and when the city of Los Angeles took over the company he became head of the Department of Water and Power.

All the time the city of Los Angeles was growing. However, that expansion was ultimately limited by a lack of water. By the end of the nineteenth century Mulholland was looking 200 miles northward to the Owens River to rectify that situation. The Owens Valley was populated by small and medium-sized farmers and orange growers awaiting a state-funded irrigation scheme. By 1905, thanks to a combination of legitimate land purchases, bribery and political chicanery, Mulholland and his allies had acquired enough land in the valley to block the scheme and divert the water from the Owens River to Los Angeles.

This, however, is where the plot thickens and more closely parallels the Robert Towne script for *Chinatown*. Mulholland and his cronies had been buying up cheap land in the waterless San Fernando Valley and it was the engineer's intention to divert much of the Owens River into his new pension scheme and make dozens of his allies extremely rich in the process.

From 1905 to 1913 Mulholland's energies and organisational abilities, both of which were considerable, were devoted to the building of the Los Angeles Aqueduct across 200 miles of desert and mountain. It was an operation akin to the laying down of hundreds of miles of railroad track in the previous century. Its completion was a triumph for Mulholland and the beginnings of the Los Angeles we know today. As one of his biographers has put it, 'He transformed a land that could not support 250,000 souls into a flourishing oasis harbouring millions.'[22]

But the citizens of the Owens Valley were not happy and they began to show their animosity in vigorous ways. In August 1924 they dynamited the aqueduct and engaged in a series of acts of sabotage for the next six months in what became known as the Owens Valley War. During the course of this guerrilla campaign, Mulholland was heard to utter his regrets at the devastation of the orange growing in the valley, 'because now there are no longer enough trees to hang all the trouble-makers who live there'.[23]

Trouble flared up again in 1927 and Mulholland sent armed guards to the valley with orders to shoot to kill. Resistance ended, however, when the Owens Valley Bank collapsed and financially ruined Mulholland's main adversaries.

The Irish engineer's ultimate triumph was short-lived. Three years after the final end of the Owens Valley War, the St Francis Dam collapsed, unleashing fifteen billion gallons of water into Ventura County and killing 500 people. Mulholland, already a controversial figure, had supervised the building of the dam. He was blamed by an official inquiry for allowing the reservoir to fill too quickly and for ignoring indications that it was leaking. He was forced to resign. He died seven years later in 1935.[24]

Joseph Murphy: *wagon maker*

In almost every movie made about the American West there is at least one shot of a wagon. Most of those wagons, in reality, would have borne the insignia 'Murphy – St Louis', the mark of the man who designed them and who built many of them himself.

Joseph Murphy was born near Drogheda in 1805. At the age of twelve, accompanied by his nineteen-year-old aunt, he left Ireland for Newfoundland. From there the two were set to travel to St Louis to link up with three Irish brothers, the Hullens. However, by the time they got to Missouri the Hullens, a dissolute trio, had already left for New Orleans. Rather than attempt to follow them, Murphy sought work in St Louis. As luck would have it he was offered a job as an apprentice wagon maker in 1819.

His main job was the construction of the traditional Conestoga wagon that had been developed in Pennsylvania in the 1700s and had been used for nearly 100 years by migrant settlers. They were large enough to hold 1,000 pounds of cargo.

In 1839, however, with Murphy by now well established in his own business, circumstances began to change. The Mexican government, which owned much of the territory along what would become the Santa Fe Trail, placed a $500 tax on each wagonload of merchandise crossing their land. As a response to this economic threat to trade and migration, Murphy set about designing a wagon that would hold up to five times the load of a Conestoga wagon, thus reducing the tax liability of traders and travellers. The Mexican–American War of the mid-1840s eliminated the tax, but by that stage the Murphy 'prairie schooner' had already taken off and was the mode of transportation of choice of thousands of settlers and traders on the Santa Fe and Oregon Trails.[25]

John Nugent: newspaperman and duellist

Nugent was born in Galway in 1829 and came to America as a boy. He was educated in New Jersey and first began to work as a journalist in New York with the *Herald*. As their Washington correspondent, he befriended influential politicians such as Stephen Douglas and future president James Buchanan. Through a Buchanan leak he managed to get hold of the wording of the secret treaty that had ended the Mexican–American War. He was jailed for refusing to reveal his source but was released from prison by the secretary of state – James Buchanan.

His first excursion into the West was as part of a group led by a former Texas Ranger, Jack Jays. He wrote a highly colourful account of the trip. It included an excursion by Nugent into hostile Apache territory along the Rio Grande accompanied by Jack Gordon, a guide who was well respected by the Apache. Subsequently, when the army surveyed the route in advance of the building of a railroad, Nugent handed over his notes on the terrain and in return had a pass in southern Arizona named after him.

However, it is for his ownership and editorship of the San Francisco *Herald* that Nugent is best known. The paper was one of more than two dozen daily journals in the growing city when it was founded in 1850. Nugent was a particularly vitriolic and uncompromising writer with a highly independent frame of mind. In 1851, for example, despite his Irish Catholic background and his adherence to the Democratic Party, he lent his newspaper's support to the efforts of the San Francisco vigilantes (a largely Nativist, Republican organisation) to clean up the lawless Barbary Coast area of the city. Later he would oppose another of their violent populist campaigns.

His virulent writing style involved him in much personal animosity. Given the more muscular approach to affront in the nineteenth-century West, Nugent was called upon frequently to provide the opposition in a duel. Most of these resulted in non-fatal wounds for the quarrelsome Irishman. In 1852 a face-off at ten paces with an alderman resulted in a compound fracture to his left thigh. Even a separation of thirteen paces didn't seem to improve his luck. In 1853, in an encounter with yet another alderman at that distance, he received a compound fracture of the arm.

He gradually lost interest in the *Herald*, which quickly slid down the slopes of San Francisco into the bay and disappeared without trace in 1869. He turned his hand to law, so successfully that he pleaded at least one case before the US Supreme Court. Nugent died in 1880. In 1959 he was posthumously admitted into the California Journalism Hall of Fame.[27]

Cornelius O'Keefe: cattleman

Another Cork man, O'Keefe had an extremely eventful life. Born on 12 September 1827, the young O'Keefe was deported to Tasmania for his political activities by the British authorities in the early 1850s. However, he managed to make his escape and arrived in New York in 1853. (Up to this point his career bears a marked similarity to a famous Irishman who once used the name Colonel Cornelius O'Keefe as a pseudonym, prompting some doubts as to the veracity of the facts of O'Keefe's early life – see Thomas Francis Meagher in Reel Seven.) Realising that the West provided more opportunity to the newly arrived Irishman than the highly stratified society of the east coast, he shipped for California via Cape Horn in the late 1850s. After a short period as a labourer he settled in southwest Montana and became a highly progressive rancher. He farmed on irrigated land and imported the first threshing machine, reaper and mower into Montana, surviving many Indian attacks as he built up his landholding.

A large man with a violent temper (he once wrecked a court after disagreeing with a judge's verdict), he acquired the nickname the Baron and never quite shook off his Irish disrespect for authority. In the early 1860s a well-organised gang known (to themselves) as the Innocents, led by Henry Plummer, who also happened to be sheriff of Bannack, Montana, was terrorising Montana mining towns. Then an equally well-organised group of vigilantes began to make inroads into the Innocents' activities and lynch many of their number. One of the most notorious Innocent gangsters, Robert Zachary, in his flight from the vigilantes, sought and was granted temporary refuge on O'Keefe's ranch. When Zachary's pursuers caught up with him, O'Keefe refused to hand him over until he had given him breakfast. He argued to the members of the vigilance committee that 'you can't hang a man on an empty stomach'. Zachary was duly fed, tried and hanged expeditiously. (For the record, Plummer was later betrayed by one of his former henchmen and himself hanged.)

O'Keefe's act of civil disobedience didn't greatly damage his reputation in southwest Montana. He became Missoula County commissioner in 1872 and also served in the state legislature. He died of Bright's disease in 1883.[27]

William Owen 'Buckey' O'Neill: lawman and rough rider

Born in Ireland in 1860, O'Neill was an accomplished gambler who earned the nickname Buckey from his habit of 'bucking the tiger' in the game of faro. He first emerged as a printer in 1879 and then an editor, one of his more exotic publications being a livestock newspaper named *Hoof and Horn*. He became a probate judge in Yavapai County, Arizona in 1886 and subsequently ran successfully for election as sheriff in 1888. One of his most celebrated *coups* while in that position was his capture of four outlaws responsible for the robbery of the Atlantic and Pacific train at Canyon Diablo in Arizona in March 1889. O'Neill and his posse chased the four train robbers for 600 miles and succeeded in bringing them back to justice.

He stood twice for Congress in the 1890s but was defeated and on the outbreak of the Spanish–American War was appointed captain in the 1st US Volunteer Cavalry (the famous Rough Riders). He served in Cuba and was killed there by a sniper's bullet in Santiago. He was buried in Arlington National Cemetery in 1899. A statue erected to the memory of the Arizona Rough Riders in Prescott, Arizona in 1907 has come to be known as the 'Buckey O'Neill statue'.[28]

Thomas Mayne Reid: novelist

Born in 1818, a native of County Down and the son of a Presbyterian minister, Reid was an adventurer before he became a highly successful writer. He entered the USA via New Orleans and quickly became involved in the activities of hunters and fur traders. He fought in the Mexican–American War and was badly wounded at Chapultepec, where the Mexican defenders of the town included members of the famous San Patricio battalion, Catholic Irishmen fed up with Nativist anti-Catholicism who had switched sides to fight with Mexico.

After spending just over a decade in the USA, mostly in the West, he returned to Europe and began to harvest his American experience as a writer. Between 1848 and his death in 1883 he wrote more than seventy adventure novels and, ironically as an Irishman writing from Britain, played a huge part in the mythologising of the West, even amongst Americans. Theodore Roosevelt was an avid young fan of Reid's novels and the writer Charles Lummis said of him that 'Reid was the very first man who taught Americans the charm of the American West.'[29]

The thrust of his approach to the West can be gauged from the titles of some of his more famous novels, many of which did not appear in American editions until well after his death. *The Scalp Hunters: A Thrilling Tale of Adventure and Romance in Northern Mexico* (1899) and *The Rifle Rangers: A Thrilling Story of Daring Adventure and Hairbreath [sic] Escapes during the Mexican American War* are but two examples from the dozens available.

The Silver Kings: the inheritors of the Comstock lode

As far as Ireland is concerned, the sad story of the failure of Patrick McLaughlin and Peter O'Riley to capitalise on their discovery of what was to become known (bogusly) as the Comstock lode is mitigated by the fact that three Irishmen, John William Mackay, John G. Fair and William S. O'Brien, along with their Irish American partner James C. Flood, made the kind of fortunes out of the lode that the former pair might have made had they been less gullible.

By the time it was finally depleted around 1880, the Comstock had produced more than $500 million worth of silver and made multimillionaires of the so-called 'Silver Kings'. Flood and O'Brien had been the original instruments of amassing this wealth. Working together in a restaurant in San Francisco, both kept their ears open for mining stories. When they heard about the Comstock discovery they liked the sound of it enough to set off for Virginia City (then growing daily above the lode). With money provided by John Mackay and Jim Fair, they acquired, over a period of time, a number of highly profitable mines.

O'Brien opted out of the partnership early after becoming merely rich. The other three went on to become fabulously wealthy. Flood, born in New York of Irish parents, went on to establish himself as a well-heeled society figure on San Francisco's Nob Hill. Fair and Mackay, the two native-born Irishmen, were contrasting characters. Both made personal fortunes that amounted to around $50 million each from mining interests mainly located in Nevada, California, Montana and Utah.

Mackay had been born in Dublin in 1831 and emigrated to the USA in the mid-1840s. He first worked in New York as an apprentice shipbuilder but was part of the California stampede of the 1850s. Mackay was a prudent man who refused a percentage of his daily wages in exchange for stock in the mines in which he worked. When they boomed he made enough money to put down his pick and shovel and become a mining engineer and investor. His first big strike netted him $200,000 and prompted him to announce that this was enough money for any man: 'the man who wanted more than that was a fool'.[30]

Mackay, by dint of a devotion to getting his hands dirty, managed to retain the affection of his employees while he was actively involved in mining. It was said of him that 'he most thoroughly understands mining in all its branches as there is nothing required to be done in a mine that he has not done with his own hands'.[31] He was also a noted philanthropist, giving away millions anonymously to a variety of charities. He is said to have secretly paid a Virginia City grocer to supply provisions to any Nevada miner down on his luck.

Towards the end of his life he moved to New York, where even his enormous affluence did not guarantee social acceptance at the highest levels. Mackay found himself more comfortable in Europe, where he mixed with the likes of the Prince of Wales, who described him as 'the most unassuming American I have ever met'.[32] A patronising old-Yankee attitude often came through in newspaper articles about Mackay and his wife, Louise. In one case, where a journalist had alleged that Louise Mackay had once been a washerwoman in Virginia City and had then descended 'even lower than that', the sixty-year-old Mackay, still a formidable, bullish presence, sought out the writer and punched him.

James Fair, on the other hand, was probably the least popular and generous of the Silver Kings. Born in Belfast in 1831, he had emigrated to the USA with his family in 1843 and settled in Illinois. He moved to California as a forty-niner and stayed there until 1860 before forming the partnership with Mackay, Flood and O'Brien. From an early stage in his mining career he acquired a reputation for double-dealing, earning the nickname 'Slippery Jim'. With the help of his Comstock millions he was elected as a Democrat to the US Senate in 1881. He served one undistinguished term, rarely speaking in the chamber, and was not re-elected.

Fair's wealth did not bring him much personal happiness. In 1861 he had married an Irishwoman, Theresa Rooney, with whom he had four children. Sometime after the Comstock investment began to pay off, the couple went through a highly rancorous divorce. Fair was given custody of one of the four children, his namesake, James, who was so unhappy living with his father that he committed suicide. He so alienated the rest of his family (and most of his friends) that in his last years he lived alone in a San Francisco hotel, solitary and embittered.

Michael and Pat Sughrue: lawmen

The Sughrues (or Sugrues) were Kerry-born twins (1844) who became Kansas cow-town lawmen. They were contemporaries of Wyatt Earp and Bat Masterson when both were operating in Dodge City. In fact, Pat Sughrue, during his election campaign in 1883 for the position of sheriff of Ford County (Dodge was the county seat), had to assure voters that, were he to be elected, he would not deputise Masterson, a previous incumbent. The future sportswriter had been booted out by the very same voters of the Kansan city in the election of 1879. Sughrue was careful to add that the former sheriff would be 'fully competent and acceptable' were it not for the fact that, since his defeat in 1879, he had become a resident of Denver. On polling day Masterson and Earp (now resident in Tombstone) both showed up in town. Their activities on the day may have had something to do with the electoral success of Sughrue.[33]

Sughrue served for four years. His most famous case was that of 'Mysterious' Dave Mather (or Mathers or Matthews). It was, in fact, two cases. Mather, a former law officer himself, was first accused of shooting dead Assistant Marshal Thomas Nixon. The two may have fallen out over a woman. Sughrue was forced to pursue Mather to Fort Worth and arrest him there. Mather was subsequently acquitted, only to be rearrested a short time later for another killing, this time after a saloon shooting. The charmed Mather, supposedly a descendant of the New England seventeenth-century writer Cotton Mather, never even came to trial for the second murder.

During Sughrue's tenure as sheriff, the nature of the job changed considerably. The town itself became less of a cow town when its role as a trail-driving destination ceased in the late 1880s. In addition, the state imposed a prohibition on the sale of alcohol that reduced the amount of violence in the town. Dodge City began its slow progress towards middle-class respectability. It was a story that would be replicated in many of the other roisterous cow towns.

Meanwhile, Pat Sughrue's twin, Michael, who briefly served under him in Dodge, had been making waves of his own. As one of his tasks, Michael Sughrue was sent to the town of Ashland to assist in a disturbance that had led to the deaths of two townspeople. Mike Sughrue managed to arrest one of the killers, Joe Mitchell, and then headed out of town in pursuit of Mitchell's accomplice, whom he never managed to capture. Unfortunately, in Mike's absence Lynch Law prevailed and Mitchell was taken out and hanged by townspeople.

Mike Sughrue's actions in neutralising the killers of two residents of Ashland led to his being offered and accepting the position of town marshal. He served as marshal and local sheriff for a total of seven years. He died in Ashland in 1900. His twin followed him six years later.[34]

The Sullivan ranch

Another unspectacular but typical Irish couple in the West, William Cleary Sullivan and Nora O'Connor Sullivan, along with her cousin Nora Buckley, started the Sullivan ranch in Converse County, Wyoming, in 1886 or 1888. William Sullivan was born in Kerry in 1848. He came to the US in 1875 and to Cheyenne, Wyoming in 1876. There he homesteaded in Granite Canyon. Nora was also born in Ireland, working in Washington, DC before coming to Wyoming. The couple were married in Cheyenne in 1886. They moved to Converse County and wintered south of Glenrock before moving to Spring Creek, where they bought and homesteaded land in 1890. Mrs Sullivan bought 2,100 acres of desert land from the government for 25 cents an acre; Nora Buckley filed on her homestead paying $3 for 159 acres. In 1891 William Sullivan built a ditch and got water rights for forty acres. He was responsible for putting many acres of land under irrigation both on Spring Creek and LaPerel Creek. They lived on Spring Creek until about 1900, when they had acquired land on LaPerel. The land is still with the Sullivan family and today they raise Hereford cattle.[35]

CLOSING CREDITS

ACKNOWLEDGEMENTS

I suppose I should start by thanking amazon.com and abebooks.com. This kind of book wouldn't have been possible until they arrived on the scene. They never let me down. Neither did all the mad enthusiasts who maintain hundreds of entertaining websites on a variety of western subjects. Entertaining, but not always totally reliable, of course.

It's probably too late to enter a caveat at this stage, but it's distinctly possible that you will find quite different accounts elsewhere of the lives of some of the characters you have just met. Sometimes I had to choose between conflicting sets of facts. I hope no one gets too offended with some of the choices I've made.

When I started out on this venture I was fortunate enough to come across a fellow obsessive at the very outset. I owe a lot to Eddie Brennan, who provided me with books, maps and photographs of his own. Quite a number of the characters who have made it into this volume did so after a chat with Eddie that began with the words 'Have you come across ... yet?' My thanks also to Pat McCartan for some loans from his extensive book collection.

Also of great help to me in getting this project underway was my good friend Professor Elaine Tyler May of Minnesota who, over the years, has sent me some intriguing material to follow up. Equally valuable material was supplied by my RTÉ colleague Brian Lynch, who allowed me to benefit from his research into the life of Paul Kane. Writer Joseph O'Connor directed me towards the truly hideous Heidi Gleim and unwittingly prompted me to rip off a wonderful idea of Montana historian Dave Walter that led to the RTÉ/National Museum *Speaking Ill of the Dead* conference in March of this year. My thanks are also due to Dave for his vetting of the Sir St George Gore extract. Sadly, Dave died while this book was being proofread.

My trip to Wyoming was ridiculously short and would have been far less useful had I not been accompanied by my favourite Washingtonian, Stacey Jones, who, in a frenzied couple of hours in the Buffalo Bill Historical Centre in Cody, must have photocopied herself into a state of temporary blindness. Thanks also to this former University of Washington women's cox for a great day at the Little Bighorn, the product of which did not make it into this volume. Next time! That trip was also made more pleasant and effective by the hospitality of the affable former governor of the state, Mike Sullivan, and his highly entertaining and hugely helpful wife, Jane.

During the writing of this book I was very happy to make the acquaintance (by mail) of Cathleen O'Neill Gear, whose work on Thomas Fitzpatrick offered me a short cut into the life of a formidable man and who has kindly allowed me to reproduce material collated by her during her tenure as Wyoming State Historian.

My gratitude is due also to Ronan Gallagher, who was in at the conception and the birth of this project, and to Edwin Higel and Deirdre Nolan of New Island, who had faith that I hope will prove to have been justified.

Thanks to my partner Dr Nerys Williams, who has patiently watched and waited while I have crossed the prairie in a Murphy wagon, descended mines in Montana, shot rapids on the Yellowstone and done all sorts of things in my imagination that I never would have been able to do in real life.

Thanks also to my kids (Amber, Rory, Lara and Ross) for watching westerns with me – way above and beyond the call of duty for their generation.

Above all, my heart goes out to all those brave Irish souls who headed west, some into totally unknown and uncharted territory, in pursuit of the decent life and decent living denied them at home in Ireland and in other parts of the USA. There were thousands of them and most of their lives were unrecorded and quietly heroic.

NOTES

PRE-CREDIT SEQUENCE

[1] Ed Buscombe (ed.), *The BFI Companion to the Western* (London, 1991), p. 350.

[2] Patricia Limerick, *The Legacy of Conquest: The Unbroken Past of the American West* (New York, 1987), p. 54.

REEL ONE – INTRODUCTION OR HOW THE IRISH REALLY WON THE WEST

[1] David Levinthal, artist, Salzburg Seminar, 1993.

[2] Timothy J. Sarbaugh and James P. Walsh (eds), *The Irish in the West* (Kansas, 1992), p. 5.

[3] David Emmons, *The Butte Irish: Class and Ethnicity in an American Mining Town 1875–1925* (Chicago, 1989), p. 9.

[4] The Know Nothings were a Nativist political alliance opposed to most types of immigration.

[5] Frederick Jackson Turner, 'The Significance of the Frontier in American

History', in *Rereading Frederick Jackson Turner*, John Mack Farragher (ed.) (New York, 1994), p. 47.

6 Michael C. O'Laughlin, 'Irish Genealogical Foundation', in *Irish Settlers on the American Frontier* (Missouri, 1984), p. 3.

7 Sarbaugh and Walsh, p. 6.

8 Ibid.

9 Emmons, p. 8.

10 Mark Wyman, *Immigrants in the Valley: Irish, Germans and Americans in the Upper Mississippi Country 1830–1860* (Chicago, 1984), p. 210.

11 Wyman, p. 231.

12 R.A. Burchaell, *The San Francisco Irish* (Manchester, 1979), p. 181.

13 James P. Walsh, 'The Irish in the New America: Way Out West', in *America and Ireland 1776–1976: The American Identity and the Irish Connection: The Proceedings of the United States Bicentennial Conference of Cumann Merriman, Ennis, August 1976* (London, 1976), p. 173.

14 Walsh, p. 174.

REEL TWO – MOUNTAIN MEN: IRISH PIONEERS OF THE FUR TRADE

1 Ken Burns and Dayton Duncan, *Lewis and Clark: The Journey of the Corps of Discovery* (London, 1998), p. 15.

2 Robert V. Hine and John Mack Farragher, *The American West: A New Interpretive History* (Yale, 2000), p. 137.

3 Hine and Farragher, p. 146.

4 Ross Cox, *The Columbia River* (Oklahoma, 1980), p. xxxi.

5 Ibid., p. 70.

6 Ibid., p. 70.

7 Ibid., p. 94.

8 Ibid., p. 103.

9 Ibid., pp. 105–6.

10 Ross Cox, *Adventures on the Columbia River* (New York, 2004), p. 96.

11 George Bird Grinnell, *Trails of the Pathfinders* (New York, 1913), p. 329.

12 Geoffrey C. Ward, *The West: An Illustrated History* (London, 1996), p. 56.

13 Ibid., p. 57.

14 Winfred Blevins, *Give Your Heart to the Hawks* (New York, 2005), p. 50.

15 Leroy R. Hafen, *Broken Hand: The Life of Thomas Fitzpatrick, Mountain Man, Guide and Indian Agent* (Lincoln/London, 1981), p. 1.

16 Ibid., p. 34.

17 John Niehardt, *The Splendid Wayfaring* (Lincoln, 1948), pp. 145–6.

18 Hafen, *Broken Hand*, p. 37.

19 Hiram Chittenden, *Fur Trade of the Far West* (Nebraska, 1986), p. 40.

20 Hafen, *Broken Hand*, p. 19.

21 Blevins, p. 171.

22 http://www.xmission.com/-drudy/cg.

23 Leroy R. Hafen (ed.), *French Fur Traders and Voyageurs in the American West* (Nebraska, 1997), p. 161.

24 Bernard de Voto, *Across the Wide Missouri* (Boston, 1947), p. 12.

25 Leroy R. Hafen (ed.), *Mountain Men and Fur Traders of the Far West* (Lincoln, 1982), p. 332. The article on Drips is by Harvey L. Carter, who describes Drips' Irish birth as being 'according to a family tradition'.

26 Stanley Vestal, *Jim Bridger, Mountain Man* (Nebraska, 1970), p. 111.

27 Washington Irving, *The Adventures of Captain Bonneville*, Chapter 4, http://www.xmission.com/-drudy/cg.

28 De Voto, pp. 83–4.

29 Chittenden, p. 304.

30 Vestal, p. 124.

31 Blevins, *Dictionary of the American West* (New York, 1993), p. 226.

REEL THREE – THE DONNER PARTY: CANNIBALISM ON THE WESTERN TRAIL

1 Virgina Reed Murphy, *Across the Plains in the Donner Party*, Karen Zeinert (ed.) (New Haven, 1996), p. x.

2 Ibid., p. 22 (Letter of James Reed to his brother, 16 June 1846).

3 Gwen Moffat, *Hard Road West* (London, 1981), p. 35.

4 George R. Stewart, *Ordeal by Hunger: The Story of the Donner Party* (Boston/New York, 1988), pp. 14–15.

5 Dale Morgan, *Overland in 1846: Diaries and Letters of the California–Oregon Trail* (Nebraska, 1963), p. 247.

6 Kristin Johnson (ed.), *Unfortunate Emigrants: Narratives of the Donner Party* (Utah, 1996), p. 130.

7 Murphy, pp. 9–10.

8 Ibid., pp. 11–12.

9 Stewart, p. 20.

10 Murphy, p. 29.

11 Ibid., pp. 33–5.

12 Ibid., p. 34.

13 Joseph A. King, *Winter of Entrapment: A New Look at the Donner Party* (Lafayette, California, 1998), p. 19.

14 Murphy, p. 37.

15 Ibid., pp. 42–3.

16 Ibid., p. 49.

17 Ibid., pp. 50–1.

18 Kristin Johnson, p. 191.

19 Ibid., p. 38.

[20] Ibid., p. 39.
[21] Murphy, p. 55.
[22] Ibid., p. 72.
[23] Ibid.
[24] Kristin Johnson, p. 229.
[25] Stewart, p. 325.
[26] Murphy, p. 72.
[27] Ibid., p. 74.
[28] Stewart, p. 332.
[29] Murphy, p. 77.
[30] King, p. 86.
[31] Ibid., p. 91.
[32] Morgan, p. 322.
[33] Kristin Johnson, p. 230.
[34] Ibid., p. 90.
[35] Ibid., p. 91.
[36] Ibid., p. 199.
[37] King, p. 110.
[38] Kristin Johnson, p. 115.
[39] Ibid., p. 172.

REEL FOUR – INDIAN AGENT: THE LATER CAREER OF THOMAS FITZPATRICK

[1] Leroy R. Hafen, *Broken Hand: The Life of Thomas Fitzpatrick, Mountain Man, Guide and Indian Agent* (Lincoln/London, 1981), p. 173.
[2] Ibid., p. 175.
[3] Ibid., p. 217.
[4] Fitzpatrick to Thomas Harvey, Superintendent of Indian Affairs, 18 September 1847, collection of Cathleen O'Neill Gear, p. 92.
[5] Ibid., pp. 102–3.
[6] Fitzpatrick to Harvey, 19 October 1847, Gear, p. 124.
[7] Fitzpatrick to Harvey, 18 December 1847, Gear, p. 146.
[8] Fitzpatrick to Lieutenant Colonel William Gilpin, 10 February 1848, Gear, p. 160.
[9] Fitzpatrick to Harvey, 18 December 1847, Gear, p. 148.
[10] Fitzpatrick to Harvey, 6 October 1848, Gear, p. 186.
[11] Fitzpatrick to D.D. Mitchell, Superintendent of Indian Affairs, 22 May 1849, Gear, p. 193.
[12] Hafen, *Broken Hand*, p. 268.
[13] Ibid., p. 271.
[14] Fitzpatrick to Mitchell, 24 September 1850, Gear, p. 225.
[15] Hafen, *Broken Hand*, p. 280.

[16] Fitzpatrick to A. Cumming, Superintendent of Indian Affairs, 19 November 1853, Gear, pp. 289–90.

[17] Hafen, *Broken Hand*, p. 321.

REEL FIVE – TOFFS: IRISH ARISTOCRATS WEST OF THE MISSISSIPPI

[1] Jack Roberts, *The Amazing Adventures of Lord Gore: A True Saga from the Old West* (Utah, 1977), p. 11.

[2] Barry Johnson, *The Life of St George Gore* (London, 1997), p. 13.

[3] David Walter, 'The Unsaintly Sir St. George Gore' in *Speaking Ill of the Dead* (Connecticut, 2000), p. 8.

[4] Barry Johnson, p. 33.

[5] Ibid., p. 35.

[6] J. Cecil Alter, *James Bridger: A Historical Narrative* (Salt Lake City, 1925), p. 267.

[7] R.B. Marcy, *Thirty Years of Army Life on the Border* (New York, 1866), p. 402.

[8] Ibid., pp. 401–2.

[9] Hiram Chittenden, *The American Fur Trade of the Far West* (Nebraska, 1986), p. 256.

[10] Stanley Vestal, *Jim Bridger, Mountain Man* (Nebraska, 1970), p. 195.

[11] Ibid., p. 191.

[12] Barry Johnson, p. 41.

[13] Ibid., p. 40.

[14] Ibid., p. 42.

[15] Marcy, p. 403.

[16] Barry Johnson, p. 46.

[17] Marcy, p. 403.

[18] Vestal, p. 193.

[19] Chittenden, p. 386.

[20] This is Barry Johnson's account of the row. The late David Walter believed that the dispute was actually with Culbertson's factor at Fort Union, James Kipp, a view supported by Jack Roberts in his book.

[21] Barry Johnson, p. 47.

[22] Ibid., p. 50.

[23] Ibid.

[24] Marcy, p. 402.

[25] Mark Brown, *The Plainsmen of the Yellowstone* (New York, 1969), p. 108.

[26] Barry Johnson, p. 50.

[27] Marcy, pp. 402–3.

[28] H. Montgomery Hyde, *Oscar Wilde: A Biography* (London, 1976), p. 50.

[29] Ibid., p. 51

[30] Richard Ellman, *Oscar Wilde* (London, 1987), p. 151.

[31] Hyde, p. 51.

[32] Mervyn Holland and Rupert Hart-Davis, *The Complete Letters of Oscar Wilde* (London, 2000), p. 123.

[33] Dee Brown, *Wondrous Times on the Frontier* (London, 1994), p. 54.

[34] Ellman, p. 186.

[35] Philippe Julian, *Oscar Wilde* (London, 1969), p. 100.

[36] Oscar Wilde, *Impressions of America* (Sunderland, 1906), pp. 26–7.

[37] Ibid., pp. 28–9.

[38] Gary Schmidgall, *The Stranger Wilde* (London, 1994), p. 378.

[39] Julian, p. 103.

[40] Grubstaking was the practice of subsidising a prospector until he made a successful strike.

[41] Virginia Hopkins, *Pioneers of the Old West* (London, 1988), pp. 66–70.

[42] Ibid., p. 70.

[43] Wilde, pp. 30–1.

[44] Ibid., p. 31.

[45] Ibid., pp. 31–2.

[46] Brown, p. 57.

[47] Rupert Hart-Davis, *The Letters of Oscar Wilde* (London, 1962), pp. 111–14.

[48] Brown, p. 57.

[49] Oscar Wilde, *Decorative Art in America* (London, 1894), pp. 8–9.

[50] Wilde, *Impressions of America*, p. 33.

[51] Brown, p. 58.

[52] Hyde, p. 71.

[53] Schmidgall, p. 377.

[54] Brown, p. 58.

[55] Trevor West, *Horace Plunkett: Co-operation and Politics, an Irish Biography* (Bucks, 1986), p. 7.

[56] Lawrence M. Woods, *British Gentlemen in the Wild West* (London, 1990), p. 2.

[57] West, p. 12.

[58] Woods, *British Gentlemen in the Wild West*, pp. 77–8.

[59] Ibid., p. 95.

[60] L. Milton Woods, *Moreton Frewen's Western Adventures* (Wyoming, 1986), p. 171.

[61] Margaret Digby, *Horace Plunkett: An Anglo-American Irishman* (Oxford, 1949), p. 35.

[62] Woods, *Moreton Frewen's Western Adventures*, p. 178.

[63] Ibid., p. 180.

[64] Ibid., p. 199.

[65] West, p. 14.

[66] Digby, p. 37.

[67] West, p. 14.

[68] Ibid., p. 231.
[69] Frank Harris, *My Life and Loves* (London, 1964), p. 96.
[70] Ibid., p. 97.
[71] Ibid., p. 100.
[72] Ibid., p. 99.
[73] Ibid., p. 103.
[74] Ibid., p. 117.
[75] Ibid., p. 119.
[76] Lord Dunraven, *Past Times and Pastimes* (London, 1922), p. 65.
[77] Ibid., p. 72.
[78] Ibid., p. 74.
[79] Denis McLoughlin, *Wild and Wooly: An Encyclopedia of the Old West* (New York, 1975), p. 508.
[80] Dunraven, p. 86.
[81] Ibid., p. 91.
[82] Ibid., p. 122.
[83] Ibid., p. 99.

REEL SIX – NOT SO GENTLE TAMERS: IRISH WOMEN STAKE THEIR CLAIM

[1] Ide O'Carroll, *Models for Movers: Irish Women's Emigration to America* (Dublin, 1990), p. 15.
[2] Don Chaput, *Nellie Cashman and the North American Mining Frontier* (Arizona, 1995), p. 3.
[3] Hasia Diner, *Erin's Daughters in America* (Baltimore, 1983), p. xvi.
[4] Melanie Mayer and Robert DeArmond, *Staking Her Claim: the Life of Belinda Mulrooney, Klondike and Alaska Entrepreneur* (Ohio, 2000), p. 19.
[5] Chaput, p. 23.
[6] Anne Seagraves, *High Spirited Women of the West* (Idaho, 1992), p. 124.
[7] Chaput, p. 27.
[8] Ibid., p. 29.
[9] Ibid., p. 52.
[10] Ibid., p. 63.
[11] Seagraves, p. 126. Both stories come from what is a colourful but not totally reliable account of Cashman's life.
[12] Chaput, p. 92.
[13] Ibid., p. 102.
[14] Ibid., p. 128.
[15] Much of the material on Belinda Mulrooney comes from the Mayer and DeArmond biography *Staking Her Claim*, cited above.
[16] Chaput, p. 105.
[17] Mayer and DeArmond, p. 153.
[18] Ibid., p. 175.

[19] Roger McGrath, from an article in *The American Irish* (New York, 1987), pp. 79–82.

[19] Anne Seagraves, *Soiled Doves: Prostitution in the Early West* (Idaho, 1994), p. ix.

[20] Patricia Limerick, *The Legacy of Conquest: The Unbroken Past of the American West* (New York, 1987), p. 64.

[21] Chaput, p. 138.

[22] Diner, p. 117.

[23] Roger McGrath, *Gunfighters, Highwaymen and Vigilantes* (Berkeley, 1984), p. 149.

[24] Robert V. Hine and John Mack Farragher, *The American West: A New Interpretive History* (Yale, 2000), p. 265.

[25] All figures from McGrath.

[26] David Emmons, *The Butte Irish: Class and Ethnicity in an American Mining Town* (Chicago, 1989), p. 85.

[27] Dee Brown, *The Gentle Tamers* (Nebraska, 1958), p.171.

[28] Seagraves, *Soiled Doves*, p. 33.

[29] James Relfe Sprigg to Elizabeth Linn, 5 January 1853, Lewis Linn Papers, Missouri Historical Society.

[30] Denis McLoughlin, *Wild and Wooly: An Encyclopedia of the Old West* (New York, 1975), p. 357.

[31] Patricia Cronin Marcello, *No Place for a Woman*, www.malakoff.com.

[32] George McMinn, *The Theatre of the Golden Era in California* (Idaho, 1941), p. 361.

[33] *Helena Daily Independent*, 26 October 1899.

[34] Ibid.

[35] Information from Seagrave, *Soiled Doves*, and Deborah Mellon, *The Legend of Molly b'Dam* (Idaho, 1989).

[36] Seagraves, *Soiled Doves*, p. 109.

[37] Ibid., p. 111.

[38] All the information on Mary Gleim is culled from Jodie Foley, 'Missoula's Murderous Madam: The Life of Mary Gleim', in Dave Walter (ed.), *Speaking Ill of the Dead* (Connecticut, 2003).

REEL SEVEN – HEROES AND VILLAINS: THE IRISH GOOD, BAD AND DISTINCTLY UGLY

[1] www.donegallibrary.ie.

[2] Ibid.

[3] J. Evitts Haley, *Charles Goodnight: Cowman and Plainsman* (Oklahoma, 1949), p. 300.

[4] Ibid., p. 301.

[5] William Cochran McGaw, *Savage Scene: The Life and Times of Mountain Man Jim Kirker* (New Mexico, 1972), p. 17. Most of the material on Kirker

has been culled from this work and from a number of websites devoted to Kirker.

[6] William R. Hunt, *Whiskey Peddler: Johnny Healy, North Frontier Trader* (Montana, 1993), p. 48. The material on Healy comes from this book and from a series of newspaper articles in the *Southern Star*, February–March 1993.

[7] Ibid., p. 51.

[8] Ibid., p. 76.

[9] Ibid., p. 85.

[10] Ibid., p. 90.

[11] Ibid., p. 95.

[12] Ibid., p. 109.

[13] Paul Kane, *Wanderings of an Artist among the Indians of North America* (Toronto, 1925 – original publication 1859), preface, p. xii.

[14] Ibid.

[15] Brian Lynch, *The Landscape of Vision, Text and Value: The Case of Paul Kane and Nicholas Point S.J.*, paper read at the Association of Art Historians Sixteenth Annual Conference, Trinity College Dublin, 26 March 1990, p. 4.

[16] Robert V. Hine and John Mack Farragher, *The American West: A New Interpretive History* (Yale, 2000), p. 185.

[17] CBC TV documentary.

[18] Ibid.

[19] Kane.

[20] Ibid., chapter XII.

[21] Bill O'Neal, *The Pimlico Encyclopedia of Western Gunfighters* (London, 1998), p. 7. O'Neal's definition of a gunfighter is one who has, verifiably, taken part in at least two firefights.

[22] Jay Robert Nash, *Encyclopedia of Western Lawmen and Outlaws* (New York, 1994), p. 231.

[23] Nyle H. Miller and Joseph W. Snell, *Great Gunfighters of the Kansas Cowtowns* (Nebraska, 1967), p. 345.

[24] Ibid.

[25] Ibid., p. 354.

[26] Ibid., p. 358.

[27] Patricia Limerick, *The Legacy of Conquest: The Unbroken Past of the American West* (New York, 1987), p. 80.

[28] Thomas Keneally, *The Great Shame* (London, 1998), p. 444.

[29] Ibid., p. 450.

[30] Hunt, p. 81.

[31] Keneally, p. 464.

[32] Ibid., p. 415.

[33] Hunt, p. 81.

[34] *The Irish Times*, 8 May 1973.

[35] All references to Strobridge as an Irishman come with a health warning. My principal source for this cameo is Stephen Ambrose's account of the construction of the transcontinental railroad, *Nothing Like It in the World*. This volume has been attacked for a number of inaccuracies by a descendant of Strobridge, Edson Strobridge, in an article (available on the web) 'The Sins of Stephen Ambrose'. However, Edson Strobridge does not challenge Ambrose's contention that James Harvey Strobridge was Irish.

[36] Geoffrey C. Ward, *The West: An Illustrated History* (London, 1996), p. 220.

[37] Stephen Ambrose, *Nothing Like It In The World: The Men Who Built the Transcontinental Railroad 1863–1869* (New York, 2000), p. 120.

[38] Ibid., p. 164.

[39] Ibid., p. 350.

[40] Ibid., p. 378.

Reel Eight – The Lincoln County War: Murphy, Dolan, Riley, Brady and Billy the Kid

[1] Maurice G. Fulton, *History of the Lincoln County War* (Tucson, 1997), p. 33.

[2] Ed Buscombe (ed.), *The BFI Companion to the Western* (London, 1991), p. 87.

[3] Frederick Nolan, *The Lincoln County War: A Documentary History* (Oklahoma, 1992), p. 39.

[4] Ibid., p. 43.

[5] Ibid., p. 494.

[6] William A. Keleher, *Violence in Lincoln County* (New Mexico, 1957), p. 15.

[7] Ibid., p. 108.

[8] Nolan, p. 73.

[9] Fulton, p. 71.

[10] Patrick F. Garret, *The Authentic Life of Billy the Kid* (Oklahoma, 1954), p. 60.

[11] Nolan, p. 98.

[12] Ibid., p. 127.

[13] Ibid., p. 140.

[14] Ibid., p. 146.

[15] Ibid., p. 127.

[16] Fulton, p. 110.

[17] Donald R. Lavash, *Sheriff William Brady: Tragic Hero of the Lincoln County War* (Santa Fe, 1986), p. 76.

[18] Nolan, p. 203.

[19] Fulton, p. 129.

[20] Keleher, p. 100.

[21] Nolan, p. 244.

[22] Garrett, pp. 60–1.

[23] Keleher, p. 115.
[24] Fulton, p. 200.
[25] Nolan, pp. 439–40.

Reel Nine – Cameos: Pioneers, Plutocrats, Popinjays and Populists

[1] Dan L. Thrapp, *Encyclopedia of Frontier Biography* (California, 1988), p. 153.
[2] Denis McLoughlin, *Wild and Wooly: An Encyclopedia of the Old West* (New York, 1975), pp. 71 and 379; Thrapp, p. 199.
[3] Thrapp, pp. 296–7.
[4] Patricia Condon Johnston, *Minnnesota's Irish* (Minnesota, 1984), p.53.
[5] John Wallace Crawford, *The Poet Scout: A Book of Song and Story* (New York, 1886), p. 15.
[6] Ibid., pp. 74–5.
[7] Thrapp, p. 359.
[8] www.bitterroot.net.
[9] Thrapp, p. 604.
[10] Thrapp, p. 691.
[11] R.A. Burchell, *The San Francisco Irish 1848–1880* (Manchester, 1979), p. 153.
[12] Jay Robert Nash, *Encyclopedia of Western Lawmen and Outlaws* (New York, 1994), p. 197.
[13] Robert M. Utley and Wilcomb E. Washburn, *The American Heritage History of the Indian Wars* (New York, 1992), p. 246.
[14] Thrapp, p. 831.
[15] Don Chaput, *Nellie Cashman and the North American Mining Frontier* (Arizona, 1995), p. 10.
[16] Denis McLoughlin, *Wild and Wooly: An Encyclopedia of the Old West* (New York, 1975), p. 299.
[17] Thrapp, p. 869.
[18] Exhibit in Wyoming Pioneer Memorial Museum, Douglas, Wyoming.
[19] Dan De Quille, *The Big Bonanza* (London, 1969), p. 24.
[20] McLoughlin, p. 109.
[21] Thrapp, p. 922.
[22] Margaret Leslie Davis, *Rivers in the Desert: William Mulholland and the Inventing of Los Angeles* (New York, 1993), p. 3.
[23] www.pbs.org/weta/thewest/wpages/wpgs400/w4mulhol.
[24] Many of the accusations made against Mulholland are disputed in Catherine Mulholland, *William Mulholland and the Rise of Los Angeles* (Berkeley, 2000), but it is worth bearing in mind that the author is Mulholland's granddaughter.
[25] Michael C. O'Laughlin, *Irish Settlers on the American Frontier* (Missouri, 1984), p. 118.

[26] Thrapp, pp. 1065–6.

[27] Ibid., p. 1077.

[28] Ibid., p. 1085.

[29] Ibid., p. 1203.

[30] Stephen Birmingham, *Real Lace: America's Irish Rich* (New York, 1973), p. 138.

[31] De Quille, p. 400.

[32] Birmingham, p. 139.

[33] Nyle H. Miller and Joseph W. Snell, *Great Gunfighters of the Kansas Cowtowns* (Nebraska, 1967), p. 293.

[34] Ibid., p. 1387.

[35] Exhibit in Wyoming Pioneer Memorial Museum, Douglas, Wyoming.

BIBLIOGRAPHY

Alter, J. Cecil, *James Bridger: A Historical Narrative* (Salt Lake City, 1925).

Ambrose, Stephen, *Nothing Like It in the World: The Men Who Built the Transcontinental Railroad 1863–1869* (New York, 2000).

Birmingham, Stephen, *Real Lace: America's Irish Rich* (New York, 1973).

Blevins, Winfred, *Give Your Heart to the Hawks* (New York, 1973).

Brown, Dee, *The Gentle Tamers* (Nebraska, 1958).

——————— *Wondrous Times on the Frontier* (London, 1994).

Burchaell, R. A., *The San Francisco Irish* (Manchester, 1979).

Burns, Ken and Dayton, Duncan, *Lewis and Clark: The Journey of the Corps of Discovery* (London, 1998).

Buscombe, Ed (ed.), *The BFI Companion to the Western* (London, 1991).

Chaput, Don, *Nellie Cashman and the North American Mining Frontier* (Arizona, 1995).

Chittenden, Hiram, *Fur Trade of the Far West* (Nebraska, 1986).

Condon Johnston, Patricia, *Minnnesota's Irish* (Minnesota, 1984).

Cox, Ross, *The Columbia River* (Oklahoma, 1980).

Crawford, John Wallace, *The Poet Scout: A Book of Song and Story* (New York, 1886).

Davis, Margaret Leslie, *Rivers in the Desert: William Mulholland and the Inventing of Los Angeles* (New York, 1993).

De Quille, Dan, *The Big Bonanza* (London, 1969).

De Voto, Bernard, *Across the Wide Missouri* (Boston, 1947).

Digby, Margaret, *Horace Plunkett: An Anglo-American Irishman* (Oxford, 1949).

Diner, Hasia, *Erin's Daughters in America* (Baltimore, 1983).

Dunraven, Lord, *Past Times and Pastimes* (London, 1922).

——————— *The Great Divide* (London, 1876).

Ellman, Richard, *Oscar Wilde* (London, 1987).

Emmons, David, *The Butte Irish: Class and Ethnicity in an American Mining Town 1875–1925* (Chicago, 1989).

Fulton, Maurice G., *History of the Lincoln County War* (Tucson, 1997).

Garret, Patrick F., *The Authentic Life of Billy the Kid* (Oklahoma, 1954).

Grinnell, George Bird, *Trails of the Pathfinders* (New York, 1913).

Hafen, Leroy R., *Broken Hand: The Life of Thomas Fitzpatrick, Mountain Man, Guide and Indian Agent* (Lincoln/London, 1981).

——————— (ed.), *French Fur Traders and Voyageurs in the American West* (Nebraska, 1997).

——————— (ed.), *Mountain Men and Fur Traders of the Far West* (Lincoln, 1982).

Haley, J. Evitts, *Charles Goodnight: Cowman and Plainsman* (Oklahoma, 1949).

Harris, Frank, *My Life and Loves* (London, 1964).

Hart Davis, Rupert, *The Letters of Oscar Wilde* (London, 1962).

Hine, Robert V. and Farragher, John Mack, *The American West, A New Interpretive History* (Yale, 2000).

Holland, Mervyn and Hart-Davis, Rupert, *The Complete Letters of Oscar Wilde* (London, 2000).

Hopkins, Virginia, *Pioneers of the Old West* (London, 1988).

Hunt, William R., *Whiskey Peddle: Johnny Healy, North Frontier Trader* (Montana, 1993).

Hyde, H. Montgomery, *Oscar Wilde, A Biography* (London, 1976).

Johnson, Barry, *The Life of St. George Gore* (London, 1997).

Johnson, Kristin (ed.), *Unfortunate Emigrants, Narratives of the Donner Party* (Utah, 1996).

Julian, Phillipe, *Oscar Wilde* (London, 1969).

Kane, Paul, *Wanderings of an Artist Among the Indians of North America* (Toronto, 1925; original publication, 1859).

Keleher, William A., *Violence in Lincoln County* (New Mexico, 1957).

Kenneally, Thomas, *The Great Shame* (London, 1998).

King, Joseph A., *Winter of Entrapment: A New Look at the Donner Party* (Lafayette, California, 1998).

Lavash, Donald R., *Sheriff William Brady, Tragic Hero of the Lincoln County War* (Santa Fe, 1986).

Limerick, Patricia, *The Legacy of Conquest: The Unbroken Past of the American West* (New York, 1987).

McGaw, William Cochran, *Savage Scene, The Life and Times of Mountain Man Jim Kirker* (New Mexico, 1972).

McGrath, Roger, *Gunfighters, Highwaymen and Vigilantes* (Berkeley, 1984).

McLoughlin, Denis, *Wild and Wooly: An Encyclopedia of the Old West* (New York, 1975).

Marcy, R. B., *30 Years of Army Life on the Border* (New York, 1866).

Mayer, Melanie and DeArmond, Robert, *Staking Her Claim: The Life of Belinda Mulrooney, Klondike and Alaska Entrepreneur* (Ohio, 2000).

Mellon, Deborah, *The Legend of Molly b'Dam* (Idaho, 1989).

Miller, Nyle H. and Snell, Joseph W., *Great Gunfighters of the Kansas Cowtowns* (Nebraska, 1967).

Moffat, Gwen, *Hard Road West* (London, 1981).

Morgan, Dale, *Overland in 1846: Diaries and Letters of the California-Oregon Trail* (Nebraska, 1963).

Mulholland, Catherine, *William Mulholland and the Rise of Los Angeles* (Berkeley, 2000).

Nash, Jay Robert, *Encyclopedia of Western Lawmen and Outlaws* (New York, 1994).

Niehardt, John, *The Splendid Wayfaring* (Lincoln, 1948).

Nolan, Frederick, *The Lincoln County War: A Documentary History* (Oklahoma, 1992).

O'Carroll, Ide, *Models for Movers: Irish Women's Emigration to America* (Dublin, 1990).

O'Laughlin, Michael C., *Irish Settlers on the American Frontier* (Missouri, 1984).

O'Neal, Bill, *The Pimlico Encyclopedia of Western Gunfighters* (London, 1998).

Reed Murphy, Virgina, *Across the Plains in the Donner Party*, edited by Karen Zeinert (New Haven, 1996).

Roberts, Jack, *The Amazing Adventures of Lord Gore: A True Saga from the Old West* (Utah, 1977).

Sarbaugh, Timothy J. and Walsh, James P., (eds.), *The Irish in the West* (Kansas, 1992).

Schmidgall, Gary, *The Stranger Wilde* (London, 1994).

Seagraves, Ann, *Soiled Doves: Prostitution in the Early West* (Idaho, 1994).

Stewart, George R., *Ordeal by Hunger: The Story of the Donner Party* (Boston, New York, 1988).

Thrapp, Dan L., *Encyclopedia of Frontier Biography* (California, 1988).

Turner, Frederick Jackson, *The Significance of the Frontier in American History* (New York, 1994).

Utley, Robert M. and Washburn, Wilcomb E., *The American Heritage History of the Indian Wars* (New York, 1992).

Vesta, Stanley, *Jim Bridger: Mountain Man* (Nebraska, 1970).

Walter, Dave (ed.) *Speaking Ill of the Dead* (Connecticut, 2000).

Ward, Geoffrey C., *The West: An Illustrated History* (London, 1996).

West, Trevor, *Horace Plunkett: Co-Operation and Politics, an Irish Biography* (Bucks, 1986).

Wilde, Oscar, *Decorative Art in America* (London, 1894).

_____ *Impressions of America* (Sunderland, 1906).

Woods, Lawrence M., *British Gentlemen in the Wild West* (London, 1990).

Woods, L. Milton, *Moreton Frewen's Western Adventures* (Wyoming, 1986).

Wyman, Mark, *Immigrants in the Valley: Irish, Germans and Americans in the Upper Mississippi Country, 1830–1860* (Chicago, 1984).

USEFUL WEBSITES

www.unm.edu/~wha/
www.pbs.org/weta/thewest
http://comehomemontana.org
www.archives.gov/research/guide-fed-records/groups/075.html
www.usu.edu/history/whq/

INDEX